'City of the Future'

Published by
Berghahn Books
www.berghahnbooks.com

© 2016 Mateusz Laszczkowski

Library of Congress Cataloging-in-Publication Data

Names: Laszczkowski, Mateusz, author.
Title: 'City of the future' : built space, modernity and urban change in Astana /
  Mateusz Laszczkowski.
Description: New York : Berghahn Books, [2016]. | Series : Integration and conflict
  studies ; v. 14 | Includes bibliographical references and index.
Identifiers: LCCN 2016024955 | ISBN 9781785332562 (hardback : alk. paper) |
  ISBN 9781785332579 (ebook)
Subjects: LCSH: Astana (Kazakhstan)—Social conditions. | Urban renewal—
  Kazakhstan—Astana. | Group Identity—Kazakhstan—Astana. | Sociology,
  Urban—Kazakhstan—Astana.
Classification: LCC HN670.23.A95 L33 2016 | DDC 307.3/416095845—dc23
LC record available at https://lccn.loc.gov/2016024955

British Library Cataloguing in Publication Data

A catalogue record for this book is available from the British Library

ISBN 978-1-78533-256-2 (hardback)
ISBN 978-1-78533-257-9 (ebook)

For Ania, with love

Contents

Maps, Figures and Tables

Maps

Figures

Tables

Acknowledgements

This book is based on my doctoral dissertation, the fruit of a fellowship at the Max Planck Institute for Social Anthropology in Halle. The research was made possible by SocAnth – Marie Curie Early Stage Training network – MEST-CT-2005-020702.

Many people have contributed to my research and the completion of this manuscript. First and foremost, I am indebted to my doctoral supervisors, Günther Schlee, Svetlana Jacquesson and Catherine Alexander, for their advice and often challenging commentary. Throughout the several years I spent working on this project, their help has been absolutely invaluable. I am grateful to the Max Planck Institute for Social Anthropology for providing me with an institutional home, and to Michael Stewart for creating and coordinating the Marie Curie SocAnth programme, which provided essential financial support.

My debt is equally great to the many people in Kazakhstan whose openness, hospitality, willingness to share knowledge as much as uncertainty, and friendship, made my fieldwork possible; in the pages that follow, many of them appear under pseudonyms. I wish particularly to thank Mira and her parents, Margarita and her mother, Chernii, Kirill and Giselle, Bella and Sputnik, Bakytgul' and Aleksandra Stepanovna and her family, but also others who are not mentioned directly in the text. A separate place must be reserved for my local research assistant, who appears in one episode below as 'Tasha'. Moreover, I am thankful to local scholars who provided me with support in getting established in the field and carrying out my research: first of all, Kul'shat Medeuova, as well as Zhanar Jampeissova and Aigul' Zabirova. I thank Paweł Jessa and Barbara Kaczmarczyk, who were consuls at the Polish embassy in Astana at the time of my fieldwork and offered me far more support than their official duties required.

Many colleagues – my peers as well as senior scholars – provided stimulating commentary on various parts of the manuscript, at different stages of its preparation. Often, beyond strictly intellectual exchange, their company simply made my life much more enjoyable during the years spent working on this project. I wish to thank Sally Cummings, John Eidson, Joachim Görlich, Joachim Otto Habeck, Bettina Mann, Stephen Reyna and Lale Yalçın-Heckmann, as well as Aida Alymbaeva, Ogato Ambaye, Echi Gabbert, Aksana Ismailbekova, Mariya Ivancheva, Patrice Ladwig, Azim Malikov, Maria Nakhshina, Zhanara Nauruzbayeva, Mihai Popa, Rita Sanders, Phillip Schröder, Hans Steinmüller, Oliver Tappe, André Thiemann, Tommaso Trevisani, Roberta Zavoretti and the participants of the research colloquia at the Max Planck Institute. Felix

Girke, Judith Beyer and Madeleine Reeves deserve special credit for sharing their thoughts on numerous occasions, covering a broad range of topics of mutual interest, and helping me develop my ideas about a great many things, also beyond the scope of this book. They became dear friends and I feel I have learned a lot from them. Natalie Koch, author of excellent articles on Astana, offered extensive, incisive and very helpful comments on earlier versions of this manuscript. I wish to thank her for that, and also to extend my gratitude to my other fellow 'Astanologists': Alima Bissenova and Adrien Fauve, for continuously rediscovering and sharing the interest for what may sometimes seem not exactly the most fascinating field-site on Earth – Astana, that dusty, noisy city with its landscapes of concrete and its climate that had once made the region a fitting site for the Gulag. In the pages that follow, I hope to have conveyed some of what we all found so captivating about the place.

I owe thanks to Manuela Pusch, Ingrid Schüler, Viola Stanisch, Nadine Wagenbrett, Viktoria Zeng, Dirk Bake and Ronald Kirchhof from the Max Planck Institute administration for all manner of logistical and organizational support; to the librarians Anja Neuner, Anett Kirchhof and Josefine Eckardt for always supplying me with whatever literature I needed; and to Jutta Turner for drawing the maps used in the book. I thank the reviewers for the Berghahn series 'Integration and Conflict Studies' for their helpful comments on earlier versions of the manuscript. Moreover, I thank Cornelia Schnepel for her invaluable help in proof-reading and correcting the final version of this book and in preparing the index.

My greatest debt, however, is to my partner Ania, without whose love, patience, understanding and forgiveness over the years I would have never made it.

Note on Translation
and Transliteration

All translations from the Russian are by the author, unless otherwise specified.

Throughout the text, for Russian and Kazakh words a simplified version of the Library of Congress transcription system with reduced diacritics is used, except for certain proper nouns that are conventionally spelled differently in English.

Introduction

Pathways into the 'City of the Future'

One wintry evening, six friends in their early to mid twenties sat around a small kitchen. Through the narrow window could be seen the courtyard below, wedged between two grey concrete apartment blocks from the mid 1970s. It was January 2009, midway through my fieldwork, and we were in my rented apartment in a Soviet-era neighbourhood in Astana, the capital of Kazakhstan. While water for tea was coming to the boil, Kirill[1] told a recent joke representing the popular genre of (post) Soviet railway travel *anekdot*:

> Some people are travelling by train from Almaty to Moscow. For days, all they can see out of their compartment's window is steppe. Boring. steppe, steppe, steppe ... Suddenly [Kirill, abruptly animated, speaking loudly] they go: 'Look, Astana! Just look at what fantastic buildings they've built! Wow, Astana!' [and just as abruptly – subdued, monotonous] And the steppe again, and steppe, and steppe, and steppe ...

It might be a risky idea to start a book with an anecdote so context-specific that few readers are likely to get it. But Kirill's joke evokes many of the themes of this book. Astana is located in north-central Kazakhstan, amidst vast plains on the outskirts of southern Siberia, swept by powerful winds that encounter little to diminish or redirect them. In summer, endless expanses of tall grasses and wheat wave under immense skies. In winter, the scenery is covered with a thick blanket of snow. The region, in the approximate middle of the Eurasian landmass, has a harsh continental climate with very hot summers and long, dry, frosty winters with temperatures dropping to as low as minus 40ºC. The river Ishim, a tributary of the larger Irtysh, which it joins on the Russian side of the border, flows slowly through the land. Astana sits at a point where the river takes a mild north-westerly turn. As travellers approach Astana by car or by train, a sheaf of glass and steel skyscrapers shine from afar amid the flat steppe landscape, flickering like a

Map 0.1 Kazakhstan

mirage. But this is a fairly recent development, connected to a set of complex and ongoing transformations in this city and in Kazakhstan more broadly.

Kazakhstan gained independence with the break-up of the Soviet Union in 1991 and Astana became the country's capital in December 1997, when the seat of government was relocated here from the much larger Almaty. Almaty, a good thousand kilometres to the south-east (Map 0.1), had been the capital of Kazakhstan throughout the Soviet period – that is, since the 1920s. The new capital, in contrast, used to be a mid-size provincial city, centre of an agricultural region. Originally established as a Russian tsarist outpost named Akmolinsk, from the 1960s the city was known as Tselinograd (Chapter 3), and then, after independence, briefly as Aqmola (1992–1998). Following the capital relocation, it received its present name, Astana – Kazakh for 'capital'.

A government-orchestrated building boom was soon to thoroughly transform the city. Beginning in the early 2000s, an expansive area of grandiose government buildings, shiny office skyscrapers, hotels, massive residential complexes, commercial venues and symbolic monuments was built – generally on previously undeveloped land on the opposite bank of the river from the pre-existent Soviet-era urban core (Figure 0.1). The pace and scope of construction were often astonishing, and the style of this new architecture was literally unseen before in Kazakhstan. The emerging built forms stood in sharp contrast to the Soviet-era box-shaped concrete apartment blocks and shabby semi-rural individual dwellings that make up the bulk of the urban built environment elsewhere in the country, including the old part of the new capital itself, as well as Kazakhstan's numerous remote villages. It was these spectacular new buildings that Kirill's joke referred to. But as the joke suggests – and as this

Figure 0.1 The skyline of Astana (photo: M. Laszczkowski)

book explores – 'the spectacular' stands in an ambiguous relationship to the mundane. The new cityscape of Astana was built to impress. Inevitably, however, it evokes questions about the nature of its – often concealed – embeddedness in the surrounding social and material landscapes, on which it depends as much for resources needed to construct and populate the new capital as for the aesthetic and ideological effect.

Paralleling the architectural transformation, Astana also underwent a sweeping demographic change. In little more than a decade after the capital relocation, the population of the city roughly tripled (from around 250,000 in the mid 1990s to between 600,000 and 800,000, according to various estimates, by the late 2000s) as a result of migration from all corners of the country. The presence of this large and heterogeneous group of migrants has engendered complex dynamics in the formation of collective identities and notions of belonging.

The changes of spatial, social and political relations underway in Astana offer a unique opportunity to explore the complexity of connections between space and diverse emerging social actors, structures and representations. The ongoing transformations in the Kazakhstani capital highlight built space as a dynamic field of the political – that is, of the processes whereby social aggregates, patterns of relations, values and horizons of the possible are defined, defied and defended; where experiments in structuring social life can be carried out, fail and be taken up again. In official discourse, Astana was dubbed the 'city of the future' (*gorod budushchego*) or 'city of dream' (*gorod-mechta*). Its construction was explicitly framed as an assertion of the rise of the new state and its place in the world.

Among Kazakhstani citizens, the developments triggered fascination, hope and enthusiasm, but also disbelief, scepticism and sarcasm. Kirill's joke above expresses that tension between enchantment and doubt. Astana's new built forms became touchstones for conflicting public feelings, imaginings and evaluations of the state, society, modernity and the future. They became foci for questions that citizens asked themselves about the material conditions, forms of social life, politics, personhood and identities that would be desirable, appropriate or even possible (Buchli 2007).

To date, a specifically anthropological, ethnographic study of Astana – one that moves beyond a focus on elite schemes for ruling and transforming space and society – has been pending.[2] This book ventures to address this lacuna. It is an ethnography of space- and place-making in the city – a study of mutually constitutive relationships between individual and collective subjects and their spatial environment. It explores the many ways in which materiality and imagination intertwined in constructing Astana – both in the literal sense of 'construction' as building and in the more metaphorical sense of 'social construction of reality'. It follows how the city's inhabitants engaged in embodied practices, discourses and the work of imagination to lend specific characteristics to space, to make and maintain places, to become particular kinds of subjects and define their terms of belonging in the social 'worlds' they constructed. And it investigates the imbrications of multiple visions of the past and the future materialized in the built environment.

In the book, I ask, inter alia, what social dynamics did the capital relocation and the building boom engender? What futures did it evoke? What possibilities for arranging social relations were opened up, or closed down? What specific qualities were inscribed in built space, and how did their inscription affect other social processes? In particular, in what ways was space constructed as 'urban' or 'rural', 'modern' or in need of 'modernization'? And how did those characteristics of space translate into individual and collective identities among the various groups of residents? I also ask what imaginings of locality and its relationship to the world at large were evoked, enabled or compelled. How were these different imaginaries enacted, affirmed and contested in spatial practices? What might be the effects of everyday engagements with old and new built forms for the formation of sociality, subjecthood, place and politics?

The making of places imbued with particular characteristics is a fundamentally political activity through which local subjects claim agency, identity and power (Gupta and Ferguson 1992; Rodman 1992; Ong 2011). This book emphasizes that this is not limited to elite projects – such as the development of Astana orchestrated by the post-Soviet regime in Kazakhstan – but involves the situated, interconnected but uncoordinated agency and aspirations of multiple actors. Hence, I follow the relationships between officially produced ideologies, discourses and images, and the details of everyday life in the quickly transforming city. This is also a book about the connections between the construction of global imaginaries, the state-inspired production of urban space and local place-making. It inquires after the spatial practices and imaginings through which residents, migrants and planners situate themselves, their collectives, their city (and, implicitly, the country of which it is the capital) in historical and translocal contexts.

The ethnography of the ongoing sociospatial dynamics in Astana emphasizes that place-making, by virtue of the tangled relationships between its participants and the constraints set by the material make-up of places, is a reiterative process and its outcomes are usually provisional and in some measure indeterminate. In particular, various actors' efforts to materialize a vision of distinctly 'urban' social and moral order – undertaken at various times and with different versions of the urban ideal in view – repetitively entail the proliferation of material forms and social practices that undermine that desired order and that are construed as 'rural'. The tension between these mutually opposed yet inextricably linked spatial categories – 'urbanity' and 'rurality' – remains at the heart of the politics of place-making in Astana and the construction of situated identities. As the discussion in this book further reveals, these are simultaneously spatio-temporal categories, for 'urbanity' is construed as tantamount to 'modernity', 'progress' and the future, while 'rurality' is associated with 'backwardness'. Thus, the material and imaginational construction of space entails also the equally political construction of alternative qualities of time.

Focusing on the changing urban landscapes of the Kazakhstani capital, I highlight the importance of built forms – their construction, their tangibility and rigidity, their fragility and need of maintenance, as well as their aesthetic properties – to social continuity and change. Subjectivities, identities and collectives, visions of social worlds and actors' particular emplacements in those worlds, are all made and remade, I argue, through engagements with space and the built environment. As I elaborate later on in this introduction, built space is also the material dimension that gives substance to contested and consequential narratives of pasts and futures. By focusing on Astana, this book highlights the enduring strength of the myths of modernism and modernization as teleological collective utopias (Berman 1988; Benjamin 1999 [1927–1939]; Ferguson 1999; cf. Buck-Morss 2002), while simultaneously making a case for the radical openness of space to plural experimentation with 'alternative social visions and configurations – that is, "worlds"' (Massey 2005; Ong 2011: 12).

Astana, Kazakhstan and the Global Lives of Modernist Urbanism

'Modernism' may be defined as the belief that present and future reality can be shaped rationally, according to plan, by means of the controlled transformation of the material and social environment. The human individual, in this mindset, becomes simultaneously the subject and object of transformation (Berman 1988). Historically, modernism entailed the emergence of new forms of power aiming to transform and 'improve' society (Foucault 1977, 1991; Mitchell 1988; Scott 1998). The building and rebuilding of cities has consistently been one of the principal ways of exercising this power in diverse parts of the globe. In introducing this book, therefore, it is instructive to place Astana in a transnational historical context of modernist urban planning ideologies, highlighting the features it shares with cities on various continents as well as what is specific to Kazakhstan and its new capital. Such a comparative view helps underscore the relevance of Astana to broader scholarly and political concerns with the burgeoning diversity of contemporary cities, and with the practices through which variously situated subjects claim their place in the world and compete to define global hierarchies of value.

Nineteenth-century European capitals were subject to massive reconstruction orchestrated by governments in the pursuit of nationalizing, modernizing or other transformative agendas (e.g., Agnew 1998 for Rome; Harvey 2003 for Paris). But modern urbanism in the sense of an institutionalized nexus of arrangements for planning and managing the social environment in cities was born, according to Paul Rabinow (1989), out of experiments undertaken by French colonial authorities in Africa and Asia (see also Metcalf 1989; Wright 1991). Soon, the newly invented technologies of urban planning and governance found application in France itself. In the second half of the twentieth century, city-building proved an attractive way for the elites of newly emerging postcolonial nations and states to assert their place on the map and their aspirations to 'modernity'. In particular, constructing new capitals not only carried much symbolic weight but also seemed a forceful practical move on the road of state-building and modernization. Between the 1950s and the 1980s, the capitals of at least ten formerly colonized countries in Africa, Asia and Latin America were relocated (Schatz 2004b: 115).[3]

The most widely known of these relocated capitals is Brasilia, the capital of Brazil built from scratch between 1956 and 1960.[4] It was also there that the ideals of 'high modernist' socially transformative city planning, as developed by Le Corbusier and the CIAM (International Congress of Modern Architecture) movement (Scott 1998: 103–46; Hall 2002: 219–61), were most fully realized. Architectural and city-planning solutions – such as the elimination of the mixed-use street and its replacement with the motorized highway and immense square, or the settlement of residents into *superquadras* – that is, gigantic apartment blocks – were introduced with the explicit goal of forcing individuals into new forms of consciousness and changing society. President Juscelino Kubitschek and the architects responsible for planning Brasilia envisioned the new capital as an 'exemplary centre' (Holston 1989, drawing on Geertz 1980) that would radiate progress across Brazil and thus help overcome poverty, inequality and technical obsolescence. The experiment, however, remained confined to Brasilia and ended in failure, from one viewpoint at least, as the forms of social exclusion that had plagued Brazilian cities were reproduced, perhaps even more maliciously, in the new capital (Epstein 1973; Holston 1989; Caldeira and Holston 2005).

From this angle, Astana is not an unprecedented case. There are suggestive parallels in particular between the Kazakhstani capital and Brasilia. Yet it is important to remember that urbanism, like other forms of modernity, does not travel unaffected 'from the West to the rest' (Roy 2011: 309–10). Rather, multiple interconnected yet often incompatible modernities and urbanisms have been produced in different parts of the world and at various historical moments, including a spectrum of 'socialist' and 'post-socialist' conditions worldwide. Astana offers a rare opportunity to study the 'social life' of urban space, first under state socialism and more recently under a regime that fuses strong central government with an embrace of the transnational capitalist market.

Arguably, the Soviet Union was where socially transformative production of urban space was undertaken at the largest scale. Cities were ideologically valued as hotbeds of modernization. The architectural milieu of a socialist city was held to provide the catalyst for producing a socialist society (Crowley and Reid 2002; Alexander and Buchli 2007). City-building (*gradostroitel'stvo*) developed into a unique discourse and institutionalized practice, a form of total social planning (French 1995; Collier 2010: 34). Especially in the 1930s under Stalin, building new cities was understood as tantamount to constructing a new social order, 'building socialism'. Multiple towns and cities were built where none had previously existed. Entire industrial cities built from scratch, such as Magnitogorsk in the Urals (Kotkin 1995) and Karaganda in Kazakhstan (Brown 2001), were expected to produce not only coal or steel but also a new kind of 'collectivist individual' (Kharkhordin 1999) and new social relations. Simultaneously, where the Bolshevik government found the need to 'modernize' particularly acute – as in Central Asia – historic urban centres were reconstructed to turn them into hotbeds of transformed society (Liu 2007 for Osh; Stronski 2010 for Tashkent). The objective, in either case, was to, quite literally, build 'a new economy, society, politics – in short, a new culture' (Kotkin 1995: 34; Hoffmann 2003). In later decades, the urban built environment in the Soviet Union retained its ideological role of social mould (French 1995: 69–95; Buchli 2000: 138–58; Gerchuk 2000). Nikita Khrushchev, who had succeeded the deceased Stalin, urged extensive and swift construction of standardized housing, materializing ideals of residential equity and 'modern living for all'. The scale of the mass housing campaign initiated in 1956 was such that apartment blocks erected under Khrushchev and his successor Brezhnev comprise to this day the bulk of the built environment of many a former Soviet city – including Astana (see Chapter 3).

Following the dissolution of the USSR, each of its former republics and 'satellite' countries followed a different, contingent trajectory of transformation of the political and economic system (Burawoy and Verdery 1999; Hann

2002; Humphrey 2002b; Jones Luong 2004). Although this was allegedly a post-ideological age (Fukuyama 1992), everywhere urban space was restructured to manifest and give momentum to the transformations (Andrusz, Harloe and Szelenyi 1996; Alexander, Buchli and Humphrey 2007; Czepczyński 2008; Darieva, Kaschuba and Krebs 2011). Spatial renewal, especially in capital cities, appealed to leaders of the newly independent states as an attractive way to perform statehood, promote new national identities and induce new political-economic relations. While Kazakhstan was the only post-Soviet state to relocate its capital, all post-Soviet capitals were refurbished (Bell 1999 for Tashkent; Grant 2014 for Baku), and in neighbouring Kyrgyzstan the capital was renamed (from Frunze to Bishkek). Many smaller cities were likewise rebuilt (Ruble 1995 for Yaroslavl, Russia; Trevisani 2014 for Namangan, Uzbekistan). In some places, like in Astana, cityscapes were subject to sweeping transformation. Turkmenistan's Ashgabat made headlines around the world for its extravagant built forms erected to represent in concrete, steel, glass and lots of marble the ideas of the country's idiosyncratic leader, Saparmurat Niyazov, better known as Turkmenbashi (Šír 2008; Denison 2009). Ashgabat is the only regional counterpart to match Astana in terms of the scale of construction (Koch 2015b). An important difference between the two seems to be that while Ashgabat was conspicuously shaped to materialize Turkmenbashi's personality cult (Denison 2009: 1175), Astana's new built environment appears rather to embody ideas of development, 'modernity' and entrepreneurial statehood (Koch 2012a; Bissenova 2014), only implicitly hinting at president Nursultan Nazarbaev's 'personality cult by proxy' (Adams and Rustemova 2009).

Kazakhstan is a presidential republic, and a series of constitutional amendments, referendums and elections, none of which has been recognized by international monitoring bodies as fair, has allowed Nazarbaev (the last Soviet-era leader of Kazakhstan) to occupy the post of president continuously since independence in 1991.[5] In 2008, the two-chamber parliament was monopolized by the president's party, Nur Otan (Bowyer 2008).[6] Opposition is weak and fragmented, its leaders (commonly former Nazarbaev cronies fallen out of favour) compromised, exiled or both. Usually, little physical violence is necessary to prevent organized expressions of dissent, although individual opposition politicians or journalists who would not be co-opted (Cummings 2005: 108–16) have been harassed, jailed or killed in circumstances of which little or nothing is publicly known (Schatz 2009: 210). However, in a rare outburst of spectacular violence, on 16 December 2011 the Kazakhstani police cracked down on striking oil workers in the Caspian town of Zhanaozen, leaving at least ten dead (Kislov 2011) and many injured. This dramatic episode provides a chilling reminder of the nature of translocal connections through which Astana is produced, since the development of the capital city depends on the political economy of Kazakhstan's oil, in which towns such as Zhanaozen are crucial sites.

The Kazakhstani regime's strategy of maintaining complacency usually relies on more structural and thus less ostensive forms of violence and on providing relative prosperity to selected constituencies (Koch 2013). Economically, following the acute crisis of the 1990s (see Chapter 1), Kazakhstan is doing relatively well compared to its neighbours in the region. It is a resource-rich country – as some citizens would sometimes boast, 'the entire periodic table of elements' is found in its territory. Major American and European companies have invested in the exploitation of Kazakhstan's oil and gas deposits. Between 2000 and 2007 – which coincides with the crucial first phase of the building boom in Astana – Kazakhstan's economy growth rate, generated primarily by the extractive industries, was an impressive 9 per cent per year (Central Intelligence Agency 2011). While residents in many areas of the countryside and factory towns across Kazakhstan that were ruined economically in the aftermath of the collapse of the USSR still find it hard to make ends meet, the fruits of oil-fed prosperity are clearly visible in the largest cities such as Almaty, the Caspian port of Aktau and, first and foremost, Astana. Alongside impressive developments of the built environment and urban infrastructure, residents in those places – at least those who can afford it – enjoy access to cosmopolitan consumer goods (Laszczkowski 2011b).

The cost of building Astana is unknown. By 2007, it was officially estimated at fifteen billion U.S. dollars, while independent scholars believed the actual price tag must have been much higher (Dave 2007: 168). The works are carried out by a range of construction companies, some Kazakhstani, others foreign – primarily Russian and Turkish. Financing comes either from the state – as with government buildings, monuments and housing for public officials and civil servants – or from domestic and international commercial investors. The financial crisis in 2007 drove a number of developers into bankruptcy. As a result, the pace of the works dropped considerably around 2008, with many projects frozen in mid construction. However, state intervention, including bailouts for bankrupt companies and subsidy programmes for would-be homeowners, soon helped overcome the crisis and put the construction back on track (Bissenova 2012: 141–58). At the time of this writing, in 2014–2015, the new part of Astana continues to expand with further residential complexes, commercial venues and public projects such as a new university campus.[7]

Official public discourse in Kazakhstan – consisting mainly of works attributed to Nazarbaev, his speeches and publications by various officials and luminaries (e.g., Dzhaksybekov 2008) – reveals considerable affinities between the construction of Astana and earlier, in particular Soviet, modernist visions of social transformation through city-building. The discourse revives the myth of modernization as linear development and progress (cf. Ferguson 2005). A range of familiar modernist topoi are reiterated. For instance, the topos of the conquering of 'nature' is invoked when it is claimed that the new capital has 'risen' out of the 'bare', 'virgin' steppe. The tropes of 'emptiness', 'bareness' or 'barrenness' of the land have been persistently invoked in subsequent 'colonizing' narratives in this area since the time of tsarist colonization (Buchli 2007: 47–48) and, as is discussed at several points below, they resurface for various political uses – also contesting official ideology – today (see especially Chapter 3). Another commonplace modernist trope in contemporary official discourse about Astana – speed – is emphasized in numerous assertions that the construction works in the new capital are accomplished at a 'miraculous' or 'record-breaking' pace (e.g., Nazarbaev 2006: 349; cf. Berman 1988: 49–50).

Nazarbaev calls Astana a 'symbol of the rise of the state' (2006: 357); 'of the renewal of Kazakhstan ... of the inextinguishable creative energy of its multiethnic [*mnogonatsional'nogo*] nation ... a symbol of the nation's belief ... in the nation's own strength' (Nazarbaev 2005: 17); finally 'a symbol of the liberated nation's hope and assuredness as to its flourishing future and the future of its descendants' (ibid.).[8] Evaluating the results of building Astana, the president adds in a clear modernist idiom: 'As a systemic mobilizing factor of the rebirth of Kazakhstan, Astana has accomplished her historical mission ... Kazakhstan today is a stable and cohesive state, firmly and irreversibly progressing along the path of socio-economic development and socio-political reconstruction of society' (ibid.: 49). Astana, moreover, is expected to radiate development out across the national territory – an effect Nazarbaev (2005: 58) calls 'resonance development'. Here, the echoes of the utopianism of Brasilia, half a century earlier, are perhaps the most clearly heard (cf. Holston 1989: 14–20).

Nazarbaev (2006: 335) suggests that the origin of the idea of capital relocation can be traced back as early as 1992, just a few months after independence. He claims this was when he first thought of then Aqmola as the future capital and writes:

> The time called for great and significant deeds. But are great deeds possible with an old burden of conservative mentality? [A mentality] basically unable to accommodate concepts such as private property, the market, pluralism, the freedom of speech and of the spirit ... Some extraordinary decision was needed to help shake the people and literally 'air' [*provetrit'*] their brains. Thus, little by little, I came to the conclusion about the necessity of capital relocation. ... Because a capital, as I had no doubt ... defines the vector of development of the state and allows to structure society in line with global trends. (Nazarbaev 2005: 27–28)

And further:

> The capital of a state is not just the brain of the country, but also its central nervous system, defining not only the mentality, but also the norms of behaviour of all strata of the population and even of individual

citizens. The capital is the place where the behavioural structures of the entire society are formed. (Nazarbaev 2005: 28–29)

In these passages, modernist tropes resonate with particular intensity. Nazarbaev positions himself as the quasi-Faustian 'developer' who sets out to destroy 'old mentality' and 'air people's brains' to create conditions for the construction of the new (cf. Berman 1988: 60–71). He declares that the capital relocation was to change the Kazakhstani society to make it more compatible with 'global trends', paving the way for private property, market relations and so forth. Just as in Soviet modernist ideology, the city is expected to serve as the engine of social transformation. Speaking of shaking off 'the burden of conservative mentality', the president simultaneously strikes an acutely modernist note, writing that the changes are expected to reach into individual citizens' consciousness in order to transform their behaviour and thus programme the 'behavioural structures' of society at large.

The echoes of Soviet modernism become even more explicit when Nazarbaev spells out the ultimate reason for the construction of Astana as follows:

The country needed a patriotic breakthrough, a feat, akin to that of the Virgin Lands Campaign. Yet this time it was related to new conditions: the strengthening of independence, the building of statehood, the deepening of socio-economic and political transformations. And we were convinced that the transfer of the capital to Aqmola would, in many respects, facilitate the accomplishment of these goals. (Nazarbaev 2006: 350)

Here, the president most openly declares the transformative agenda associated with the construction of Astana. The Soviet past is invoked in an ambiguous claim of simultaneous denial and renewal. Although elsewhere in this discourse 'Soviet' is at times synonymous to 'outdated' – as in the phrase 'to turn a Soviet town into a contemporary capital' (Nazarbaev 2006: 351) – in the passage just quoted Nazarbaev likens the building of Astana to the Virgin Lands Campaign, the Tselina. That had been a massive agricultural development scheme carried out under Khrushchev in the 1950s and 1960s to transform the steppes of north-central Kazakhstan into an enormous grain-producing region for the USSR (M. Pohl 1999). As I describe at more length in Chapter 3, the campaign had also boosted the growth of Tselinograd – a crucial stage in the history of today's Astana.

Yet, I argue, it would be a mistake to write off the Kazakhstani government's Astana project and attendant ideological discourse as mere reinvention of Soviet ideology. Without necessarily believing in President Nazarbaev's commitment to the values of 'pluralism' and 'the freedom of speech and of the spirit', it is worthwhile situating Astana in a broader, transcontinental pattern. Over the recent decades, governments variously allied with particular class constituencies and corporate interests have continued to restructure cities in China (Zhang 2006; Bellér-Hann 2014), South and South East Asia (Askew 2002; Herzfeld 2006; Roy and Ong 2011; Schwenkel 2013), the Middle East (Koch 2014), Africa (Mbembe 2004; cf. Simone 2001), the Americas (Cooper 1999; Rutheiser 1999; Low 2000) and in Europe (McDonogh 1999; Herzfeld 2009; Weszkalnys 2010). Of course, these different cases cannot be reduced to instantiations of a single politico-economic or cultural logic. While ideals, benchmarks and models travel across cities on different continents, each local case of urban transformation is a 'particular engagement with the global' (Ong 2011: 2). In late-socialist Kunming, for instance, the goal has been to 'speed up' growth and 'catch up' with other, more developed areas (Zhang 2006); in Manila, the objective of restructuring the downtown is to nurture a class of residents fit to form the managerial corpus for a desired knowledge economy (Shatkin 2011); and in Berlin, it is to regain 'European' identity, supposedly lost during the decades of socialist rule over one half of the city (Weszkalnys 2010: 49–61). However, this worldwide perspective suggests that the modernist 'will to improve' (Li 2005) by means of spatial transformation (usually for the benefit of some groups and to the detriment of others) endures in this supposedly postmodern, non-ideological world.[9]

In her introduction to a recent collection of studies of contemporary Asian cities, Aihwa Ong (2011) identifies two master prisms through which urban life in what until recently used to be called the Third World has usually been studied. What she calls the 'political economy approach' subordinates the plurality of urban experience on several continents to generally a single factor: the global spread of the forces of (originally 'Western') capitalism. In turn, the 'postcolonial' approach applies the similarly singular logic of the struggle of the 'subaltern' against colonial domination. But, Ong contends, none of these approaches does justice to the plurality of creative experiments with urban forms, through which subjects across Asian cities seek not only autonomously to assert their own identities, but also to lay claim to define what counts as 'modern' and re-establish the distribution of 'centres' and 'peripheries' in the geography of the global production of 'modernity'.

Kazakhstan belongs to a part of Asia that lies beyond the scope of Ong's argument. The urban experience in this part of the continent has been interpreted by scholars through another master trope, one that links it to specific other world regions: 'the post-socialist city' (Andrusz, Harloe and Szelenyi 1996; Alexander, Buchli and Humphrey 2007; Czepczyński 2008; Darieva, Kaschuba and Krebs 2011). While the category 'post-socialist' clearly has much merit in emphasizing common characteristics that link places in, say, East Germany, Kazakhstan and Vietnam and make them different from other areas that might be located much nearer but have not had that kind of historical experience with 'socialism'

(Humphrey 2002a; cf. Kandiyoti 2002; West and Raman 2009), I suggest that the post-socialist trope can be as limiting as the reductive effects of the tropes of 'capitalist globalization' and 'the postcolonial condition' identified by Ong.

Instead of reducing the multiplicity and diversity of cities to one or another of a handful of master narratives, what is needed is ethnographic attention to what Ong calls 'worlding practices' – 'constitutive, spatializing, and signifying gestures that variously conjure up worlds beyond current conditions of urban living. They articulate disparate elements from near and far, and symbolically re-situate the city in the world' (Ong 2011: 13). As the chapters in this book make clear, these situated practices include the agency of leaders and planners as well as so-called 'ordinary citizens'. The relevance of the Astana experience to our understanding of the diversity of hybrid urbanisms proliferating in the world today stems from the polyvalent mixing of such signifying practices: some akin to those in operation elsewhere, some drawing on the specific legacies of Soviet urbanism, and some context-specific instances of local innovation.

While the bulk of this book explores this heterogeneity of place-making practices in Astana through foci on a range of everyday experiences by residents, hybrid approaches are notable also in the work of local political and professional city-planning elites. Despite the pronouncements of the government discourse as cited above, members of the architectural establishment in Astana whom I interviewed for this research rejected the idea that the massive state-orchestrated construction campaign in Kazakhstan's new capital served goals of social transformation. They shunned Soviet modernist ideology in favour of a liberal approach, postulating permissive 'user-friendly' planning (Chikanaev 2008; cf. Rutheiser 1999: 327). In 2001, a General Plan for the city was commissioned from the Japanese architect Kisho Kurokawa, merging references to the 'East' and 'West', 'nature', 'tradition', abstract geometric symbolism and hi-tech futurism (Chikanaev 2008: 85–89; Bissenova 2012: 34–67). The late Japanese master explicitly set his ideals in opposition to those of Le Corbusier's modernism, which had guided the design of Brasilia and influenced Soviet urbanism (Kurokawa 1997). As time went by, Kurokawa's plan was repeatedly corrected by AstanaGenPlan, a planning institute established to supervise its implementation and adjustments, until no more than basic general ideas were preserved from the original vision. Anthropologist Alima Bissenova (2014), who has followed the work of AstanaGenPlan, argues that the Kazakhstani authorities' goal in hiring Kurokawa – next to securing the considerable sums from the Japanese international cooperation funds that came with his plan – was to buy 'cultural capital' (Bourdieu 1984) associated with his expertise and thus help position Kazakhstan in a global 'economy of appearances'.

I suggest that the paradoxes of simultaneous break and continuity between Soviet-era and present-day production of space in Astana are themselves socially and politically productive. They enable a range of creative constructions of the past and the future by the ruling and city-planning elites as well as by individual citizens. Contradictions such as reiterating key tropes of Soviet modernist city-planning ideology and rejecting it, or hiring the Japanese star architect and subsequently thoroughly changing his master plan, highlight the complexity of 'worlding' in a place like Astana. Creative reworking of Soviet ideological and institutional legacies and re-appropriating heterogeneous neoteric ideas and flows of symbolic as well as financial capital are but some of the ideological and politico-economic practices involved in the ongoing emergence of Kazakhstan's capital.

By having Astana built, the Kazakhstani government put forth a particular vision of the national future within a global context. This does not imply that the vision was completely explicit or coherent, let alone hegemonic. But, as the chapters below explore, various actors' imaginings of self, place, time, sociality and politics were articulated in relation to that vision and its material realization in built forms. Buildings gave 'modernity' a specific look and texture. Individual residents of Astana variously, performatively and creatively engaged with those material forms to claim a place for themselves in the local social environment as well as in an imagined world at large. Exploring these engagements ethnographically entails revisiting anthropological perspectives on place and space, the local and the global, from a novel angle afforded by the particularities of Astana's past and ongoing development.

Anthropology's Space

During the 1990s and 2000s, a 'spatial turn' occurred in anthropology. While space had always formed a part of the background against which anthropologists crafted their accounts of social organization, in this more recent period space began to be increasingly brought to the foreground as a constitutive dimension of social life (Lawrence and Low 1990; Low and Lawrence-Zùñiga 2003). Anthropologists have come to appreciate how place and space are constitutive of social relations, personhood and subjectivity, as well as various forms of social organization and political processes – in short, of culture. Scholars in the discipline recognized that, as geographer Doreen Massey put it, 'it is not just that the spatial is socially constructed; the social is spatially constructed too' (1984: 6). Anthropology's spatial turn drew on earlier developments in geography (e.g., Massey and Allen 1984; Agnew and Duncan 1989) and on a range of philosophical theories spanning from a focus on the human body and the sensory perception of space (e.g., Merleau-Ponty 1962; Casey 1996) to neo-Marxist analyses of the political economy of space production (Harvey 1973; Lefebvre 1991 [1974]).[10] While the turn has been immensely productive, anthropology also inherited from these various intellectual currents a number of binary distinctions and habits of thought that, I would argue, may impede the understanding of the social dimensions of space (or the spatial dimensions of the social). It is some of these dualisms that I aim to reconsider.

One fundamental distinction is that between 'space' and 'place'. Much ink has been spilled by theorists trying to define these two categories and their mutual relationship. Broadly, scholars agree with the common-sense view that space is general while place is particular; that places are where objects and events are distributed across space. However, phenomenologist Edward Casey (1996) argues, for instance, that while it is conventionally assumed that places are secondary subjective constructs carved out from objective space, the actual experience is the opposite: the abstract and general concept of space is an elaboration of the direct perception of particular, concrete places by the human individual (see also Tuan 1977). In contrast, Michel De Certeau (1984) reverts the terms. 'Space is a practiced place', he writes (1984: 117), by which he means that places are abstract geometrical positions enlivened and thus transformed into spaces by being used: 'the street geometrically defined by urban planning is transformed into a space by walkers' (ibid.).

In general, as geographer John Agnew (2005) notes, 'space' lends itself to objectivist interpretations, while 'place' to subjectivist ones. That is to say, the analyses of 'space' tend to focus on political economy and planning, while those of 'place' highlight subjective 'meaning', personal experience and intimate communities. Connected to this is a political dualism. Space is often conceptualized as the domain of planning, control and uniformity, while place tends to be seen as the locus of particularity, difference, spontaneity and, more or less implicitly, resistance.[11]

This dualism is reflected, inter alia, in Henri Lefebvre's seminal work on the social production of space (1991). Lefebvre's fundamental thesis – on which numerous other authors have drawn and on which I also build in this book – is that space is produced by social actors, purposefully and within the structures of political economy. Simultaneously, space is what enables and conditions social relations. It sets constraints and opens up possibilities for action. In other words, space 'is at once result and cause, product and producer; it is also a stake, the locus of projects and actions deployed as part of specific strategies, and hence also the object of wagers on the future' (Lefebvre 1991: 142–43). It follows that a transformation of space is a necessary condition of social change. This is clearly relevant to Astana, where the development of built space was linked to a reconstruction of state order following the demise of the Soviet Union and Kazakhstan's independence, and to a transformation of the economy (Laszczkowski 2014). According to Lefebvre, each new politico-economic formation (mode of production) requires qualitatively new spatial relations. For instance, capitalist space is 'homogenous' and 'fractured' – that is, divisible into formally equivalent abstract units that can be subject to trade. Also 'the state', as a condition of its own emergence and operation, establishes a particular kind of space appropriate for its objectives: a space that is bounded by borders, hierarchically organized into centres and peripheries, and hardwired with infrastructural networks that support the maintenance of control and production (Lefebvre 2003a).[12] Lefebvre sought the bases of resistance against the imposition of abstract state-capitalist space in the memories, representations and practices rooted in an older kind of space that the state and capital colonize: the supposedly more authentic, concrete and lived 'space of places', so to speak (Agnew 2005: 90).

Anthropology, at least since the 1960s, has been distinguished by a sensibility to practise, to the particular, the irregular and the 'bottom-up', to the indeterminacy of social action and the partiality of its outcomes (Ortner 1984; Moore 1987). The anthropology of place and space has been informed, alongside Lefebvre, also by phenomenology (Richardson 1982; Ingold 1995; Feld and Basso 1996; Richardson 2008), semiotics (Fernandez 2003 [1984]) and various theories of practice (Bourdieu 1977, 1990; De Certeau 1984). By the turn of the century, the prevailing anthropological view seemed to be of places as shifting, provisional constructs of a plurality of situated agencies (e.g., Raffles 1999). While taking into account the structuring impacts of 'the state' and other 'large-scale' forces, anthropologists tend to emphasize how places are continuously constituted as meaningful realities through everyday practices, repeated bodily movement, language, narratives and symbolization. Places, in the anthropological perspective, are 'multivocal' – constructed by a multiplicity of actors who claim 'voice' in shaping particular locales and defining the relations between them (Rodman 1992).

These various inspirations are brought together, for instance, in the way Setha Low expands on Lefebvre's work by introducing the concept of the 'social construction of space' as a counterpart to 'social production':

> The *social production of space* includes all those factors – social, economic, ideological, and technological – that result, or seek to result, in the physical creation of the material setting. The materialist emphasis of the term *social production* is useful in defining the historical emergence and political/economic formation of urban space. The term *social construction* may then be conveniently reserved for the phenomenological and symbolic experience of space as mediated by social processes such as exchange, conflict, and control. Thus, *the social construction of space* is the actual transformation of space – through people's social exchanges, memories, images, and daily use of the material setting – into scenes and actions that convey meaning. (Low 2000: 127–28, italics original; see also Low 1999b)

I argue that the distinction between 'production' and 'construction' – despite its analytic usefulness, best proven in Low's own work – reiterates the same kind of dualism expressed in the place-space dichotomy. 'Production' is about political economy and the agency of structural forces such as the state and capital; 'construction' is about the everyday, personal attachment, community and, implicitly, resistance.

Taking the perspective on places and spaces as complex, multivocal and dynamic for my starting point, I want to question that resilient dualism and shake up the relative ease with which the complexity of the mutually constitutive relationships between social forms and space is analytically divided into material 'production' and phenomenological, linguistic or symbolic 'construction', and space itself is split into seemingly separate planes of matter and 'meaning'. In making this critical move, it is helpful to draw on the work of geographers and anthropologists who scrutinize the dichotomies of place and space, the local and the global (Tsing 2000; Massey 2002, 2005; Agnew 2005; Cresswell 2011). This is not to say there is no difference in meaning between these terms, but to emphasize how place and space are intricately related. The distinction between place and space, as much as that between the local and the global, is not a qualitative difference, but rather an oscillation between figure and ground (Strathern 2002), a matter of perspective. Attempts at stopping this oscillation and fixing boundaries between these spatial categories are themselves profoundly political acts on which projects of domination (for example, state control over a designated 'territory' and all the places that it encompasses) are founded (Mitchell 1990, 1991). This is why it is important to keep those categories in motion.

In Massey's formulation, for instance, places remain particular, yet each is constituted as a node of translocal, space-spanning relationships. Places are 'constructed on a far larger scale than we happen to define for that moment as the place itself, whether that be a street, or a region or even a continent' (Massey 1994: 154). They are open and unbounded, integrating 'in a positive way the global and the local' (1994: 155; see also Tsing 2000). Space, on the other hand, remains, in a sense, general, but it is 'concrete and embedded too. It is no more than the sum of our relations and connections … and, like place, it too is continually being made' (Massey 2002: 25).

Issues of scale and politics are connected to this. I argue that a sharp analytic separation between 'the state' and other 'large-scale actors' producing space 'from above' and, on the other hand, individuals or 'local communities' constructing place (or, 'constructing space' in Low's sense) on the intimate scale of the everyday is untenable.[13] In the chapters that follow, my ethnographic focus shifts back and forth between panoramic vistas of the design of Astana and close-ups of the details of everyday practice and the capillaries of the built environment. This does not so much mean moving across scales, as following how scalar imaginations – perceptions of the 'large' and the 'small'; the 'global' and the 'local'; the 'general', the 'collective', the 'particular' and the 'individual'; the 'total' and 'the partial' – are themselves produced in a plurality of situated practices (Marston

2000; Latour 2005: 184–85). For instance, in Chapter 1 I explore the tensions between individual migrants' personal experience of living in Astana and more totalizing visions of the city and its place in the world, in which they have affectively and materially invested; Chapter 4 studies how contests over the qualities of the city played out within the more restricted boundaries of central squares; and in Chapter 5 I look at how cross-currents of broad-ranging flows of people, ideas and materials were provisionally stabilized to make up the local milieu of a neighbourhood. Astana, I argue, is continually constructed by planners on their drawing boards and by excavators and cranes raising new buildings and monuments, as much as by residents engaged in quotidian conversations, encounters in the street and maintenance jobs inside back alleys and courtyards. Simultaneously with this ongoing construction of the city, in all those situations other scales are being produced and contested: from face-to-face relationships within apartment blocks and neighbourhoods, to national identities (Chapters 2 and 3), to electronically connected transnational networks (Chapter 6) and global cartographies of value (Chapters 1).[14]

Politically, these processes are hardly reducible to the bipolar dynamics of domination and resistance. Sometimes, the residents' place-making and world-making practices are aimed to resist or contest schemes imposed by government officials (Chapters 3 and 5); more often they are not (e.g., Chapter 6). Rather, what goes on is a complex interplay of heterogeneous agencies whose objectives may or may not overlap and that contingently collide or collude, opportunistically drawing on one another. It is through such translocal relationships that place and space, from the intimacies of the 'local' to the immensity of the 'global', are constituted in a proliferation of diversely situated performances and encounters.

Following Massey (2005), I emphasize the radical openness of space to heterogeneity, change, improvisation and possibility, and its simultaneous material concreteness. Space, I argue, is inherently hybrid: far from the fantasies of Cartesian 'realism' and, at the other extreme, a post-structuralist obsession with free-floating signifiers, space is an ever-morphing assemblage of material and imaginational elements (see also Cresswell 2011). It is generated through the multiplicity of situated practices, which it enables, evokes and endures. In Astana, various images and imaginations of the city and the world, in the future and in the past – produced as much by professional 'imagineers' (Rutheiser 1999: 322) as by 'ordinary' residents – are particularly significant in motivating social action (see especially Chapter 1 below). Simultaneously, these images become concrete, are reaffirmed or compromised by the particular material qualities of the surfaces of buildings, streets and squares, and specific building materials. In Astana, glass and steel, for instance, epitomize 'modernity' and 'urbanity' while mud-brick is the stuff of 'rurality', obsolescence and 'underdevelopment' (Chapters 1–3). As brought to the fore most clearly in Chapter 5, material elements of the built environment not only induce specific interpretations of social life, but can actually modify human agency and partake in the constitution of places, persons and collectives (see, e.g., Buchli 2000; Latour 2005; Thrift 2008).

The challenge for contemporary social theory is to productively bridge 'social-constructionism' – the emphasis, that is, on the imaginative and discursive aspects of social formation – and the recognition of the social efficacy of non-human material actants, as found in a range of novel theories that have been termed 'the new materialisms' (Coole and Frost 2010; cf. Navaro-Yashin 2012). This challenge becomes especially clear in researching space- and place-making, that field of mutually constitutive relationships between human individuals, groups and their material spatial environments. The task is to recognize the significance of objective spatial relations and the agency of material elements, and at the same time capture the difference made by the specifically human work of imagination, representation and narrativization.

The complexity of space and its openness to coexisting plurality of actual and virtual alternatives – what, following Victor Turner (1988), can be called subjunctivity – requires a theoretical approach equally prepared to simultaneously embrace disjunct perspectives, operate across (seemingly) incompatible planes and speak a plurality of languages – a kind of theoretical and methodological surrealism that has always been the lifeblood of ethnography (Clifford 1988). The chapters below are an attempt to perform such ethnographically informed hybrid theorizing, bringing together materialist, social-constructivist, semiotical, human-centred and thing-centred perspectives. The arguments of this book are simultaneously powered by attention to everyday practices, the phenomenology of spatial experience, materiality and by a loosely post-structuralist (but also Benjaminian) emphasis on imagination, discourse and representation (e.g., Baudrillard 1983; Foucault 1986; Zukin 1992; Soja 1996; cf. Benjamin 1999 [1927–1939], 2002 [1936]) – for these are all consequential dimensions in the making of place, space and selves.

Space and Time

One of the key themes addressed in this book concerns the entanglements of space and time in the built forms and social dynamics in Astana. Constructing pasts and futures in the material form of the built environment is a crucial element in the politics of space and place. It is a classic topos in anthropological theory that time – like space – is a social construct, imbued by human groups with various qualities (Hubert 1999 [1905]; James and Mills 2005; cf. Gell 1992). Particular qualities of time are materialized in the landscape and the built environment (Ingold 1993; Bender 2006). The meanings of various periods and of time's flow itself change along with the material condition and social uses of places and buildings, while within the material structures of the built environment national and personal temporalities clash (e.g., Herzfeld 1991; Edensor 2005; Navaro-Yashin 2012; Schwenkel 2013). Post-socialist cities subject to reconstruction – the selective erasure of architectural and monumental legacies of the past, their replacement with new *lieux de mémoire* (Nora 1996) to establish new versions of history (Wanner 1998; Forest and Johnson 2002) and the simultaneous construction of new cityscapes expected to embody desired futures (Pelkmans 2003; Alexander and Buchli 2007; Czepczyński 2008; Weszkalnys 2010; Grant 2014) – are among those places where the politics of spatio-temporal entanglement are especially clearly foregrounded.

In Astana as elsewhere, new visions of the state and social order are articulated in relation to the past and past versions of futurity that remain materially present in the architectural tissue of the city (cf. Street 2012; Stoler 2013). This book explores how the co-presence of old and new elements in the built environment enables constructing the city as multiple overlapping and frequently incompatible time-spaces, or 'chronotopes' (Bakhtin 1981). The city's Soviet-era incarnation, Tselinograd, is kept alive in multiple ways (Chapters 3 and 4). Different futures and pasts not only take shape through architectural design and officially produced images of the cityscape (see Chapter 1), but crucially their specific meanings emerge from everyday embodied practices by situated actors. The new parts of Astana are explicitly constructed to materialize a particular vision of the future, yet their construction depends – conceptually as well as materially – on the very conditions of the present that it denies. As I point out in Chapter 1, for the individual actors involved, this creates a paradoxical situation of a temporal limbo where the future seems almost at hand yet perpetually suspended in (literally) mid construction.

At the same time, as the Chapters 3 to 6 highlight in various ways, the enduring presence of Soviet-era spatial forms and imaginations, and their ongoing transformation through residents' practices, enable alternative constructions of the past and the future. This sometimes implies critique of dominant city-planning and state-building discourses and of the political economy of the post-Soviet state. In old-time neighbourhoods, where most lifelong residents as well as recent migrants live (Chapter 2), change occurs every day, from one mundane instance to the next (Chapter 5), and the watersheds of official history are blurred by the continuity of dwelling (Chapter 3). Industrial ruins unexpectedly become the venues of creative performances by young people that spawn astonishing collages of materialized spatial and temporal imaginings (Chapter 6). But of course all of those places are also enmeshed in and affected by the material and ideological dynamics of the 'building of the future'.

Theorizing the City Anthropologically

By declaring my work an ethnography, I express a methodological choice – the choice of a style of research and writing that aims to speak to broad theoretical questions through an evocative and relatively detailed description of forms of everyday social interaction in a particular place at a particular time. But writing an ethnography of a city – especially a city being actively and thoroughly trans-formed, like Astana – singularly reveals the challenges and contradictions inher-ent in this methodology. As discussed above, places are rarely, if ever, bounded or stable (Raffles 1999), and neither does the turbulent flow of time lend itself to slicing into handy snapshots (Sanjek 1991) – rather, it carries with it uprooted fragments of former configurations and bits of knowledge, creating often unexpected juxtapositions and new forms always-already in motion.[15]

Like any large city, Astana is dizzyingly dynamic and complex – by which I mean a condition where 'phenomena share a space but cannot be mapped in terms of a single set of three-dimensional coordinates' (Mol and Law 2002: 1). Geographers Ash Amin and Nigel Thrift describe the city (any city) as 'a complex imbroglio of actors with different goals, methods, and ways of practice' (2002: 92). Cities, according to them, 'are truly multiple. They exceed, always exceed' (ibid.: 30). Or, as one character in Salman Rushdie's *The Satanic Verses* percep-tively notes, 'the modern city … is the locus classicus of incompatible realities' (2006 [1988]: 314). For these reasons, cities are – and, since the inception of modern social science, have always been – both exceptionally compelling sites for inquiring into the maelstrom condition of 'modernity' (Berman 1988), and extremely challenging settings for social research (Sennett 1969).[16]

The formidable difficulty in researching cities is 'to see the totality as well as the parts' (Harvey 2003: 18). For anthropologists, this took the form of the dilemma over whether their goal was an 'anthropology of the city, or only in the city' (Hannerz 1980: 248; cf. Fox 1972, 1977; Jackson 1985; Gulick 1989; Low 1999a). Most of the time, anthropologists have preferred to study vari-ously defined enclaves within cities – ethnic ghettoes, occupational groups, reli-gious communities, particular spatially delimited districts or kinds of place (e.g., Hannerz 1969; Burdick 1993; Bourgois 1995; Caldeira 1996; Baumann 1996; Bestor 1999; Low 2000; Herzfeld 2009).[17] More 'panoramic' anthropological studies of cities have tended to focus on political economy and planning (e.g., Epstein 1973; Holston 1989; Rabinow 1989).

Recent theory in social science, rather than being overwhelmed by the immense complexity of the phenomena it seeks to study, embraces the dynamism and incoherence or 'messiness' of social life (e.g., Deleuze and Guattari 1987; Mol and Law 2002; Law 2004; Latour 2005; Massey 2005). In this context, the unique heuristic potential of anthropology's beacon method – ethnography – comes to the foreground in new ways. The challenge of urban ethnography has long been the incompatibility of the traditional requirement of a spatially bounded 'field' as a necessary condition of the ethnographic enterprise (Gupta and Ferguson 1997; cf. Candea 2007) with the empirical unboundedness and turbulent nature of city life. But, as mentioned above, ethnography also means a commitment to an epistemology that values partial truths and ever shifting perspectives and recognizes its object of study – 'culture' or 'social life' – as an always-already changing configuration of partially connected fragments (Clifford 1986; Strathern 1995, 2004). What anthropologists do is inquire as to how those bits and pieces come to be arranged and rearranged; how the connections among them are provisionally stabilized and unmade.

Thus, despite the challenges, I would argue that anthropology may be particularly well equipped to explore and theorize cities as heterogeneous and constantly morphing sites of abundant, open-ended action. Low (1999a: 2) postulates that 'the city' in anthropological writing should not be a 'reification', but a focus of study, a heuristic frame for research. The methodological objective, then, is to observe performances and processes that occur within and constitute the city treated as a necessarily 'unstable and shifting frame of reference' (Latour 2005: 24). In certain ways, such an approach resembles the manner in which city dwellers experience their cities: from the innumerable particular interactions with space, built forms and other human actors arises a shifting, indeterminate sense of the city as a whole.

As AbdouMaliq Simone (2004) ethnographically shows with several African examples, the city is usually a perpetual 'work in progress', contingently assembled by residents and other actors who creatively, and with a lot of effort, draw on local and translocal resources to patch up the social and material fabric of place. Similarly, the recent ethnography of Berlin's central square, Alexanderplatz, by Gisa Weszkalnys (2010) conveys the notion of the city as an ongoing becoming, composed of spatial and temporal elements and perspectives that 'relate but don't add up' (Mol and Law 2002: 1). Weszkalnys speaks of Alexanderplatz as 'multiple' (drawing on Mol 2002) – that is, an object distributed across time and space; a place simultaneously constituted by events of diverse kinds, occurring within its shifting confines as well as far away: planning symposia in the town hall, political rallies, artistic happenings, informal get-togethers, hanging out.

Such an understanding of cities is congruent with the approach to place and space as continually crafted through a plurality of disparate, connected but not necessarily compatible, diversely situated practices. It also jibes well with the discussion of scale earlier in this introduction. For the perennial anthropological difficulty in studying cities was essentially a matter of scale. The city was just too big for the ethnographer to get a grip on, while on the other hand studies conducted inside neighbourhoods or with particular resident groups seemed inadequate as bases of inferences regarding the totality of city life. Yet the approach to cities as 'multiple' offers a way not so much out of this conundrum as to thrive on it. It consists in seeing all scales, both infra-urban and supra-urban – say, from a relationship between flatmates to a transcontinental network of migration or exchange – as mutually reflected in one another, sort of fractal-like (cf. Gleick 1988; Strathern 2004), and continually reproduced in interactions occurring in far-flung locations. 'The city' is then one of those scales, ever provisionally stabilized, and embedded in the ongoing productivity of places and spaces. Studying it ethnographically entails exploring the very multiplicity and heterogeneity of the situations in which it is being constructed, and of the locales where that occurs.

Rather than focusing on any one site, my book expands outward from a range of different locations within the built texture of Astana, such as the kitchen described in the opening vignette – or a courtyard, a street, a square, a ruined factory – and from the quotidian practices that they enable, such as joke-telling, socializing, walking or participating in spectacles. This plurality of viewpoints helps grasp the complexity of the city as it is lived and imagined – the variety of ways in which heterogeneous performances and processes specifically interweave in forming these diverse sites (Askew 2002). Moreover, this choice of a kind of 'multi-sitedness' (Marcus 1995) within one city – 'one' and simultaneously 'multiple' – highlights that each particular perspective, every individual location within Astana acquires its specific meanings through relations to other sites; each moment – actual or virtual – acquires its qualities by being imbricated with plural pasts and futures co-present in the built environment. Together, these sites and moments – each of which is itself multiple, a criss-crossing – give rise to 'Astana' as the ever-shifting, incoherent and open-ended 'whole', not a system but rather an assemblage (Deleuze and Guattari 1987) that becomes the focus of political and personal projects, the reference frame for imagining selves and worlds, and for wagers on the future.

Fieldwork in the 'City of the Future'

This book draws on thirteen months of continuous ethnographic fieldwork in Astana between June 2008 and July 2009, supplemented by several short visits later on. An approach to city life that deliberately adopts a plurality of foci, as outlined above, creates specific challenges when translated into a fieldwork methodology. The perspectives explored in the chapters below are all partial, all more or less loosely connected fragments. This has been a conscious choice that I, as researcher, made. In part, however, this multiplicity of partly disjointed viewpoints was imposed upon me by the conditions of urban fieldwork. Living on my own in a rented apartment (in a Soviet-era neighbourhood), I was often alone and with not much in particular to do – paradoxically, perhaps, given the maelstrom of activity that defines the urban. I was concerned about the lack of that round-the-clock intimacy with informants that forms a part of the romantic image of ethnographic fieldwork. When all my local friends and acquaintances were busy at work or university (where I could rarely follow) and I was not having an appointment with a city planner or a neighbour for a more or less informal 'interview', I often kept myself busy walking the city street by street.

Partly, it was these walks that made me realize the importance of space and its complexity – from the newest monumental plazas to the dusty semi-rural back alleys – for the dynamics of social formation underway in Astana. (Initially, I had thought this would be a book about time, and more narrowly focused on the most recent buildings as futuristic fantasies. Only gradually did I realize that time itself was 'messy' – that is to say, that the 'future' was plural and could not be easily separated from multiple 'pasts' and 'presents' – and inextricably entangled with material space.)

Basically, I built three open-ended networks of informants. One, which began with Mira, the daughter of my first host-family during a pre-fieldwork trip, consisted of young people, roughly between eighteen and thirty years of age: ethnic Russians, other Slavs and Russophone Kazakhs, with broadly 'middle-class' backgrounds (through, economically, there was a world of difference between, say, Sputnik – the son of a high-ranking government official, and Kirill – the son of a working-class family, who had not finished higher education, worked as a salesman, moonlighted as a taxi driver and lived with his wife and child in a dorm provided through his wife's work; see Chapter 2). The parents of some of these young people became important informants too, such as Sasha and Olga in Chapter 1. My second network included Kazakh migrants from small towns and villages scattered across Kazakhstan. What brought them together was that they were all low-ranking employees of a biotechnological research institute (mostly, lab hands or administrative clerks rather than scientists) where my other early host, Bakytgul' – a female migrant from the east Kazakhstani countryside (see Chapters 1 and 2) – worked. They earned little by local standards (say, the equivalent of one hundred and fifty Euros a month), and most of them occupied rented rooms in the old part of the city. The third network consisted of the residents of the apartment block where I lived. I characterize this group at some length in Chapter 5 – basically, they were Russians or other Slavs, between their forties and seventies, and most of them had lived for most or all of their lives in Tselinograd/Astana. Finally, there were also people I met casually beyond these networks and then followed (for instance, Sultan in Chapter 1); local university contacts; and experts such as city planners and architects. Other than my own observation and the analysis of public discourses (media content, officials' speeches and the like), the bulk of my knowledge of Astana derives from 'deep hanging out' (Geertz 1998) with members of these different groups, sharing with them the experience of various places across the city, and from hours upon hours of conversations in which they generously shared with me their reflections about living in Astana.

Initially, I worried about the compartmentalization of my informant networks. However, I gradually came to accept that this reflected the fact that most urbanites, as James Ferguson notes, know one another in a specific way: 'some quite well, some only in passing, others in special-purpose relationships that [can give a researcher] detailed knowledge of some areas of their lives and almost none of others' (1999: 21). Had I decided to access other groups (for instance, non-Russian-speaking poor Kazakh rural migrants; or members of the professional elites) this would have become a very different book. But such relativity of perspectives is, as noted, a feature of both city life and the ethnographic enterprise.

* * *

It remains briefly to outline the chapters that follow. Chapter 1 begins by exploring how Astana is constructed – both materially and imaginatively – as a utopian place; a social environment designed to transcend the constraining conditions of the past and the present and to materialize a desired future. The outline of the official ideology accompanying the city's development since the capital relocation, begun in this introduction, is complemented in Chapter 1. I reconstruct a historical narrative common among post-Soviet urban residents that depicts the period immediately after the collapse of the Soviet Union as a time of breaking social ties, disrupting material connections and the almost literal decomposition of 'modernity'. Against that background, I follow individual actors in Astana pursuing their own projects of 'modernity' and 'modern' personhood in relation to images and expectations of 'the city of the future' and amidst heterogeneous material landscapes. This casts in sharp relief some of the ambiguities and contradictions inherent in the emergence of the new capital.

In Chapter 2, the ethnographic focus remains attuned to the personal experience of migrants engaging with the material and social environment to perform their desired styles of personhood. Drawing on five personal accounts that cover a range of different experiences of gradually settling in the city, I highlight the relationship between contemporary expectations of 'modernity' and 'urbanity' and Soviet-era ideals of 'modern' urban 'culture'. I follow how individuals' efforts to perform particular models of personhood were reciprocally related to constructing Astana as a place imbued with specific, though variously defined, characteristics: 'modernity', 'worldliness', or 'rurality' and 'backwardness'; and how constructing 'urbanity' entailed also the inscription of the 'rural' into the urban social and material landscape. Moreover, this is linked to dynamics of collective identification, as individuals' efforts to become 'modern urbanites' involved drawing distinctions between groups. While scholarly discussions of collective identity in post-Soviet Central Asia have usually emphasized such ascriptive categories as ethnicity and nationality, my analysis highlights a notion of identities as embodied, performed and intrinsically linked to the qualities of place.

Chapter 3 shifts from the narratives of recent migrants to long-standing, Soviet-era residents. The analysis reaches back in history to reconstruct the reiterative efforts, over decades, to create urban 'modernity' in Tselinograd – underscoring the ambiguous relationships between contemporary and Soviet-era visions of modernity. The chapter examines how long-standing residents, confronted with spatial and social transformations in the wake of independence and the capital relocation, draw on narratives of Soviet-era modernization to assert their belonging in the city and, I argue, in 'modernity'. Nostalgic discourses emphasizing the residents' intimate connectedness to place and quotidian spatial practices such as walking help reconstruct Tselinograd in the present as an alternative chronotope of collective belonging. Moreover, the chapter highlights the ambiguities inherent in the category of 'rurality': on the one hand, in a sequence of different colonizing narratives over decades (or indeed centuries), rurality is recurrently construed as the bothersome condition that requires a modernizing intervention to overcome it; yet simultaneously, in the present-day nostalgic reconstructions of Tselinograd by its former residents, rurality is emphasized to enhance the sense of intimate local 'community'.

Chapter 4 further elaborates on the relations between long-standing urban residents and more recent migrants, and how those relations connect to the material and imaginational constructions of city space in the past and the present. Concentrating on public holiday celebrations in the central squares of Tselinograd and Astana, a more specific spatial focus is adopted in this chapter. Accordingly, the chapter compares Soviet-era and present-day meanings and uses of 'public space' in the city, exploring a novel angle from which to consider ongoing scholarly debates on this topic. I argue that official holiday celebrations in central squares serve to communicate to audiences of primarily rural migrants an image of Astana as the 'city of the future' and a collective identity of 'Astanaians' (*astanchane*). Yet the absenteeism of long-standing urbanites and certain other groups of migrants implies a challenge to official meanings of who can claim being 'modern' and 'urban' subjects. Thus, public holidays, although ostensibly monopolized by official discourse, become an arena in which contests over collective identities, belonging, the qualities of place and the shape of the future are played out.

In Chapter 5, the focus then shifts away from 'public' space and into the nooks and crannies of a Soviet-era residential neighbourhood. The chapter illustrates how place, local actors and the specific temporal rhythms of place-making emerge out of a plurality of contingently interweaving translocal agencies, alongside, apart from, despite and sometimes against official city planning. This analysis underscores the unruliness and instability of place and emphasizes the roles of heterogeneous material items in enabling and constraining human performance in place-making. I ethnographically follow a group of long-standing residents engaged in patching up the infrastructure of their apartment block and the adjacent courtyard out of available scraps, at a time when the attention of city-planning authorities was concentrated on producing the new urban landscape elsewhere in the city. Through the residents' improvised creative labour, place was constructed at once materially and as imbued with memories and meanings. However, a conjunction of factors – including shifting legal and economic conditions, migration, changes within the city administration, personal relationships among neighbours and the recalcitrance of material elements of the infrastructure – eventually led to the residents' losing what little control they had over their block. To the committed residents, that meant an unravelling of locality.

Finally, Chapter 6 follows the players of 'Encounter', a game that consists in exploring industrial ruins, incomplete buildings and other dark 'capillaries' of the city, and staging outlandish, surrealistic scenes in public space. Playing Encounter was a particularly engaging research method that gave me a visceral, sensorial kind of knowledge *of* (rather than *about*) Astana's material space – a knowledge that it has been a challenge to translate into text. If I have ever 'gone native' (Kuhn 1970, cited in Tresch 2001: 313) for brief moments, it was surely during these games. Although played by only a couple hundred (mostly young and relatively affluent) people, I argue that the game offers an especially revealing perspective on the themes of this book. The bulk of the book examines various actors' attempts to stabilize visions of place, time and social order through engagements with the built environment. The Encounter game and its players, in contrast, inject the surreal and the subjunctive into the 'archi-texture' of the city (Lefebvre 1991 [1974]: 118). Exploding the cultural codes of built space into a flurry of ephemeral hybrid configurations, the game brings a radically open horizon of possibility to the fore. Moreover, by enlivening industrial ruins and other parts of the city more usually deemed obsolescent or abandoned, and by enacting fantasies drawn from Soviet historical themes, Encounter animates Tselinograd not just as a nostalgic retrospection but rather a living material-and-imagined time-space. Thus, Chapter 6 emphasizes the radical openness of urban space to the heterogeneity of creative social performances. This is followed by a brief conclusion in which I chart some of the broader implications of the case of Astana for the study of urban transformation and power.

Notes

1. The names and nicknames of all informants appearing in this book are pseudonyms, unless otherwise specified. Most informants are referred to with their (fictionalized) first names only, yet – following the custom in the Russian language – those informants who were considerably older than me and with whom I maintained more formal relations are called with their first names and patronymics (e.g., in Chapter 3, Maria Pavlovna, or in Chapter 5, Mikhail Petrovich).

2. A forthcoming book by anthropologist Alima Bissenova (n.d.) based on her doctoral dissertation (2012) studies the liaison between the aspirations of an emerging urban middle class in Kazakhstan's largest cities, including Astana, and the 'state' that caters to those constituencies by developing 'modern' urban environments. Other than Bissenova's work, an early exploratory article by Victor Buchli (2007), and my own work (Laszczkowski

2011a, 2011b, 2014, 2015, 2016, forthcoming), the scholarly attention that Astana has attracted so far comes primarily from political science and geography. This work has tended to focus on elite discourses and strategies of state-building and government (Schatz 2004b; Koch 2012a; Fauve 2015). Scholars have also inquired about the official and unofficial motives that led President Nazarbaev and his allies among the ruling elite to relocate the capital. Official explanations centre on geopolitics (the old capital Almaty's dangerous proximity to China), logistics (Astana's geometrically more 'central' location, the argument goes, being more suitable for creating a transportation and communication hub) and even seismology (Almaty lies in an earthquake-prone zone at the foot of the Tian Shan). Unofficially, commentators have spoken about reshuffling power-elites (Schatz 2000a, 2000b; Cummings 2005) and about plans to diminish Russian domination in Kazakhstan's north – the legacy of Soviet-era resettlements – and pre-empt the threat of separatism (Kaiser and Chinn 1995; Kolstø 1998; Wolfel 2002; Anacker 2004). Astana has, moreover, been interpreted as an attempt to legitimate the regime through an ostentatious display of wealth (Matveeva 2009: 1105) and as a central element in Kazakhstan's 'branding' as a successful, progress-oriented 'Eurasian' nation-state (Marat 2010). In general, the project has been seen as an attempt to rally the citizenry around a 'national idea' and thus tackle the 'identity dilemma' with which, according to many scholars, the old-new elite was confronted (Akiner 1995; Svanberg 1996; Holm-Hansen 1999; Kolstø 1999; Malkova, Kolstø and Melberg 1999; Odgaard and Simonsen 1999; Olcott 2002; Dave 2007).

3. Additionally, in 1999, the capital of Malaysia was relocated from Kuala Lumpur to Putrajaya; in 2005 the capital of Myanmar (Burma) was transferred from Yangon to Naypyidaw; and in 2006 the Pacific island republic of Palau changed its capital from Koror to Ngerulmud. In turn, looking back in history, Turkey's Ankara (1923) (Çinar 2007; Batuman 2009) and Australia's Canberra (1927) (Beer 2008) can be considered antecedents of that trend. Strictly speaking, Turkey had of course never been colonized. However, Ankara was built to assert the change from the Ottoman imperial regime, nineteenth-century Europe's (in)famous 'sick man', to the youthful, progress-oriented Republic. The nationalistic rhetoric of the republican government prefigured the postcolonial nation-building ideologies of the latter half of the twentieth century (Bozdoğan 2001).

4. It should be noted that Brazil had since 1822 been an independent state, and so its capital relocation did not occur in an immediately postcolonial context as was the case elsewhere (Schatz 2004b: 115).

5. For a general overview of the Kazakhstani political system, see Cummings (2005); Olcott (2002); Schatz (2004a).

6. The marginal presence of two other parties was restored in the 2012 elections, which nonetheless returned an 80 per cent vote for Nur Otan and were characterized by international observers as 'orchestrated' (Radio Free Europe 2012).

7. On the latter project, Nazarbaev University, see Koch (2015a).

8. Calling Kazakhstan's population 'multi-ethnnic' refers to the fact that, as a legacy of its complicated history (especially during the Soviet period), the country is inhabited by over a hundred officially recognized 'nationalities and ethnic groups'. The Kazakhs numbered 53 per cent in 1999, and 63 per cent ten years later; the second largest group are Russians, with 30 and later 24 per cent (Agentstvo 1999: 11, 2011a: 20; see Chapter 2).

9. It is worth noting that in the late twentieth century large architectural projects were sometimes undertaken not to reinforce domination, but to represent and help empower

previously disenfranchised peoples such as the Kanak of New Caledonia, the Australian Aborigines, the Black natives of South Africa or the Blacks of the U.S. South (Findley 2005).

10. See also, with regard specifically to urban space and built forms: Castells (1977, 1978, 1983); Harvey (1985a, 1985b, 1989); Hillier and Hanson (1984); King (1980); Lefebvre (2003b [1970]).

11. The political implications of the place-space binary are ambivalent. As Agnew also remarks (2005: 83), 'place' is often assumed to be the locus of nostalgia and conservatism, while 'space' represents the transcending of the past and is seen as open to progress.

12. Although in the Soviet Union and other officially socialist countries built space was explicitly produced with the goal of constructing an altered future society (Kotkin 1995; Crowley and Reid 2002; Humphrey 2005), Lefebvre pondered whether 'state socialism' had managed to produce its proper, qualitatively specific space. 'The question is not unimportant', he argued, for 'a revolution that does not produce a new space, has not realized its full potential; indeed it has failed in that it has not changed life itself, but has merely changed ideological superstructures, institutions or political apparatuses' (1991: 54). Yet, Lefebvre found himself constrained to leave the question unanswered (ibid.). Similarly, as I have outlined above, it is ambivalent to what extent the developments in Astana break with Soviet patterns in space production. However, as explored in the chapters that follow, the government-orchestrated production of space significantly creates conditions for multiple, multifaceted and indeterminate dynamics of social change.

13. On the problems entailed by the concept of community, see, e.g., Creed (2006).

14. In this sense, place-making practices are worlding practices, in Ong's (2011) sense cited above.

15. One practical challenge during writing has been the quickly changing material landscape of Astana. New buildings and vast neighbourhoods have continued to grow, while old squares have been refurbished, monuments removed and replaced, and so forth. The forms of social action enabled by those various sites have been shifting as well. The past tense used generally in the bulk of this book refers to the main period of fieldwork from 2008–2009. Occasionally in the text, however, I have decided to highlight this continuously morphing character of the site and subject matter of this research.

16. Early classics of urban sociology sought to construct rational coherent models of the city (Simmel 1969 [1903]; Spengler 1969 [1922]; Weber 1978 [1905]; also Redfield 1969 [1947]; Redfield and Singer 1969 [1954]). However, both Georg Simmel (1969 [1903]) and Max Weber (1978 [1905]) identified heterogeneity, diversity and excess as defining features of urban living. Sociologists of the Chicago School later attempted to sort out and map that diversity and dynamism, depicting zones of different qualities and the flows and relations between them, similar to ecological models or meteorological charts (Park 1968 [1925]; Wirth 1969 [1938]; see also Hannerz 1980: 19–58). Yet, in 1970, Henri Lefebvre, seeking to define 'the urban problematic', again emphasized movement, contradiction, the proliferation of difference and the impossibility of closure (2003b: 171–78).

17. Recently, this approach has developed to produce studies of transnational, deterritorialized, mobile or 'floating' groups within and between cities (e.g., Appadurai 1996; Ong 1999; Zhang 2001).

Chapter 1

Materializing the Future
Images and Practices

On 6 July 2009, at ten in the morning, the bright sun was high above Astana.[1] Despite the scorching heat, large crowds had gathered to watch the show 'Astana: The Music of Life', a highlight of the three-day-long central pageantry of Astana Day – a national holiday that had been added to the official calendar the year before to celebrate the anniversary of Astana's capital status.[2] The broad, monumental stage was decorated with large silhouettes of a selection of the city's most recognizable new buildings. Each of those was initially in pieces: the bottom half on one side of the stage, the top half on the other. In the forefront, there were colossal mythical winged horses. In the background, scaffolding supported a giant image of two ancient Turkic warriors and a *shanyrak* symbol[3] such as in the city's emblem. People were taking their seats.

When it was announced that President Nazarbaev was approaching, the audience stood up to watch and to welcome him with an ovation. Then, the show began with the sound of bells tolling. Young men and women wearing neat and clean construction workers' outfits started appearing on the stage. Their number grew steadily until they were as many as a hundred. They danced a lively modern dance while the great silhouettes began moving, each half towards its counterpart, so that the buildings were becoming whole. The music was loud and aggressive, uplifting and triumphant, an industrial warrior dance incorporating the sounds of construction work. Flashing plumes of sparks and smoke spurted out intermittently from tubes mounted high on the scaffolding. This lasted for some time. In a culminating moment, the poster with the warriors slid down to reveal a different background: a giant green map of Astana, with the city's emblem on top and big red letters reading, in Kazakh, 'Happy Birthday, Astana!' (*Tughan kuningmen, Astana!*). Behind this theatrical representation of construction works, actual buildings in mid construction – with scaffoldings and cranes – could be seen (Figure 1.1).

Figure 1.1 'Astana: The Music of Life', 6 July 2009 (photo: M. Laszczkowski)

As soon as the 'building work' on the stage was complete, all the dancer-workers stood in rows at the back, and the president stepped up to a rostrum. He spoke first in Kazakh and then in Russian. He said Astana Day was already well established as a 'true holiday' for 'the entire nation', celebrated 'in all corners of Kazakhstan'. The president emphasized Astana's economic role: he spoke about nationwide progress stimulated by the development of the capital, about the jobs it created and about Astana's rapidly rising share of Kazakhstan's GNP. He underscored that Astana was the 'centre of Kazakhstan, of Central Asia and of all Eurasia'. Nazarbaev argued that the Kazakhstanis had 'accomplished the impossible': built 'a new city in the steppe' in just a decade. Hence, he concluded, they were ready to face any challenge and Kazakhstan's future was 'even brighter' than the present. Finally, the president wished Astana and the entire country well-being, prosperity and further development.

The show took place in a recently created monumental area. The stage was placed in front of the pyramid-shaped Palace of Peace and Reconciliation (Figure 1.2), which sits in a riverside park amid a carefully arranged landscape of gentle green hillocks, fountains and streams, and against an impressive vista of the bright, architecturally eclectic government quarter across the river.[4] The stands for the audience were arranged at the foot of another recent landmark, the Monument to the Kazakh Land, officially inaugurated on Astana Day 2008 – a white marble obelisk reaching 91 metres (for 1991, the year of Kazakhstan's independence), topped by a golden eagle-like bird (Samruk) spreading its wings.

Figure 1.2 Palace of Peace and Reconciliation, 'the Pyramid' (photo: M. Laszczkowski)

Behind that monument, there was the deep blue glass trapezoid of the Palace of Independence with a lattice of white pipes on the facade, reminiscent of the support structure of a yurt – the traditional dwelling of Central Asia's pastoral nomads. Nazarbaev said he found it 'deeply symbolic' that the event was taking place amid these buildings, which, according to him, reflected eternal key values for the Kazakhs: first, 'the land, which had always been hospitable to more than a hundred nationalities'; second, independence; and third, 'peace and accord amid the population'. Although the Palace of Independence had been ceremoniously opened in December 2008, half a year later construction work was still in progress both there and at the neighbouring, similarly coloured, crater-shaped futuristic Palace of Creativity. As of summer 2009, this area was flanked with top-end apartment estates under construction. Although envisioned as Astana's future centre, currently it occupied a rather peripheral location along the southern margin of the city. Just several years ago this used to be a suburban dacha area, and garden plots, some of them abandoned, doomed to be cleared for further development, still lay near the palaces before they gave in to untamed grasslands. Thus, the venue for the Astana Day show had an exciting feel of newness, a 'first furrow' not just of nation-state monumentality but also, and crucially, of a new architectural modernity, an unfolding skyscraper civilization on the borderland between the city and the steppe.

This chapter draws both on the excitement and the uncertainty of that moment, taking up the themes of construction and its representation to begin exploring the social and political effects of building work and the built environment in Astana. As the show suggests, Astana was constructed as a 'real-and-imagined' place (Soja 1996) through a process in which actual building work intertwined with 'construction' in a more metaphorical but not less important sense of the work of images and performances, discourse and imagination. As though one of Italo Calvino's (1978) *Invisible Cities*, Astana seemed to have a double nature: imagined and material reality mirrored, pervaded, supported and determined one another. Unlike in Calvino's case, though, this was not a matter of poetic metaphor; rather, the 'two Astanas' were aspects of a single social reality, complex and ridden with implicit contradictions.

As indicated in the introduction, from the viewpoint of government ideology, the construction works in Astana were tantamount to state-building, mobilizing citizens around an elite-defined imagery of progress. Astana was to be an exemplary capital. It was also to become a 'rational and critical utopia' (Holston 1989: 85) – a model for the transformation of the country and its citizens, a harbinger of 'modernity' and a 'locomotive' to drive Kazakhstan into the desired future and away from present conditions and past burdens.[5] But what the show as described above obliterates is the role of spectators as crucial and wilful performers. Just as a theatrical performance would make no sense without viewers, so the performance of statehood requires active involvement of the citizen public (cf. Navaro-Yashin 2002; Reeves, Rasanayagam and Beyer 2014)', and so the construction of Astana depended on the wilful involvement of hundreds of thousands of individual residents and incomers. More generally, as Marshall Berman (1988) shows, 'modernity' is not just a project of rulers. Rather, the condition of modernity implies that 'everyone' becomes a 'developer' who struggles with shifting conditions to make oneself at home in the maelstrom of social and material transformation and lend particular qualities to one's self and one's environment. The work of crafting alternative social 'worlds' consists of everyday situated practices.

For these reasons, to follow how Astana was constructed as an environment at once material and imagined, in which to work out new visions of social order and agentive personhood, requires shifting between several sets of lenses: describing the new architectural landscape; analysing official discourse and visual representations; and following personal narratives by migrants who moved to Astana hoping to partake in the city's development. On Astana Day, the bleachers were filled with a thousand spectators who had come to participate in the celebration of the construction of Astana and all that it stood for, and further thousands swarmed behind the perimeter fence the police had put up around the venue. Every day, individuals arriving to Astana from all corners of Kazakhstan strove and desired to make themselves and their own environment meaningfully and satisfyingly modern. State-orchestrated building work and imaginational construction of Astana entangled in complex, mutually conditioning ways with their quotidian agency. This chapter charts how individual actors engaged with the process of material development of the city, its various images and constructions of the past and the future. The building boom and the growth of the city offered them possibilities for employment, a career and personal improvement – in short, the realization of a desired future in the present. As I outline in the next section, construction seemed to offer a way out of the incapacitating state of disorder that had ensued in the wake of the collapse of the Soviet Union. Yet, as the rest of the chapter demonstrates, the material realities of actually living in Astana were often much more ambiguous. Although the show just described suggests the 'city of the future' miraculously materialized within the time span of a well-choreographed dance, the personal narratives that follow show how in the everyday experience of individual residents the building of the future was rather a protracted, contingent and far from simply linear process marked with a variety of improvised rhythms.

Deconstruction, Reconstruction

To most residents of Kazakhstan, as of most other parts of the former Soviet Union, the early and mid 1990s were a time of decay, atrophy, deprivation, rapid disappearance of vital safeguards and the questioning or outright abolition of values previously taken for granted (Bridger and Pine 1998; Burawoy and Verdery 1999; Humphrey 2002b; McMann 2007; Alexander 2009a, 2009b). Still today, a common way of referring to the post-perestroika period is 'when everything was collapsing/tumbling down/falling into ruin' ('*kogda vse valilos'* / *rushilos'*"). In Tselinograd, as today's Astana used to be known in the late-Soviet period, a number of large industrial establishments (such as the TselinSel'Mash, an agricultural-machinery producer renowned throughout the Soviet Union) were shut down and split up. Similarly, rural and urban enterprises, often the sole basis of a town's or a region's subsistence, collapsed across the former USSR. This affected the majority of the urban population because entire living quarters had been managed by those enterprises. Former employees of the factories and of many related establishments – including teachers, nurses and accountants, especially women – took to petty bazaar trading. Rural inhabitants found themselves backed into even tighter corners (Yessenova 2003). Virtually all of my informants old enough to have been professionally active in the late 1980s and early 1990s recall those events with dread or grief.

Previously, under the Soviet order, people, things and meanings had been knitted together by networks of fixed relations, generally familiar to the citizens. 'The state' found ubiquitous material presence in infrastructures, utility networks, workplaces, kindergartens, schools and hospitals, and even family housing with adjacent playgrounds (Alexander 2004, 2007a; Collier 2004, 2010; Humphrey 2005). The presence and functioning of the Soviet state was also manifested in the performance of fundamental, everyday forms of social relations that those material forms enabled and mediated. Functioning material connections in the built environment epitomized social connection. Associated with this was a teleology according to which society was developing towards communism as a version of modernity (cf. Hoffmann 2000). Such development entailed a sequence of progressive transformations of the material environment as well as of citizens' subjectivity. While neither the citizens nor the ideologues themselves necessarily believed in it on any fundamental personal level, the narrative provided a conceptual framework with which to go about social life (Yurchak 2006). Social reality was riddled with contradictions (ibid.), yet it was relatively known and navigable.

In the wake of perestroika and the subsequent break-up of the Soviet Union, those vital relationships among people, things and ideas were reshuffled. The Soviet state was abolished and its new incarnation, the independent republic, long seemed highly uncertain. To this day, many former Soviet citizens, while not necessarily 'nostalgic' about the Soviet reality – too aware of its many dark sides – recall the foregone time as one when there at least used to be some order and sense of purpose. Afterwards, as one of my neighbours in Astana – a chain-smoking, choleric retired operator of heavy construction vehicles – would frequently grumble, post-Soviet Kazakhstan seemed a total 'mess' (*bardak*). Another elderly informant succinctly summarized the change that had occurred, playing on the root meaning of the Russian word 'perestroika', derived from the verb 'to build' (*stroit*): 'Everything's been taken apart, with this ... *rasstroika* ... *stroika* ... [deconstruction ... construction ...]. Something was divided, where's it gone? Now there's nothing, nothing. Where have things gone? Who took them away? ... Nothing's left'. Social order was undermined and – much as James Ferguson (1999) describes for Africa – 'modernity', in the sense of that future state of advancement always almost at hand, seemed cancelled.

While the narrative of 'post-Soviet chaos' (Nazpary 2002), or 'bardak', is a familiar one, and the role of 'mess' or disorder as the conceptual precondition of order has often been highlighted by scholars for colonial, socialist and post-socialist contexts (Mitchell 1988: 80–82; Ssorin-Chaikov 2003: 136–37; Alexander 2009b; Weszkalnys 2010: 68–88), the words of the gentleman just quoted additionally point to the salience of construction as a key metaphor in Soviet and post-Soviet thinking about social order – and to that metaphor's inherent ambiguity (see Pelkmans 2003). Construction is a particularly convenient, even compelling, figure for the social processes of transforming reality by creating stable and coherent forms out of multiple elements – as much for social scientists (as in 'social construction of reality') as for real-life actors on the ground. In the Soviet Union, the Party and the citizens were ever 'building socialism' – at least so the official ideology had it (Kotkin 1995; Ssorin-Chaikov 2003: 110–39). Finally, Gorbachev's attempt to 'reconstruct' (*perestroit*) the system inadvertently led to its 'chaotic' deconstruction. Yet, as the spectacle described above suggests, in Astana the construction metaphor was to make a spectacular comeback. It was in the context of the mid 1990s economic collapse and social atrophy that President Nazarbaev announced his wish to relocate Kazakhstan's capital to

Aqmola. Initially met with confusion and disbelief, the idea of constructing a new capital, however, responded to many citizens' desire for renewed ordering.[6]

Let us look at the story of post-Soviet destruction, the subsequent Kazakhstani capital relocation and the construction boom in Astana from the point of view of the biographic experience of individual participants. Sasha and Olga are construction engineers. They were in their forties and had been living in Astana for about ten years when I met them there in 2008. They were originally from Temirtau, a town in central Kazakhstan, approximately 200 kilometres south-east of Astana, just north of Karaganda. By the end of the 1990s, Temirtau had fallen into the worst state of post-Soviet decline. The town had been dependent on an enormous metallurgical complex that had collapsed. Unemployment was rampant, while those who managed to hold on to their jobs received only irregular and delayed pay. Electricity shutdowns and water shortages had become the bothersome norm rather than annoying intermittent disruptions, and drug addiction rates skyrocketed. Sasha and Olga had completed their education and married right at the time when the USSR fell apart. They spent the 1990s struggling to hold on to their jobs and mastered new survival skills such as exchanging the cigarettes or factory-issued coupons for food; baking bread at home; saving water for drinking and washing, and so forth. Olga remembers that period as a 'total nuthouse' (*durdom polneishii*).

In 1998 Sasha got a temporary assignment as a technical supervisor at a housing development project in Astana. He did well and the following year was offered a permanent position. In 2000 his wife Olga and their school-age son joined him. It was difficult at first: no friends or relatives, unfamiliar places, worries about the child finding his way in a new school, a new setting, a new city. Perhaps hardest of all was that for the first time in many years Olga was unemployed and forced to stay at home. The family was nearly penniless: they had sold their Temirtau apartment for $500 (U.S.), but as Olga evocatively puts it, that amount of money in Astana 'could buy you no more than a doormat', for which they had no door to lay it in front of anyway. They eventually rented a flat, but the rent ate up Sasha's entire salary, the monthly equivalent of $100 (U.S.).

Astana at that time was still not much different than it had been in Soviet days: 'a villagy-village [*derevnia-derevnia*], even worse than Temirtau!' Olga recalls. But soon, she adds, '… within just one year, the city grew as fast as mushrooms, so much was being built!' In 2001 the couple sometimes took walks in the new development areas. With their knowing eyes of professionals they watched foundation pits being dug and poles driven in. Earthworks were being started where the new administrative centre of the capital was to be erected. Olga recounts:

> Those pits, foundations, a hell of a lot of machinery, so many people! …
> I had had no job for a year. And so we walked, Sasha and I, and I said:
> 'Oh my God!' And they were showing it on TV, they were showing
> massive construction work, that hell of a lot of excavators, yeah, the

earthworks, they were still only digging, showing plans, this and that, it was nowhere near any framework anywhere, nothing yet. When I saw all that, that endlessness, everything dug up, I said: 'Sasha, I wanna go to work! I wanna contribute to this with my skills' [laughs]. And so, I got a job, and the city grew in the blink of an eye. Literally within a few years.

This is a personal perspective on the development that was theatrically represented in the spectacle described earlier in this chapter. Discussing Soviet 'frontier villages' in subarctic Siberia, Nikolai Ssorin-Chaikov (2003: 134–39) writes of the disorderliness of mid construction as a signifier of the beginning of progress, implying a promise of completion which, however, may be perpetually deferred. He calls this the 'poetics of unfinished construction'. Yet, Olga's words and the above-described spectacle suggest rather a poetics of quick accomplishment in Astana: change appears rapidly, and the work continues at a fast pace. For Olga and her family, the construction boom following the capital relocation was a turning point. With new career opportunities came a decent income and prospects for a satisfying life. Soon, Olga and Sasha bought a two-bedroom flat in an apartment block of good Soviet quality (in one of the 1960s 'sleeper districts' of old Tselinograd). The couple could afford to dream again: they began saving to purchase a plot of land and get a suburban house built. Crucially, their lives acquired a renewed sense of meaning, progress and direction.

As mentioned in the introduction (and as Chapter 2 elaborates), hundreds of thousands of migrants from across Kazakhstan similarly came to Astana during the 2000s. The main reasons for migration were more or less clearly specified career prospects connected to the development of the new capital. People have been flowing to Astana to study or take up employment offered by state institutions or private businesses, big and small – from oil giants to cigarette kiosks and bazaar stalls. The construction sector had a seemingly insatiable demand for labour, not just for engineers such as Sasha and Olga, but also for thousands of low-skilled or even unskilled labourers from the countryside. To many migrants, such as Sasha and Olga, the construction boom in the new capital offered an unprecedented chance to break away from the incapacitating condition of their home towns and villages – often as badly hit by the post-Soviet social and economic crisis as Temirtau, or perhaps worse – and to regain a sense of personal agency. The migrants' input – not only of those directly involved in building work – was vital to the emergence of 'the city of the future'.

The Cityscape of the Future

The migrants helped create the new cityscape and transform Soviet-built Tselinograd into Astana. The city, a gem of Soviet modernist planning in the

Figure 1.3 The Ishim waterfront (photo: M. Laszczkowski)

1960s (see Chapter 3), thirty to forty years later was just an ordinary mid-size regional industrial centre, unimpressive among the many similar cities scattered across the former empire. The capital transfer to Aqmola/Astana required upgrading the cityscape. Buildings around Central Square and in Prospekt Respubliki (Republic Avenue; formerly Prospekt Tselinnikov [Avenue of the Virgin Land Campaigners]), the city's broadest, most central north-south avenue, were given a face lift, roads were renovated, and an entirely new picturesque waterfront ambience was created on the right bank of the Ishim (Figure 1.3). However, in the 2000s, dynamic architectural growth concentrated primarily on previously undeveloped grounds across the river and on the south-eastern (topographically right-bank) outskirts of the late-Soviet 'sleeper districts'. The unofficial term 'Left Bank' came to be commonly used to designate this entire area of new development beyond former city limits, regardless of which bank of the river a given site was actually located (see Map 1.1).

At the time of writing, Astana is still quickly growing. During the main period of research for this book, the heart of the new cityscape was found on the left bank of the Ishim, along the newly charted, picturesque, pedestrianized, axial Nurzhol Boulevard ('The Way of Light'), with fountains, flower beds, low stone walls and brick paving. This Left Bank 'centre' is enclosed on the east by the massive, barbican-like shining white wall of the House of Ministries, with a narrow opening in the middle guarded by two cone-shaped golden office towers. Behind it, there is the government cluster (Figure 1.4), featuring the skyscrapers

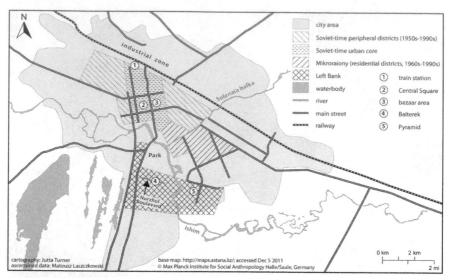

Map 1.1 The growth of the city, 1950s–2000s

Figure 1.4 The buildings of the government, the parliament and the Supreme Court on the Left Bank (photo: M. Laszczkowski)

of the two chambers of the parliament and the council of ministers, the pseudo-classicist colonnaded Supreme Court, the presidential palace under a sky-blue dome and a vessel-shaped turquoise concert hall.

Along Nurzhol Boulevard, east to west, are arranged other grandiose buildings such as the twin elite apartment estates, Nur Saia, with small columns

Figure 1.5 Left Bank housing (Nur Saia) (photo: M. Laszczkowski)

fancifully decorating their facades, and expensive stores and restaurants in the ground floors (Figure 1.5); the large 'Singing Fountain' between them; the army-green dome of the National Archives; an extensive blue-and-white striped office complex comprised of several cubistic buildings; the emerald towers of the residential estate 'Northern Lights' that appear to flicker and swing gently in the wind, the twin skyscrapers of the national railway administration; and the copper-coloured futuristic Ministry of Transport and Communication. At its western end, the boulevard is closed by an ensemble of majestic buildings with brownish glass and tile facades, including the headquarters of the national gas and oil company KazMunaiGaz with a gargantuan passageway in the middle (Figure 1.6). Behind the latter, across a park, stands the semi-transparent tent-shaped shopping centre Khan Shatyr ('Khan's Tent'), one of the world's largest tensile structures, completed in 2010 and signed – like the Pyramid – by the United Kingdom's Norman Foster.

Astana's single most important architectural icon, however, stands midway along the Nurzhol: Baiterek, a vaguely tree-shaped 100 metre tall tower of white metal lattice, with a golden glass orb on top (Figure 1.7). Its form and name allude to a Turkic myth of the Tree of Life and the bird Samruk cyclically laying its egg – the sun, kernel of all life – high in its branches. Virtually ubiquitous in various media in Kazakhstan, the silhouette of Baiterek serves as an icon of the building of the future underway in Astana.

The surfaces of Left Bank buildings are shiny, made of glass, aluminium and synthetic materials. The architectural ensembles feature a variety of sometimes

Figure 1.6 KazMunaiGaz headquarters (photo: M. Laszczkowski)

quite whimsical shapes, colours and stylistic juxtapositions. An 'aesthetic of super-fluity' (Mbembe 2004) dominates the area, which overflows with domes, turrets, decorative columns, loosely Arabian, Persian, Chinese and European-classicistic ornaments, as well as abstract geometrical shapes and hi-tech forms. As Aihwa Ong notes, in the rapidly growing cities of the 'developing world', the produc-tion of material and aesthetic forms intended to prove that the given city and country are truly 'modern' and at least on a par with what are seen as the leading centres in global hierarchies of progress (what she calls 'worlding') often relies on 'promiscuous borrowings [and] shameless juxtapositions' of heterogeneous ideas and images (Ong 2011: 23). In Astana, the architectural collage adds to the city's utopian quality, invoking the fantastic exoticism of the foreign against the shoddiness of the familiar. It is through living in this material utopia – a place of the future today and the abroad at home – that many individuals have hoped to transform themselves as persons.

Becoming 'Contemporary'

Writing about nineteenth-century Parisian shopping arcades built of glass and iron – at that time cutting-edge materials in architecture – Walter Benjamin (1999 [1927–1939]) observed that the aesthetics of built forms were fundamen-tal to the formation of modern political subjectivities. Modernity, to Benjamin, spelled a 're-enchantment' of the world (pace Weber) by the projection of col-lective utopias – visions of social, cultural, economic and political arrangements

Figure 1.7 Baiterek (photo: M. Laszczkowski)

transcending present reality. He argued that those visions were made real inter alia through construction technology. Seeing and touching steel and glass architecture, modern citizens directly experienced the fantastic artificial world – thus aesthetics lent reality to modern utopias (see also Buck-Morss 1983; Cohen 1989).[7] Similarly, the new cityscape that emerged in Astana, largely owing to its unusual materials and forms, materialized a vision of the future in the present. Individual residents and migrants engaged with this utopian 'architexture' (Lefebvre 1991 [1974]: 118) to become new kinds of 'modern' subjects, at home in that vision.

As Michel Foucault (e.g., 1977, 1983) has shown, modern power aims to produce individuals who are not just subject to authority and regulation, but actively reproduce themselves through their everyday practices as productive subjects. Modern city planning contributes to this production of individual subjects by creating ordered environments in which individuals can see themselves fit, find their proper place and be able to act in organized and productive ways (Mitchell 1988; Rabinow 1989). As discussed in the introduction, Soviet city-building was a particularly compelling case in point. In post-Soviet Kazakhstan, the ideological discourse about the construction of Astana revived the idea of moulding citizens through city planning and construction work, although this time the subjects produced were no longer to be socialist but rather adapted to a new vision of capitalist modernity. President Nazarbaev writes about changes to citizens' consciousness brought about by the new cityscape of Astana:

> Ideas of patriotism and citizenhood [*grazhdanstvennost'*] receive their content namely owing to the example of the construction of this city. Thousands of young boys and girls go to the new capital in quest of prospects. … Citizens have developed faith in themselves and their strengths, an awareness of the fact that one's future as well as the future for one's children can and must be built with one's very own hands. (Nazarbaev 2006: 357)

According to Nazarbaev, the transformation of Kazakhstan by means of the building of the capital entails the formation of a new kind of individual citizen subjectivity. While emphasis is placed on individual work ethic (the future is to be worked out 'with one's own hands'), the concept of grazhdanstvennost', which I have found no better way to translate than the admittedly awkward 'citizenhood'[8] (Laszczkowski 2014: 158), ties the desired model of subjectivity clearly to state-building. However, as noted above, the construction of an urban milieu 'of the future' could not be effected by the president's fiat alone. Rather, it depended on the involvement of individual citizens – many long-standing residents of Astana and even more migrants – who strove in their everyday lives to 'become new persons' and make their own environment adequately 'modern'. This of course implies that myriad mundane contradictions, constraints and hesitations rendered the process much more complicated than President Nazarbaev's triumphalist enunciations might suggest.

To numerous citizens, moving to Astana opened opportunities for improvement and a life that would be morally as well as materially satisfactory. It spelled material conditions that could allow those who managed to make it in the new capital to live 'normally' (*normal'no*): to live adequately, as one should (Buchli 2007: 65). Sasha and Olga reckoned that settling in Astana had allowed them to develop as persons. In Olga's words, moving to the capital changed the 'condition of their souls' (*sostoianie dushi*). In comparison, Sasha said that their friends who had stayed in Temirtau had become 'like frogs in the mud'. This dehumanizing metaphor implies that it was only thanks to the active life they were able to lead in Astana that Sasha and Olga, in their view, managed to become properly human. This seems to resonate well with Nazarbaev's above-quoted narrative of Astana transforming citizens' selves, and with Foucauldian analyses of the production of modern individuals as self-reproducing and productive subjects.

But selves are not simply moulded following dominant design, nor freely self-fashioned (Battaglia 1995a). Rather, they emerge out of reiterative encounters and performative practices over time (Butler 1999), as individuals strive to constitute themselves through relationships with their social and material environment. That ongoing effort entails taking advantage of opportunities as well as dealing with constrains – a dialectic of will and hesitation, failure and reprise, making-do and temporary solutions. The role of the built environment is not that of a mould for producing individuals following a template, but rather a complex tissue, both malleable and intransigent, imagined and material, with which individuals engage in mutually constitutive ways, constrained by the skills and resources at hand (Buchli 2000). The personal narratives in the remainder of this chapter complement Sasha and Olga's story to evoke how migrants might imagine their own transformation enabled by the urban environment in Astana, and what difficulties they might come across. By the same token, these narratives highlight how the above-discussed ideological notions of transforming society through architecture and producing 'modern' individuals played out and were transformed in the material practices of everyday life in Astana.

Oraz was born and raised in a former kolkhoz village in a remote southeastern corner of Kazakhstan. After he finished school, he moved to Astana to study biotechnology. When I met him, he lived with his sister in a cheap rented apartment and worked as a lab hand, doubling as a night watchman at a car park. He told me about his past experience and his motives for trying to settle in Astana:

Where I used to live, life had once been at least a bit civilized [*tsivilizo-vanno*]. There used to be kolkhozes, sovkhozes[9] – back in the times of the Soviet Union. ... And then, when the USSR collapsed, everything was taken apart. There was emptiness. Nothing was left. And so we lived, not knowing anything. Then I moved to Astana, the city, only then did I understand what urban life was, no sooner. ... I've gotten to like the city life, all along. ... I don't want my children to grow up like I did, in a village. ... I came [to Astana], saw high-rise houses, new architecture, investments from other countries ... saw this kind of life. This was attractive, because ... you enter, you can see new things there, as if ... your mind receives something new, and you see the new, and you become a contemporary person [*stanovishsia sovremennym chelovekom*].

Further on, Oraz spoke in quite concrete terms of what, in his mind and experience, constituted the urban lifestyle as opposed to village life. One such detail was the habit of showering daily, which had not been possible in his native village. Another was the freedom from coal dust, so ubiquitous in the coal-heated rural houses that, Oraz said, it went unnoticed unless one had experienced living in a city home, where heat was provided from a power plant.

Oraz's narrative is an extremely dense piece of discourse that is necessary to unpack little by little. First, a point where the translation seems to stumble needs to be clarified: Oraz does not make clear what or where it is that 'you enter'. Is he referring to one of the new buildings he just spoke of, or to the city, or perhaps to the new kind of life associated with them? I think this lack of clarity is in fact evocative of a crucial point: the built forms are imagined to encompass, embody and epitomize a set of aesthetic, moral and social qualities. This set remains vaguely defined, yet it goes literally without saying that it is incomparably better than Oraz's way of life back in the village. The architectural forms in Astana epitomize a 'utopian object of impossible fullness' (Hartman 2007, citing Žižek 1999) where 'normality' resides, an ideal of the self and the social. The city is imagined as a locus of an improved future attainable in the present. The improved social relations ('city life') that Astana is expected to foster are to be visually and tangibly reflected in built forms (Oraz's 'high-rise houses, new architecture') and everyday practices.

Let us look at the temporal structure of Oraz's story. There are two different pasts invoked: the distant 'once upon a time' period when the stability of Soviet rural economy ('kolkhozes, sovkhozes') had meant that life had been 'at least a bit civilized'; and the more directly remembered time of collapse, 'emptiness' and confusion ('not knowing anything'). Thus Oraz's account returns to the narrative of post-perestroika destruction of social order discussed above. Upon his arrival in Astana, however, this time of atrophy and hopelessness is replaced by a new temporality that blends the present with an attractive, hope-invested futurity (the time that will belong not only to Oraz but also to his, as yet hypothetical, children). There is no distinction in the Russian language between 'contemporary' and 'modern'. Both translate as *sovremennyi*, literally 'co-temporal', coeval, and this is the word used by Oraz.[10] It is this category – *sovremennost*', modernity/co-temporality (Humphrey 1984: 314) – that is applied to Astana to articulate normative expectations as to the city's material outlook and forms of social life. Oraz's account makes evident that materialities, aesthetics (particularly, of architecture), bodily practices such as cleanliness, lifestyles and subjectivities are all entangled with this notion of modernity, understood at once as a desired social and personal condition and as an evaluative variable.

As is usually the case in modernization narratives, time, both past and future, is spatialized by this evaluative mindset (Ferguson 2005). The past, to be discarded, belongs to the countryside. Sometimes this can be taken quite literally, as by Oraz and other rural migrants whose personal pasts were in the village but whose futures will be, fingers crossed, urban. The future, by contrast, is abroad: it is the abroad's present. Contemporariness (or modernity) is elsewhere – a state of arrangements that lies at a distance, yet to be achieved. Astana is expected to become 'modern' by catching up (becoming 'coeval') with an imaginary world abroad – note Oraz's reference to 'investments from other countries'.[11]

The Roots of Disenchantment, and its Limits

As is implicit in Oraz's narrative, those who see themselves as 'catchers-up' on the road to 'modernity' must creatively deny coevalness to their own societies (Grant 2001; Fabian 2002 [1983];): in order to build the future, they need to accept first that their present is a matter of the past (see also Zhang 2006). However, such a self-denial of coevalness may be difficult to exercise or sustain while real-life actors confront every day the conditions of the present. In Astana, contrasting temporalities became material and seemed to clash directly, as the city was divided into the 'Left Bank' and old former Tselinograd, or even as new glass and steel buildings rose right next to grey concrete apartment blocks from the 1960s or 1970s and clusters of detached mud-brick (*samannye*) dwellings – a situation that was not uncommon in partly reconstructed areas of the right-bank city (Figure 1.8). Many migrants' experience of disconnect between their expectations of Astana and the lived reality they found upon arrival gave rise to disenchantment, from which stemmed critical evaluations of the 'Astana myth' (as one informant put it). Despite that, those migrants, having invested in becoming 'modern' in Astana, made various efforts to sustain the effect of the future in the present. This involved hard quotidian labour to pay rent and make ends meet, as well as stretching the imagination and suspending disillusion.

Sultan, a young X-ray technician originally from a rural area in southern Kazakhstan, spoke about the sense of disparity between the architectural milieu of

Figure 1.8 Old and new buildings side by side in Astana (photo: M. Laszczkowski)

the Left Bank and its representations on the one hand, and his actual experience on the other:

> [If one lives on the Left Bank] then you can say: I live in Astana. …When guests come from back home, we show them the Left Bank right away. Otherwise, they would be like … shocked – around the train station, there are village-like houses all around, no one would have thought! … Even I, when I first came there, first time to Astana – I couldn't see Astana! Only Baiterek was barely visible in the distance! … This is the old city, and that's the new city. … Only when seen on TV, they show it as if everything was beautiful. They use the greatest megapixels, the colours … And people think: 'Oh, oh, oh! Astana's great!' So we show [the guests] precisely what the TV set shows; we show them the same places – that's Astana. And this, the rest, what's this simple something …?

Benjamin (2002 [1936]) noted that the reality-effects of modern utopias ('dream-worlds') were amplified by means of the mechanical reproduction of images, which rendered the experience of modernity collective. In the passage just quoted, Sultan refers to expectations of Astana shaped by images of the city that were widely circulated in various media across Kazakhstan, reproducing and considerably amplifying the effect of the future in the present achieved by architecture. Thus he brings this chapter's argument full circle to the theme of the construction of Astana through images, introduced by the holiday show described at the outset.

Images of selected new buildings from Astana, with a particular emphasis on Baiterek, appeared on television, in the news and in short videos played between programmes; in propaganda visuals displayed in the city's streets and along roads throughout the country; on souvenir knick-knacks; and on every Kazakhstani banknote.[12] Importantly, only a limited number of buildings and locations were always featured, all either Left Bank sights or, less frequently, such picturesque right-bank locations as the new Ishim embankment lined with shiny high-rises. The visuals tended to offer suprahuman vistas, with frequent use of aerial perspectives and broad angles. These were views of vast empty streets or squares with few people present in the frame.[13] The general image conveyed by those visuals was of a pure city of perfect design. For instance, a 2009 series of roadside posters unfolded an impossible panorama composed of out-of-scale images of buildings that in reality are far apart. There was no actual vantage point from which their relative positions could appear as they were in the posters. In short, such visuals created a selective collage of new, decontextualized and displaced extravagant buildings that were to represent Astana; a hyper-reality in Jean Baudrillard's (1983) sense of an order of representation where images precede and determine that which they supposedly represent. It was this image that Sultan had expected to find upon arrival, and he was disappointed to realize that the city also included many parts that were markedly different – and much more mundane.

In the quotation above, Sultan refers also to the practice of showing guests from back home around Astana. He says the sites chosen on such an occasion would be those that always appear on television. A visit to Baiterek would be a highlight of all such tours. At the viewing platform inside the tower's crowning golden orb there was an encased miniature model of the very same landscape stretching down beyond the golden glass bubble.[14] In the words of literary critic Susan Stewart, 'the reduction in scale which the miniature presents skews the time and space relations of the everyday lifeworld', creating 'an "other" time ... which negates ... the flux of lived reality'; it thus 'serves to skew the experience of the social by literally deferring it' (1984: 65–66, emphasis removed).[15] Yet crucially, from high above, the surrounding city itself looks like a miniature model: neat and perfectly organized (Figure 1.9). The decontextualizing 'god-like' (De Certeau 1984: 92) view from above is the perspective of the planner and the ruler; it erases the swarming confusion of actual social relations in favour of a legible order and turns the material environment into a utopia (Scott 1998: 57–58; Lefebvre 2003b: 129–30): at once a perfect place and a place that is not.[16] The views from high up subtly, silently, almost imperceptibly situate the viewer in a utopian position. From the top of Baiterek, no other reality can be perceived but the vistas that combine an attractive variety of shapes and colours with an imposing geometric organization and legibility. Thus, the spatial organization centred on the axis mundi of Baiterek suggests a

Figure 1.9 A view from Baiterek (photo: M. Laszczkowski)

perfect social order – always-already achieved. Few details can be seen, and in particular the Soviet-era part of Astana is blurred in the distance. The city as seen from Baiterek corresponds to the collages of television videos and roadside visuals enhanced by 'the greatest megapixels'. But, as Sultan soon learned, the life on the ground looks much different – though he preferred not to share this bitter awareness with his guests.

Likewise, Bakytgul' recalled that when she had gotten news from a friend about a job for her in Astana, she imagined herself living amid the Left Bank cityscape. She felt disappointed when upon arrival she realized her new work-place was in the old city – and right next to the bazaar, to add insult to injury. The bazaar was just a few blocks from the Soviet-era city centre, but also near to where the rundown industrial zone began, with clusters of semi-legal shabby huts rigged up on every available patch of muddy land. Shortly before Bakytgul''s arrival, in an attempt to 'civilize' the market, the authorities had ordered the building of several box-shaped 'shopping centres' upon the former bazaar rows, and most vendors moved either into those or to a much larger and less regulated bazaar just outside the city limits. Even within the new 'centres', the spaces were tiny and crowded, the goods jumbled, and the cries of hawkers, carriers and cleaners rose above the general hum of the sellers and buyers. Outdoors, a couple of alleys remained, with shipping containers or crude-looking com-partments of bare grey hollow brick for shops, in front of which vendors dis-played their stocks of food, cheap clothes, household utensils, pirated DVDs, sunflower seeds by the jar or the kilo and lengthy plastic tubes filled with the green *nasvai*, a local tobacco-based chewing mash popular among rural men. In the midst of such crowded conditions, buyers elbowed past hawkers and, on a busy day, honking cars crept through the pedestrian crowd. To Bakytgul' the market was the inverse of a 'civilized', 'European' and 'modern' urban form of sociality. By contrast, the Left Bank with its spacious if lightly used prome-nades seemed 'like a European city', which implied proximity to the apex of a global cultural hierarchy of value (see Herzfeld 2005: 66).[17]

Based on what she had seen on television, Bakytgul' had not suspected that a large part of Astana could be so old and unattractive. She found it worse and uglier, she said, than Karaganda, where she had spent several years. She expressed a sense of Calvino-esque disconnect between that 'real-and-imagined' Astana and the broader city: 'At the Left Bank, I still today have a feeling that it's a different city. ... I like it there, it's all beautiful, all good, one wants to be there. ... But to me, it seems that Astana is over there, and this here is simply the right bank'. It was as if a gap was opening between the city of the desired future – already present in the Left Bank – and the immediate lifeworld of the everyday, and individuals such as Bakytgul' and Sultan strove to bridge that gap by stretching their capacity to believe.

In particular, the materiality of one's dwelling played a crucial part in 'becom-ing modern' and evaluating the experience of Astana.[18] As Victor Buchli (2007) demonstrates, the materiality of houses has steadily been a contested index of appropriate or inappropriate social relations at the site of present-day Astana over at least the last two hundred years, and it continues to be interpreted that way today. Sultan, who at the time of this conversation worked two full-time jobs at state hospitals and lived with his wife and a baby in a rented room in the so-called *chastnyi sektor* – an area of 'village-style', coal-heated houses with outside toilets on the fringe of the city (Figure 1.10) – brought this point home:

> If I had a house to myself, my own apartment, then I could say: I live in Astana. As of now, I can't say so ... When my school-time buddies come to visit, I don't even want to show them my place. They think that because I so-called live in Astana, I surely have such a huge pocket, stuffed full of money; they think I live well. But we barely live, to tell the truth.

To improve his condition, Sultan entered a state-run housing programme for young incomers to Astana on the public payroll. His two jobs were not enough to support his family, even with a very basic rented room for a home, so he borrowed money from friends and bought a nineteen-year-old Volkswagen Golf to join the army of Astana's unofficial taxi drivers, working at nights and on weekends. The completion of the housing programme was repeatedly

Figure 1.10 A *chastnyi sektor* house (photo: M. Laszczkowski)

delayed, yet he persisted, seeing himself in a 'waiting room' before entry into a true 'Astana' lifestyle. Sometimes, not dwelling but even the process of having a house built is a claim on belonging in a place (Melly 2010) – or, as in this case, in the future. Sultan's dedication to become a 'modern' person 'truly' belonging in Astana constituted what Pierre Bourdieu (2000) calls illusio: whole-hearted investment in a 'game', immersion in a field that defines the horizon of possible action. As he scrambled to make ends meet in Astana, Sultan kept sending remittances to his relatives back home. When his sister was getting married, he bought her a television set and contributed a thousand U.S. dollars to the wedding – roughly triple his monthly salary. Thus he upheld the belief in the Astana utopia with which he himself was becoming disillusioned. With the family down south as his audience, he carried on with the performance of his new personhood.

To Bakytgul', as mentioned, the greatest disappointment was to find out that her new workplace was located in an unattractive right-bank area next to the bazaar. She had been vaguely promised a new apartment when the company made its planned move to new facilities on the Left Bank, but as the months passed, that plan continued to be postponed, and it was becoming increasingly clear that only the most favoured employees would receive housing. Bakytgul' started learning English to raise her professional skills and thus increase her admittedly minimal chances, but meanwhile she had to put up with basic rooms, rented on a temporary basis, in the dodgier parts of the city (see Chapter 2 for details). Despite becoming increasingly resigned, she wished she had more time to go for walks in the Left Bank (as she did on Sundays), to remind herself that she lived in Astana – already in the future, as it were.

Azamat, a colleague of Bakytgul''s, also hypothetically eligible for one of those Left Bank apartments, reflected on his and Bakytgul''s shared experience in more abstract terms. Equally dissatisfied with the present state of social life in Astana and in Kazakhstan at large, he realized that those many apartments would not solve the greater issue of economic underdevelopment, which he saw as tangential to 'cultural' progress:

> Economic development is one thing, and there's also a matter of cultural development. In these terms, we're at a very primitive stage yet. It must take time. You can't just tell people: from now on, be clever! – and expect they will, right away. It will take time before we stop spitting in the street, or dropping cigarette butts, or seed-shells ... They don't do such things in Europe, right? You've been going to theatres for a long time there ... It's a matter of time.

He paused, gazing at the noisy construction site across the street from his office window, and added: 'I hope it is. And the other option, the pessimistic option, is that this is just it, this is what we are, already done'.

These examples highlight the ambivalence inherent in experiencing the contrast between the propagandized utopia of Astana and the practical realities with which most newcomers to the city, as well as its native inhabitants, were confronted. For Sultan as for many others, the material conditions of living in Astana failed to match utopian expectations. On the one hand, that experience led to disenchantment and provoked criticism of official images and of the political economy that had produced the disparity. On the other, as most evident in Azamat's words, such critiques failed to transcend the logic of the modernization myth that was the political economy's ideological backdrop. Politically, the new model of entrepreneurial, development-oriented citizenhood (grazhdanstvennost') promoted by president Nazarbaev and his ideologues was not easily practicable for individuals who struggled with low salaries, high rents and, as a consequence, disappointing living conditions. In practice, endurance rather than enthusiasm often turned out to be the key attitude that gave substance to citizenhood. However, the patience and perseverance those persons invested in achieving the imagined 'Astana life', despite deferral, were instrumental in reproducing a relationship between citizens and 'the state' founded on the promise of the material development of the capital city.

Although not everyone felt an equal participant in it, some growth was clearly visible in Astana, and the greater the contrast between the 'old' and the 'new', the more seductive the latter seemed. As Timothy Mitchell (1988: 162–65) argues with regard to colonial Arab cities, to present itself as orderly and modern, the city must maintain its own opposite: a disorderly, pre-modern 'Oriental' city. In Astana, the co-presence of new and old buildings and the potential attainability of 'modern', 'European' lifestyles strengthened the commitment of aspiring migrants to the self-directed denial of coevalness: it always seemed to be necessary to work just a little more to become 'contemporary'. It was the migrants' commitment to those ideals that at once rendered the utopian imaginations of Astana critically relevant and the dissonance between utopian visions and material reality excruciating.

The often uneasy imbrications of diverse Soviet and post-Soviet temporalities, visions of the past and the future, and past versions of futurity will come to the foreground again in later chapters. In Chapter 2, the focus remains on the personal experiences of several migrants imagining and working to make themselves and their environment 'modern' and to establish themselves in the emergent social configurations in Astana. Housing will again come to the fore as a key material dimension of these aspirations. A new facet added to the analysis is how collective identities were crafted around the dichotomous pair of concepts: 'urbanity' and 'rurality', articulated in relation to the material environment, in particular to build forms, and everyday bodily practices.

Notes

1. Parts of this chapter were published in Laszczkowski 2011a and 2014.
2. The date of Astana Day commemorates the adoption on 6 July 1996 of a resolution by the Kazakhstani government to transfer the country's capital to the city then still known as Aqmola. As mentioned in the introduction, Aqmola effectively became the capital on 10 December 1997. In 1998, Aqmola was renamed Astana (6 May) and an official presentation of the new capital was held (10 June). Nonetheless, the first nationwide celebrations of Astana Day on 6 July 2008 took place under the banner of Astana's 'tenth anniversary'. As commentators frequently point out, the 6 July holiday coincides with President Nazarbaev's birthday. (For a discussion of other state holidays in post-1991 Kazakhstan, see Chapter 4.)
3. A shanyrak is the circular frame of bent wood placed in the opening at the top of a yurt. A central symbol in Kazakh and Kyrgyz nomadic cosmologies, it is frequently evoked in nation-state symbolism in Kazakhstan as well as in Kyrgyzstan (see Buchli 2007: 52–54).
4. The 'Pyramid' is one of several buildings in Astana signed by the world-famous British architect Norman Foster. However, according to informants cited by geographer Natalie Koch (2012b: 2452–53), the pyramid shape for the building was actually designed by a Kazakh architect, but the government preferred, for publicity, to be able to attach a foreign name of world renown to the structure. So, allegedly, Norman Foster was invited, and he assumed the pyramid form as he redesigned the Kazakh architect's original project.
5. Note, however, how the show above tacitly bypasses not only the Soviet period but also earlier colonial history, linking a projected future directly to an unspecified, semi-mythical past of ancient warriors and winged stallions.

6. On the concept of post-Soviet 'ordering', see Beyer (2009: 18–20).
7. Benjamin understood 'aesthetics' primarily as sensory perception, true to the original Greek meaning of the term (Buck-Morss 1992: 6).
8. Grazhdanstvennost' is different from 'citizenship', *grazhdanstvo.*
9. 'Collective farms' and 'Soviet farms', respectively. Those two forms of organization of Soviet farming differed in the details of their legal status and administration, but especially since the 1960s the differences were increasingly blurred (see Humphrey 1998: 13–14). As a result, the two terms are often used interchangeably.
10. In intellectual discourse, the noun '*modern*' (Cyrillic: модерн) is sometimes used to refer more specifically to 'modernity' in the sense of a cultural-historical epoch. This is, however, not a widespread term, and its use is generally restricted to scholarly texts.
11. Multiple 'abroads' were referred to for comparison. Often, my informants invoked Europe or 'European standards' as a reference point to evaluate the local developments, probably in part because in their eyes I, as a European, could meaningfully verify their comparative imaginations of Europe. President Nazarbaev's writings contain frequent references to other Other-lands, most prominently Malaysia, Kuwait and the United Arab Emirates – probably because these countries with their politico-economic systems fusing strong, centralized and personalized rule with resource extraction-based capitalism provide his preferred models to follow.
12. All banknotes have an image of Baiterek printed on the back, but this is not the only one of Astana's recent buildings to be represented on money. The 200 tenge bill carries images of the buildings of the Ministry of Transport and Communication and the Ministry of Defence; the 500 tenge bill shows the Ministry of Finance and the Astana City Hall (now housing the Ministry of Agriculture); the 1,000 tenge bill features the Presidential Cultural Centre; and the largest denomination – 10,000 tenge – displays the Presidential Palace. Every Kazakhstani banknote also carries a reproduction of President Nazarbaev's golden handprint exhibited at Baiterek. As a local friend of mine once pointed out, in order to enter Baiterek, one must hand across the counter a blue 500 tenge note carrying an image of that same monument – a curious case of intertextuality.
13. The perceived 'emptiness' of the Left Bank sometimes served as a focal point of criticism of the new capital and the political economy that produced it. See Chapter 5 for more on this topic.
14. Miniature models of Astana were displayed at a number of other prominent locations in the city. A special case was the Atameken Park, a 2,000 square metre 3D 'map' of Kazakhstan peppered with miniatures of landmark buildings and monuments, with disproportionate emphasis on Astana's Left Bank (see Medeuova 2008). An important feature that these miniatures shared with billboard collages and television spots, in addition to visual attractiveness, was their decontextualizing effect. They not only allowed for spatial decontextualization (the cherry-picking of selected buildings or areas instead of modelling the entire city as it stands, and freely shifting the relative positions of buildings), but also enabled temporal displacement as well. Miniature cityscapes often included buildings that had not yet been built and might in fact never be. Thus a detemporalized landscape was created. Spectators pointed at the model of one or another building and said to their companions: 'Look, this is the one I showed you yesterday' or 'Can you recognize that one? That's where auntie works'. To cite an enthusiastic report in the newspaper *Vecherniaia Astana* (13 June 2009: 6), miniatures 'allow one to view the present and the future of the capital at a single gaze' (see also Koch 2010).

15. I thank Natalie Koch for drawing my attention to Stewart's work.
16. 'Utopia', as many authors remind us, is a play on the Greek root meanings of a 'good place' (*eu-topos*) and a non-place (*ou-topos*) – see, e.g., Crook (2000: 206).
17. Michael Herzfeld (2006) proposes the term 'spatial cleansing' to denote practices whereby the former kind of spaces, crowded yet suited to indigenous practices of trade and socializing, are replaced by new ones, devoid of indigenous sociality yet conceding to an aesthetic imperialism with its imperative of 'monumental vacuity'. What he fails to acknowledge is that such 'cleansed' areas may become spaces of desire for ordinary citizens – heterotopias (Foucault 1986) well arranged to counter the jumbledness of the everyday.
18. See Bissenova (2012: 81–85) for an ethnographic account of how decorating urban apartments according to a set of stylistic norms (so-called *evro-remont*) served as an essential performance of 'modernity'.

Chapter 2

Performing Urbanity

Migrants, the City and Collective Identification

Early on in my fieldwork, in June 2008, I was invited to Bella's birthday party. Bella, an economics undergraduate at a prestigious university, was turning nineteen. I had met her during my pre-fieldwork pilot field trip as a friend of my first host-family's daughter, Mira. Bella lived with her parents, a brother and a young cousin in an apartment in a new large brick apartment block at the Ishim embankment, commonly known as the Titanik. Residence in the Titanik indicated 'upper middle class' to 'elite' status – among Bella's neighbours was the Speaker of the Senate, for example. The apartment was spacious and decorated in a modern, somewhat extravagant style: light beige wallpaper, golden curtains through which the sunset light filtered in, a big white leather sofa next to a matching armchair, a huge flat-screen television, a painting of Kazakh warrior horsemen on the wall and a crystal lamp under the ceiling. Thick volumes with elaborately designed covers lined a bookshelf, accompanied by family memorabilia: photographs and souvenirs from trips to Istanbul, Prague and Venice. A rich collection of elegant plates and glasses were displayed behind the glass doors of a black wooden cabinet. When I arrived, only three of Bella's friends were there, helping her prepare the salads: Russian girls named Pasha, Tasha and Katiusha. 'You're gonna have a lot of names to remember tonight!' they laughed after Bella had run through the introductions. And indeed, a lot of names I soon heard: eighteen guests showed up, all but one were Bella's university classmates (the other, a Russian girl, was her high-school friend). Among them, there were five Kazakh girls and six Kazakh boys, and five Russian girls and a Russian boy. As for Bella, she was Russophone like all the others. Her father was a Kazakh academic economist and her mother a successful lawyer, originally from one of the small titularly Muslim republics of the northern Caucasus. The family had moved to Astana several years before from Aktau, Kazakhstan's oil hub on the shore of the Caspian.

After a few rounds of drinks, a tall, long-haired Kazakh nicknamed Sputnik waved at me to join him and a few others for a smoke on the balcony. Sputnik was a native of Almaty and had moved to Astana with his family in 2003, when his father, a top-echelon official in one of the ministries, was transferred here. Sputnik, who was a fan of classic Soviet rock bands such as Kino but also of Metallica, Nirvana and The Who, did not like it in Astana: he missed the '*roktusovka*' ('rock-crowd') of Almaty. Out on the balcony, Sputnik and his friends asked me about living in Europe and how it compared to Kazakhstan. After listening for a while, Sputnik changed the topic and asked: 'And what do you call people who have moved to the city from the countryside?' Before I could answer, he exclaimed: 'Here such people are called *mambet*! You should remember this word!'

Mambet sprang up frequently throughout my stay in Astana, always informally, somehow improper, often tongue-in-cheek and sometimes outright cheeky, but clearly a word that mattered. That night on the balcony, Sputnik explained to me that a mambet was 'a person who had migrated to the big city from the countryside or a small town', but then he indicated that there was more to it than that. He pointed at two of his companions and said that although they had come from the relatively small town of Petropavlovsk they were not considered *mambety*. It was a matter of one's ways; a mambet was someone who had come from a village and now 'made a lot of fuss about living in the big city and being rich'. One's place of origin was not enough to determine whether a person was mambet or not. In Sputnik's words,

> It's a matter of the social [*vopros v sotsiume*]. A mambet is someone who has grown in the countryside where there's nothing but sheep, and he watches TV every day and sees how people live in the capital, and he gets jealous. And then his father goes to the capital and gets rich. And this mambet, he doesn't know how to live in the city, he's used to being poor, and now he's so proud, he's so cool, he lives in the capital! He walks like this – 'uuuhhh!' [Sputnik raising his chin and assuming a haughty expression] He's no longer like 'ooohhh!' like before [now sneaking a sideways glance] No, he's like 'uuuhhh!' So proud!

Later I learned that not everyone considered wealth a factor in whether one was mambet or not, but in any case the term had to do with one's rude or 'uncultured' behaviour on the one hand, and one's presumably rural and often southern Kazakhstani origins on the other.[1] There was also a political edge to it. Once, when I deliberately mentioned the word during a meeting at the philosophy department of the Eurasian National University, an elderly Kazakh lady protested vigorously: mambet was nothing but a 'meaningless', pejorative word intended to offend people. It was used in particular by Russians and Russified Kazakhs to depreciate the Kazakh culture and language, she insisted, as those 'Russians and Russified Kazakhs' could not bear the fact that the Kazakh culture and language had finally been accorded the respect they deserved in Kazakhstan. Another member of the faculty tried to smooth over the situation by explaining to me that mambet was the opposite of *mangurt*, a person who had forgotten, rejected or betrayed their native cultural identity (see Aitmatov 1988). A little later, when answering another question, I told the story of how I had been attacked and beaten at a bazaar a few weeks before. The elderly lady commented on the behaviour of the perpetrators: 'That's what *mambetizm* means!'

The birthday-party vignette and the brief outline of the controversies surrounding the term mambet point to the themes of this chapter. I present five further personal narratives of migrants striving to become 'modern' urbanites. Their efforts, it shall be seen, largely focused on material elements that were understood to define modern, urban personhood – primarily apartments. These stories serve to evoke images of a new urban order gradually taking shape and to build an argument about connections between everyday individual performance, the materiality of the urban environment and collective identities. Highlighting 'urbanity' and 'rurality' as salient identity categories among the heterogeneous population of Astana, I argue that the contests among various groups of long-standing residents and migrants over collective identities were simultaneously contests over the defining characteristics of the city as a place. Astana was being reiteratively constructed as 'modern', 'urban' and 'worldly' or 'rural', 'backward' and 'provincial' (each of these and related terms meaning different things for different people) not only discursively, but first of all materially, through individuals' bodily performances, living arrangements and styles of comportment. 'Urbanity' was closely associated with progress and civility, while 'rurality' carried associations with uncouthness and lack of modern infrastructures.

Identities beyond Representation

Against the grain of the abundant scholarly literature about ethnic and national identities in post-Soviet Kazakhstan and elsewhere in the former Soviet Union,[2] in the context of rapid mass migration in Astana urbanity and rurality, rather than ethnicity, came to the fore as the most compelling dimensions of identity. The vignette above, for instance, suggests that young 'urban' Kazakhs and Russians tended to group together, pointing to the 'rural' as their common 'spatial other'.[3] By deploying salient identities such as mambet and mangurt various actors in Astana strove to define the terms of their own and others' belonging in the city as a place of 'modernity'. Notions of national identity were entwined with those other categories, which were deployed to align people regardless of ethnicity (as suggested by the composition of Bella's group of friends) and introduce divisions cutting across an ethnic group (such as between rural and urban Kazakhs). My ethnographic focus is restricted to Astana. However, elsewhere in urban Central Asia analogous vernacular categories have appeared – for instance, the term *myrk* in Kyrgyzstan, virtually synonymous with the Kazakhstani mambet (Schröder 2010) – while anti-rural stereotyping and fears of 'ruralization' have been salient across many post-Soviet cities (e.g., Alexander, Buchli and Humphrey 2007; Alexander 2009b; Lemon 2011), suggesting a broader relevance of this analysis.

In theoretical terms, my argument draws on the constructivist approach, seeing collective identities as socially constructed representations endowed with normative appeal and rhetorical force (Schlee 2008; Donahoe et al. 2009). The term 'identification' refers to various actions and processes whereby identities are engaged with by social actors (Donahoe et al. 2009: 2). Identities may be used, for instance, to construct, maintain, redefine or challenge groups and their mutual relations. Yet, I move beyond this well-established approach by considering how identities are not only deployed as semantic phenomena but are moreover embodied in everyday practices through which actors constitute themselves as (particular kinds of) subjects.

James Ferguson's (1999: 93–110) concept of 'cultural styles' is helpful in exploring this path. Ferguson defines cultural style as a 'performative competence' and a 'signifying practice'. Individuals learn, with considerable effort and at the expense of time, resources and foregone opportunities, to use their attire, speech, body carriage, consumption practices, leisure activities and so on, to signify differences between social categories and position themselves in thus structured fields. This is 'an active process ... situated both within a political-economic context and within an individual life course' (Ferguson 1999: 101). It involves 'both deliberate self-making and structural determinations, as well as such things as unconscious motivations and desires, aesthetic preferences, and the accidents of personal history' (ibid.).

The scope of Ferguson's analysis can be productively extended by emphasizing the embeddedness of stylistic performance in concrete places. The practices through which actors work out desired models of subjecthood (realize desired identities) simultaneously draw on the social and material environment in which they occur and are constitutive of it. In seeking to define themselves, actors simultaneously aim to imbue the places where they live with corresponding qualities. Thus, a broadened perspective on processes of identification is needed; one that includes the reciprocal relationships between individual and collective human subjects and place. Specific identities and corresponding qualities are inscribed in places discursively, symbolically or through material intervention, while places also lend their qualities to substantiate the identities people construct for themselves and others. They are the significant material-and-symbolic substrate that both enables and constrains performance.

The five personal narratives below highlight how 'urbanity' and 'rurality' were constructed and emphasized as identity variables (Schlee 2008) and variously applied by actors engaged in self-making in relation to the shifting characteristics of the city. Identities served to evaluate one's own and others' performance; and on that basis to construct group boundaries and hierarchies. Before turning to the narratives, however, a brief sketch of the history of urbanity and rurality in Kazakhstan, as well as an overview of the dynamics of migration to Astana during the 1990s and 2000s, is in order.

Urbanity and Rurality in Kazakhstan

In his classic work, Raymond Williams (1973) shows that stereotypes of city and country have been variously deployed to serve the interests of competing groups since the antiquity. The grand narrative of 'modernity', first born in Western Europe and spread during the twentieth century the world over, decidedly tilted the odds in favour of the urban. The Bolsheviks' enthusiasm for the city at the expense of the countryside was a particularly acute expression of this more general trend.

In Soviet Kazakhstan, a cultural dualism between the city and country was produced, with increasingly polarized moral and ideological evaluations attached. At the heart of the rural-urban opposition lay a normative, morally charged concept of culture as 'culturedness' (*kul'tura, kul'turnost*), 'a gradient of refinement and sophistication' (Boym 1994; Hoffmann 2003; Sneath 2005: 156). As mentioned in the introduction, the city was viewed as the 'engine of progress' (Alexander and Buchli 2007: 1) and the hotbed of 'culture'. The Bolshevik modernization ideology and economic policy favoured the city and ignored or even discriminated against the village. The countryside was treated as a resource base for urban growth, expected to supply food and manpower – the peasant masses to be quickly transformed into industrial proletariat. The villages remained underprivileged economically and in terms of accessibility to healthcare and education. Disparities in living conditions between city and country widened.

The city-country dualism in Soviet Kazakhstan was moreover sharply ethnicized. Modernity was associated with urbanity and with the Russian language and ways of living. Rurality, in contrast, was associated with essentialized, 'orientalized' (Said 1978; Martin 2001: 125) Kazakh 'tradition' and with 'backwardness'. The cities were inhabited mainly by Russians and other Slavs.[4] The trend towards Russian demographic and cultural domination in urban Kazakhstan, already clearly marked by the 1940s, continued throughout the post-war period (Yessenova 2003). Across Kazakhstan's north-central and north-eastern provinces, Russians and other Slavs formed a regional majority as a result of immigration during the Tselina campaign.[5]

Simultaneously, beginning with the disastrous sedentarization of nomadic pastoralists and collectivization in the 1930s and continuing in later decades (1960s–1980s), economic inequalities between rural and urban areas were a powerful stimulus for Kazakhs to leave their villages and seek urban futures. Urban industrial workers and specialists ranked among the highest income categories in the Soviet economy, while peasants were at the bottom of the wage scale, if receiving wages at all. Urban residence and employment provided access to supplies and services unavailable in the village. The goods available through urban token distribution systems, and otherwise very scarce, included, at different points in time, sugar, meat and butter (Yessenova 2003: 73–74). For all these reasons and others, Kazakh presence in the cities grew steadily.

The seeds of a rural-urban divide among Kazakhs, clearly in evidence to this day, were sown (Abylkhozhin 1997: 306). Migrants to the cities were forced to adapt to a Russian linguistic milieu and cultural style. In Soviet cities, Russian-dominated elites controlled access to career trajectories and vital resources. Russians set the benchmark for advancement and were seen as the agents of modernization (Martin 2001: 126). Russianness (or Russification) carried cultural capital – the kind of 'prestige and renown' attached to a person or a family name and readily convertible into other kinds of capital, not least economic (Bourdieu 1977: 179).

The rural-urban divide among Kazakhs was sharpened in the 1970s and 1980s (Yessenova 2003: 79–80). Upward mobility within the city was contingent upon competence in the Russian language and cultural norms. Moreover, in Kazakh families with migration history, the city-born generation tended to sever or at least limit ties with their rural kin, solidifying the boundary between the (Russophone) Soviet city and the Kazakh *aul* (village; ibid.: 120–21). Furthermore, migrants tended to concentrate in smaller towns, while the largest cities remained destinations beyond the reach of many of them. Thus, during the Soviet period, among Kazakhs, urbanity and rurality (temporalized as 'modern' and 'backward', respectively) became salient categories of identification. The former was associated with cultural proximity to Russian fellow urbanites (which some scorned as Russification, going mangurt), while the latter carried the equally ambiguous implications of a 'cultural intimacy': cultural traits recognized as forming the core of a national being, while at the same time felt as sources of embarrassment (Herzfeld 2005).

In the late 1990s and the 2000s, the construction of Astana triggered a new wave of mass rural-urban migration and renewed the salience of urbanity as an ideal and an identity (cf. Zabirova 2002a). By the same token, these processes re-emphasized the ambiguous weight of 'rurality' as urbanity's opposite.

Migration to Astana

On the eve of the capital relocation, Aqmola (the former Tselinograd) had approximately a quarter of a million inhabitants. Most were Russians and other Slavs, largely descendants of the Virgin Land settlers (*tselinniki*) from the

Table 2.1   Population growth in Astana 1998–2009

Year	Population in thousands
1998	275
2001	435
2009	687

Sources: Zabirova (2002b); Sotsial'no-Ekonomicheskii Pasport Goroda Astany (2012).

1950s–1960s (see Introduction and Chapter 3; M. Pohl 1999). As can be seen in Table 2.1, during the eleven years that followed, from 1998 to 2009, the population of the city (meanwhile renamed Astana) grew by some 250 per cent. This growth was the result of migration from other parts of Kazakhstan.[6] Immediately after the capital relocation, migration was at its peak, with over 60,000 individuals arriving in Astana each year between 1999 and 2001 (Tatibekov 2005: 27). Subsequently, yearly migration rates decreased, yet remained substantial. Table 2.2 offers an overview of migration dynamics year by year. According to unofficial estimates, by 2009 the population might have reached over 800,000, including unregistered migrants.

Ethnically, the incomers were almost exclusively Kazakh – perhaps over 97 per cent (Tatibekov 2005: 100) – while those leaving were mostly Slavs or Germans departing for their 'historic homelands' – Russia, Ukraine, Belarus, Poland and Germany. The incomers differed by region of origin, rural or urban background, class, economic standing, education and proficiency in Russian and Kazakh – in short, by kinds of social and cultural capital (Bourdieu 1977, 1990). A vast majority were of working age.[7] Most brought their families along, either right away or within a few months of the family head's arrival, yet there was also a significant proportion of lone male migrants, presumably originating from the

Table 2.2   In- and out-migration dynamics in Astana (in thousands)

Year	In	Out	Net
1998	13.2	2.9	10.3
1999	61.8	8.5	53.3
2000	68.8	11.1	57.7
2001	62.4	11.0	51.4
2002	15.2	8.5	6.7
2003	15.2	9.9	5.3
2004	24.6	10.4	14.2
2005	26.8	11.1	15.7
2006	29.4	11.7	17.7
2007	31.5	12.2	19.3
2008	43.9	19.0	24.9
2009	49.9	18.0	31.9

Sources: Agentstvo (2004: 99, 2007: 124, 2011b: 86); Tatibekov (2005: 27).

most economically disadvantaged rural strata and in search of quick, if often only seasonal, income (Zabirova 2002b: 20–21).

Early wave migrants, such as Kumano, the protagonist of the first of the stories below, were usually government officials, relocated from Almaty along with their jobs, and their families. Along with other highly educated migrants from large cities (oblast capitals) they were the most 'resource-strong' group (Zabirova 2003: 217). They occupied white-collar jobs, were upwardly mobile, and tended to live in newly built or good-quality Soviet apartment blocks. Migrants from smaller towns tended to obtain lower white-collar or blue-collar positions in administration, retail and service. The most 'resource-weak' were rural migrants, who usually occupied positions in petty trade and services of the 'bazaar' type, or physical jobs requiring little or no professional education, very often in construction (ibid.: 219–21). Those worst off could only count on extremely unstable black-market employment based on an oral agreement with their own relatives or fellow villagers (ibid.: 240–41). As is generally the case in situations of migration to large cities, rural migrants tended to inhabit the semi-rural fringe of Astana, where the infrastructure and the patterns of economic activity it allowed resembled the conditions they were familiar with from their native villages, while the inhabitants also benefited from the proximity to urban occupations, supplies, health and educational services and transportation networks (Abu-Lughod 1961). The subsistence base of a typical family in the 'rural-urban fringe' typically combines a city-earned salary or salaries and domestic production such as crop-growing and livestock-breeding. In Astana such areas include the *chastnyi sektor*: clusters of mud-brick dwellings unconnected to urban utilities.[8]

Comprehensive statistical data as to the ratio of migrants coming from rural areas compared to those coming from cities was unavailable. It seems reasonable to suppose that the proportion of village or small-town migrants increased with the post-2002 construction boom that created demand for low-skilled manpower. What is clear is that many migrants belonged to the comparatively weakly Russified strata of the Kazakh population, as testified by such facts as that 70 per cent of the migrants claimed at least conversational proficiency in the Kazakh language, and most preferred Kazakh-language television to Russophone channels (Tatibekov 2005: 99, 102). While in the early years following the capital relocation the greatest share of rural and small-town migrants came from the northern oblasts surrounding Astana (Zabirova 2003: 215–16), soon the southern Kazakhstan oblast (commonly called Shymkent oblast, after its capital) became one of the most prominent 'sending areas'. Colloquially, a 'Shymkenti' (*shymkentskii*) came to stand for the stereotypical uncouth rural migrant in Astana (see Koch and White forthcoming). Although Almaty is also in the south, the term 'southerner' (*iuzhanin*, female *iuzhanka*) usually excluded people from Almaty and implied 'rurality' (cf. Nazpary 2002: 169). Recognized rural or small-town migrants were conspicuous in Astana. Just as in Almaty in the 1990s (Alexander 2009b: 153–56), so in Astana in the 2000s it was a common complaint among established urbanites that they found themselves under siege by 'rurals', disrespectfully called *kolkhozniki* ('kolkhoz-members').

In sum, migration almost tripled the population of Astana over little more than a decade. From a mid-size provincial industrial town that had been shaped in the Soviet period (Chapter 3), the city turned into a booming capital dominated by Kazakh migrants. Among those, some were long-established, highly educated Russophone urbanites, former residents of the Soviet-era capital Almaty and other large cities, yet others arrived from all sorts of places across Kazakhstan, including remote corners of the vast, impoverished countryside. In the ensuing identification dynamics, a set of interconnected binary categories rose to salience, including 'local' (*mestnyi*) or 'native' (*korennoi*) and 'newcomer' (*priezzhii*); 'urban' (*gorodskoi*) and 'rural' (*sel'skii*); 'northerner' (*severianin*) and 'southerner' (*iuzhanin*); and 'Russian-speaking' (*russkoiazichnyi*) or 'Russified' (*obrusevshyi*) versus 'Kazakh-speaking' (*kazakhskoiazichnyi*). Given the ideological emphasis put on visions of urban modernity in the context of the rapidly developing urban environment (Chapter 1), urbanity and rurality became the key pair among these identity variables. The personal narratives that follow – although by no means representative of the full diversity of migrants' experience – reveal how those identities played out as cultural styles in everyday practice as migrants with various backgrounds strove to make themselves at home in the city.

Migrants' Stories

Kumano: A Pioneer Settles Down

A heavyset, cheerful Kazakh man in his thirties, Kumano, headed a small public relations agency housed in several rooms in an office building on the edge of the Left Bank development area. The company thrived on his vast network of informal connections to influential people in various state and municipal administrative organs. Kumano was not the man's real name, but part of his literary pseudonym, under which he had written a half-memoir, half-satiric novella about the lives of people like himself – young bureaucrats in the first months and years after the relocation of their jobs from Almaty to Astana.

Kumano had graduated from a diplomatic academy in Almaty and in 2000 found himself among the first cohorts of young state cadres summoned to the new capital. Collectively dispatched on a train from Almaty's main station, the young people were seen off in a pompous Soviet-style ceremony, complete with a brass band playing military farewell marches. After the twenty-four-hour journey, they were welcomed in Astana with matching pomp and presented with salt and bread – the traditional Slav symbols of hospitality, reflecting the still predominantly Russian outlook of northern Kazakhstan at that time. By then, the entire pioneer echelon was suffering from head-crushing hangovers, save those who were still drunk. Years later, Kumano still laughed when recalling that he and a friend had managed to empty two bottles of vodka within the journey's first twenty minutes. The end result was a somewhat humorous juxtaposition of official pomp and intoxicated bacchanal.

According to Kumano, bacchanal dominated in the first few years upon relocation. Hundreds and thousands of young people enjoyed the frontier liberties of the new capital, where most things seemed in flux with very little fixed. All were uprooted, freed from the bounds of family and other social relations, able to roam the world of possibility that lay open to them in this northern steppe city. Men and women enjoyed a phase of promiscuity that those in their thirties and forties, particularly, found rejuvenating: 'Out of the blue, you're a *komsomolets*⁹ again!' as Kumano put it. Astana in the early 2000s was still a rather small town, especially compared to Almaty, and its nightlife was limited to just a handful of bars and clubs that were therefore frequented by everybody. As other early wave settlers from Almaty were also later to remark, the quality of service at those few establishments reminded them that this was a provincial town on the margins of the 'civilized' world. For example, the bartenders had to be taught that beer ought to be served chilled. On the other hand, the limited supply of bars and clubs added to the intensity of emerging relations, with so many of the same people often crossing paths. All in all, from Kumano's memories emerges an image of the early capital years in Astana as quite liminal, in a sense not far from Turner's (1995 [1969]): a 'betwixt-and-between' condition of licence and spontaneity but also uncertainty, where social structures are fluid, and persons are being constituted anew through intense experience.¹⁰

Out of such liminal flux, new social forms eventually emerge. Thus in Astana families were established, jobs gradually became more permanent, institutions more fixed, and as the years passed, the bureaucrat-settlers came to realize they now had new selves, comfortably accommodated in the city that had once seemed so frenzied. Many, admittedly, never planned to stay long: they intended to wait until they received their state-allocated newly built apartments, privatize them, sell, and move back to their true home, Almaty. For some, this is exactly what happened; but Kumano, despite initially considering his stay in Astana an 'extended business trip' (*dlitel'naia komandirovka*), came to find himself settled in the new city. He worked at the Ministry of Foreign Affairs and other public institutions before going private in the mid 2000s. His company's staff comprised five young Kazakh women and a male driver. Among the women, one was originally from Almaty, like Kumano, while the others had migrated to Astana from various cities much more recently than he had. Only the driver was a Tselinograd native.

Kumano lived with his wife and children on the Left Bank and liked it there: he praised the area for its relative peacefulness and comfort. He felt at home in Astana and missed the city when visiting Almaty. With the passage of time, he had developed his own localized habits, found his favourite shops, salons, schools for the children and so on. Most of his friends and acquaintances were educated Kazakh professionals with Almaty backgrounds. Economically, as mentioned, he thrived on his contacts with colleagues in various branches of the public administration, presumably former pioneer-bureaucrats from Almaty like himself. They lived either on the Left Bank, like Kumano, or in such affluent right-bank neighbourhoods as the Mikroraion Samal, built soon after the capital relocation specifically for this category of residents. Kumano noticed his children were growing up to become a new kind of person altogether – 'Astanaians', *astanchane*, to whom both Almaty and the old, Khrushchev-era sectors of former Tselinograd would feel quaintly foreign.

Kumano's reflections on the social developments in Astana convey a sense of mutually reinforcing ties between the spatial qualities of different parts of the city and the types of subjectivity predominant among their respective inhabitants. He held clear views on the diverse population categories in formation in Astana. First, an 'Astanaian', *astanchanin* (fem. *astanchanka*), was the kind of person Kumano believed he had gradually become, within two or three years upon his arrival: professional, under forty, 'definitely a newcomer', as Kumano underscored (*'obezatel'no priezzhii'*), and possessed of a certain ambition for personal development and material growth. An astanchanin, according to Kumano, also harboured a certain sense of disillusionment and cool, sharp-eyed detachment: having abandoned initial enthusiasm for change and become accustomed to real-life constraints, astanchane worked hard and relied on personal effort rather than on whatever anyone may have promised them.[11]

According to Kumano, former residents of Almaty contributed to the 'advancement' of Astana with their cosmopolitan manners: 'Being from the capital city, one always carries some, say, capital-city stuff (*stolichnye veshchi*): you've had more opportunities to read, to see things, and you carry this along', Kumano explained. Recently, however, in his opinion Astana had 'backslid' due to the overwhelming influx of an entirely different sort of newcomer: 'very many who-knows-whos, "kolkhoz", as the saying goes, [newcomers] from so-called underdeveloped areas, from the villages, from all those provincial towns'. Kumano explained that those rural newcomers were 'too many for the city to digest':

> There is a certain limit for the capital city to be able to soak in, process, and in due time to produce capital citizens. And now, it's such a huge stream that the city just can't keep pace. And those people … who are marked with a certain characteristic corresponding to the level of those

places they come from, those people fail to develop morally, or spiritu-
ally, and therefore they keep on throwing waste past the bins and spit-
ting around [in the street], because the culture [kul'tura] here in the city
has not managed to rise high enough yet.

In such evaluations, not uncommon in local everyday discourse, 'modernization' clichés resonated, such as the concept of developmental levels pertaining
to particular locales and social forms. Moreover, expressing value-laden ideas of
'rurality' versus 'urbanity', Kumano employed a normative concept of 'culture'
as a measureable quality unevenly distributed among rural and urban milieus.

As for the pre-capital population, tselinogradtsy, Kumano believed that as
the years passed these Soviet-era urbanites were in decline and on the verge of
'extinction'. In his novella, the only native Tselinograd character, indeed the only
Russian, was thus a ghost, or perhaps more properly a spirit: liftovoi, fashioned
after the classic household spirit domovoi of Russian folklore. As a true Soviet-
modern urbanite, liftovoi resided not in the hearth of a wooden hut but in the elevator of an apartment block.[12] To Kumano, tselinogradtsy in present-day Astana
were Russians, 'over forty', and 'people who have been completely indifferent to
the capital relocation and anything that came with it', 'who couldn't be bothered about all this "city of the future"': 'They live where they used to, they have
their own time-cemented habits, their shops and their jobs. They have by now
acknowledged that there is Astana and all, but they live their lives just as they
did before, and the new is alien to them'. Kumano easily identified particular
areas where Tselinograd in this sense continued to exist: along the Khrushchev-
era avenues north of the old centre and towards the train station, and in some of
the late-Soviet 'sleeper districts' in the south-east (see Map 1.1; Chapter 1). He
depicted the tselinogradtsy as relics marking the (vanishing) Soviet past from the
future-oriented present. Thus, looking from his viewpoint of the Left-Bank 'city
of the future', Kumano reversed some of the perspectives cited in Chapter 1: he
'denied coevalness' (Fabian 2002 [1983]) not to migrants aspiring to 'modernity',
but to the Tselinograd-era urbanites, whom he earmarked as 'people of the past'.

Kirill and Giselle: Love on the Move
Kirill, an ethnic Russian, was the son of a bus driver and a seamstress from Almaty.
The family had lived in an individual house in a green old district outside the
city centre. Kirill was eighteen when he met, for the first time, the girl living in a
neighbouring household, the daughter of a skilled stonemason and a professional
folk dancer (another ethnically Russian family). As Kirill boasts, he always had
many girlfriends back then, usually a few at a time. But when that neighbourhood girl asked him for a cigarette, after he ran into her quarrelling with her
then boyfriend in the peaceful, almost bucolic street, he knew she was somehow
special. Kirill quit all of his previous relationships and soon started dating her.

Their nascent love was to face a formidable challenge. The girl, whom I will call Giselle, graduated at age seventeen from the prestigious Almaty ballet school. It was 1999, not even two full years after the decision to transfer the capital to Astana. Reportedly, President Nazarbaev had personally decreed that the new capital ought to have a proper ballet and opera theatre, as one of the essential trappings of metropolitan culture. The Tselinograd railway employees' house of culture (*dvorets zheleznodorozhnikov*) was hastily adapted for that purpose, and a cohort of young graduates from Almaty were shipped north, Giselle among them. Despite an inadequate theatre infrastructure, accommodation in filthy, cold and humid dorms with collective showers, and plagues of mosquitoes and locusts during the Astana summer, she recalls the thrill she and her colleagues felt: they were pioneers, freed from parental control and on a mission to bring high culture to this new capital that was emerging in the midst of the untamed steppe.

Kirill remained in Almaty, working double shifts for six long months before he could afford a train ticket to visit Giselle. In spring 2001, about to be drafted to the army, he travelled to Astana a second time, to bid farewell to his ballerina. To his surprise, she welcomed him with the news that she was expecting his child. Kirill found his way into the favours of an influential officer at the replenishment command, and soon he was free to join Giselle in Astana. To make ends meet, he was prepared to take any job. Luckily, basic jobs were not hard to come by in those early capital days. Thus, Kirill soon found employment as a night guard at a newly established pizzeria just outside the Soviet era town centre. Once the couple were married, Kirill was allowed to move into Giselle's room at the ballet dancers' dorm.

Little by little, their life 'normalized'. The ballet crew relocated several times to other dorms scattered about the city, before finally settling in a relatively comfortable 1960s building near the train station. Here, each family was provided an individual one-bedroom apartment with a private bathroom. The artists had been promised new, bigger and more modern apartments that they would be allowed to privatize under a special state programme, but the fulfilment of that promise was repeatedly deferred, leading to an unprecedented strike by the ballet team in 2008. Kirill, Giselle and their two small daughters continued to live in that 'small family-type dorm' (*malosemeinoe obshchezhitie*). Moneywise, things were tight, but Kirill was a hard-working optimist. In 2005 he found a job as a salesman with a foreign company. The salary, combined with Giselle's theatre earnings, sometimes proved too little to support the family, so Kirill took up odd jobs on the side: night-time taxi driving and DJ'ing at a highbrow club where even the president would sometimes entertain his international guests.

Extremely communicative, cheerful and amiable, Kirill relied on vast networks of friends and acquaintances for favours and, when necessary, material support. Kirill's network branched out in several directions, arranged around his different past and present jobs, relations with neighbours at the dorm and other nodal points he had accumulated over the years.[13] I never had the chance to explore those networks in all their reach and complexity, but I was aware that they included people from diverse backgrounds and walks of life: Russians and Kazakhs, natives and migrants, ballet dancers and car mechanics, lawyers and salesmen. If the reach and operational capacity of networks are a measure of an individual's integration in an urban environment (Mitchell 1969: 16–19, 40; Hannerz 1980: 178–80), then Kirill was clearly well integrated.

Little wonder, then, that Kirill and Giselle, who considered themselves 'as Almaty as one gets' ('almatinskie-almatintsy') by origin, felt very much at home in Astana, especially in those right-bank areas where they had lived. They recalled that in the early years the city had been much more homogeneous in terms of its social composition. Almaty migrants stood out from the crowd and were initially perceived by locals as competitors for jobs. Not only were many of them highly skilled professionals, but also accustomed to the accelerated pace of metropolitan life; they had a seemingly natural advantage over the somewhat 'slow' provincial urbanites. Simultaneously, as some of our mutual Tselinograd-native friends recalled, the almatintsy were looked upon as bearers of a more sophisticated urban 'culture', with their fashionable attire, hairstyles and manners. In the words of one such friend, Mira, the Almaty people 'knew what a beauty parlour was! They brought us culture, which we had indeed been lacking!'

More recently, Kirill claimed, rural Kazakhs 'came to conquer the capital'. Invoking a widespread 'orientalist' cliché (Herzfeld 2005: 62), urbanites in Astana (including former Almaty residents) complained about the southern rural migrants' nepotism and proclivity to corruption: allegedly, such newcomers used any position they managed to obtain to provide multiple relatives and former co-villagers with jobs, even though in most cases their protégés lacked the most basic skills – 'as if car-building was the same as sheep-herding', as Kirill put it.[14] The implicit axiom underlying this comparison was that (especially southern) Kazakh migrants were bearers of rurality. According to Kirill, the southerners' rurality was also expressed in their bodily and socializing habits: 'Migrants from southern Kazakhstan, or from some poor aul [Kazakh for 'village'] in Shymkent or Kyzylorda oblast, are characterized by increased seed-snappability, squattability and a shala-Kazakh accent', he explained. 'Seed-snappability' (semechkoshelkabel'nost) is Kirill's invented word referring to the habit of eating sunflower seeds (semechki) as a snack. One 'snaps' (shelkat) the seed shells with one's teeth. This habit is common across nearly all population groups in many areas of the former Soviet Union, and Kirill and his friends engage in it too. However, a sense that it is not quite 'cultured' to snap seeds, and that 'Westerners' do not do it, is equally widespread, and therefore the degree of 'seed-snappability' becomes a measure of distance from an imagined cosmopolitan blueprint of 'culture'. 'Squattability' (nakortakhsidenie) is likewise a mock-academese neologism of Kirill's and refers to the habit of squatting down in public, sometimes for long periods, commonly attributed to southern Kazakhstani rural dwellers. Finally, shala-Kazakh (*shalakazakhskii*, literally 'half-Kazakh') is a popular informal word used to refer to the Kazakh language spoken with multiple Russian borrowings, often comically altered to the Russian ear by adaptation to Kazakh phonetics, syntax and inflection. By invoking these stereotypes, Kirill and Giselle – migrants themselves, and not very affluent – associated themselves with other former almatintsy as well as other urbanites (across ethnic lines) against the groups constructed as 'rural', hence 'unmodern' and 'uncultured'.

Simultaneously, what seriously impeded the couple's becoming successfully 'Astanaian', in their own eyes, was the housing question. The issue of the promised but perpetually deferred apartment stubbornly returned in conversations with Kirill and Giselle. As the months and years passed, the couple grew increasingly desperate to finally own the home they desired. Apart from practical necessity – the family having grown – it was a matter of desire for a certain vision of urban modernity. In Giselle's words, as long as the dream apartment failed to materialize, it often felt as if they were living in a 'dusty little piss-smelling town', cosy and familiar as it might have become, rather than in the future-looking capital.

Bakytgul': Caught Up in Deferrals

Bakytgul', introduced in Chapter 1, was born in a Kazakh only rural area in the eastern-Kazakhstani Semipalatinsk (Semei) oblast. She spent her youth and young adulthood, fifteen years in total, in Karaganda, a large Russian-dominated mining city in central Kazakhstan, some 200 kilometres south-east of Astana. There she received her education and obtained a degree in chemistry before moving to Astana in July 2007 when, with the help of a former Karaganda neighbour and friend, she got a job at a newly established state-run research centre.

Bakytgul''s motivation for pursuing an urban life rather than retreating to her native village is perhaps best understood by comparing her life trajectory to that of her younger sister. Like Bakytgul', her sister had finished school with distinction ('*s krasnym diplomom*'), but then, at twenty, despite the entire family's advice to the contrary, she married a 26-year-old man and moved in with his parents somewhere in the countryside. Things soon got so bad in her new household that she fled from her husband. Somehow, she was eventually persuaded to return and she became the household's sole wage earner. With her education, she was given a teacher's job at the village school. This salary, supplemented by the household's own agricultural produce, was the basis of subsistence for herself, the husband, the mother-in-law and the latter's three grandchildren, whose mother was dead and whose father lived elsewhere with his second wife. Apart from her school job, Bakytgul's sister had to do all the housekeeping: not only the cooking and the cleaning of the family's ten-room house, but also milking and taking care of eleven cows. The husband's three elder brothers lived separately with their own families, but apparently contributed little to the care of the elderly mother. Bakytgul', wishing her sister had chosen to move to the city, lamented: 'She milks those eleven cows there! And I told her, "where are you gonna live, in a village?!" She was educated … I was raised in a sovkhoz too, but I wouldn't go back. There's civilization in the city, and in the village there's nothing [*v gorode tsivilizatsiia, a tam nichego netu*]'.

As explained in Chapter 1, however, Bakytgul''s own life in Astana fell rather short of her expectations. When I met her, she lived alone in a four-bedroom flat in a dilapidated Soviet apartment block in Zhukovka, an ill-reputed 'bad neighbourhood' (Figure 2.1). I stayed with her for a week during my pilot trip. The apartment belonged to Bakytgul''s relatives, who had moved back to their more reliable source of subsistence in Karaganda once the old uncle got sick and ceased to earn an income. The adult son of those relatives, with his own family in tow, would show up on Saturday mornings to shower; I felt reluctant to inquire, but perhaps they lived in a house that had no running water. In addition, shortly after my arrival, a friend of the relatives moved in, a middle-aged Kazakh woman named Aigul'. She was a doctor and worked at two medical establishments simultaneously because one gave her a relatively good salary, and through the other she was enrolled in a state housing programme (*gosprogramma*) and expected to

Figure 2.1 Bakytgul''s neighbourhood (photo: M. Laszczkowski)

receive an apartment in the near, if unspecified, future. The latter detail was to prove significant for Bakytgul', as will be revealed shortly.

Bakytgul' had other relatives in Astana, including some who were rather affluent, but she had limited contact with them and received no financial support or other assistance from them. The daughter of her aunt and uncle had married 'a rich one' ('*za muzh vyshla za bogatogo*'), the director of a major pipe factory, who subsequently bought his new mother- and father-in-law an apartment in the extremely prestigious and accordingly expensive HighVill [*sic*] estate, about whose high-tech comforts legends circulated. The pipe factory director and his wife additionally owned a restaurant and, according to Bakytgul', several apartments in the Left Bank. Bakytgul' never visited them – she was never invited. There was also a university department head who lived in an apartment in Trinadtsataia Magistral', another, though less prestigious, recently developed area. Finally, there was a cousin who seemed to be the only relative in Astana with whom Bakytgul' maintained some sort of a regular relationship. Roughly twice a month he gave her a lift to Karaganda (in exchange for a contribution to the fuel costs), where she shopped for foodstuffs, cheaper there than in Astana. In short, contrary to the widespread opinion about the Kazakh migrants' extensive kin-based support networks, Bakytgul' was largely left to her own devices in the city. Shy as she was, she never made many friends in Astana either.

When I met her she spoke with much anticipation about the new complex being built on the Left Bank for the research institute where she worked. It was expected to include housing for some of the staff, and, as mentioned in Chapter 1, Bakytgul' worked hard, hoping she would receive an apartment. However, as the months passed, no further details were announced, and the completion of the project seemed repeatedly deferred. Slowly, Bakytgul''s hope faded, and she brought up the issue less and less.

At some point, she was forced to move out of her relatives' apartment in Zhukovka. The relative who used to come to take showers every week moved in with his wife and two children, and they divided the four rooms among themselves. Bakytgul' was embittered, but had no recourse. A period of frequent address changes began for her. First, she rented a flat in a similarly rundown area further down the road from the city centre, but it was too far away to walk to work every day, as was her custom (Bakytgul' preferred to economize on the bus tickets). Then she found shelter for some time with some relatives of her younger sister's husband in a small self-built hut in Uch-Khoz, a rural-like suburban settlement on the outskirts of the city. There was an outside toilet, and water had to be fetched from a well some distance away. In early 2009 she lived close to her work, paying fifteen thousand tenge a month (roughly equivalent to seventy-seven euros at the time, but also representing half of Bakytgul''s monthly salary) for a room she shared with a stranger, a woman from southern Kazakhstan who worked as a security guard. Bakytgul' did not like her roommate: '*mne ne nravitsia iuzhanka*', she said, literally 'I don't like a southerner'. In spring of that year, Bakytgul' finally moved in with Aigul', the friend of her relatives, who had recently received the apartment she had been promised under the gosprogramma, in a brand new nine-storey building of yellow brick, pleasant looking and with spacious rooms, though situated in a dodgy area between the back of the former TselinSel'Mash factory and an unfinished bridge over railway tracks.

Bakytgul' did not like Astana. She was disappointed with how her life had gone materially, but also thought Astana – save the Left Bank dreamland she rarely visited (see Chapter 1) – lacked 'culture'. This she blamed on the dominating presence of southern Kazakhs, *iuzhane*. At the research centre, she avoided southerners, whom she found rude and uneducated. She considered the way southerners dressed in public disgraceful: they wore socks with sandals, slippers or flip-flops, and put on dressing gowns for a walk along the street or when shopping at the neighbourhood store. In short, reflecting a normative cultural cliché that the reader will already find familiar, she considered the southerners the bearers of whatever was anti-urban and 'uncultured'.

Bakytgul' did not feel integrated in Astana. Shortly before my departure, in July 2009, I asked her if she considered herself an astanchanka, now that two full years had passed since she had moved to the capital. She replied briefly and firmly 'no', before adding: 'I don't like this Astana. It doesn't suit me. Maybe one can like it on TV ... I don't know the city, I never go anywhere. So I'm not an astanchanka. When I go to Karaganda, they're all like "Oh, she lives in Astana!" And I don't feel such an Astana person'.[15] When I asked who she thought she was, if not an astanchanka, she smiled hesitatingly and said: 'I don't know, *priezzha*' – a 'migrant', 'newcomer'. She still rented a room from Aigul' for fifteen thousand tenge a month. 'Maybe if I had an apartment ...' – she would perhaps consider herself an accomplished 'Astanaian'. Relatives often asked Bakytgul' if she had someone who might become her future husband. She commented: 'I don't. I never go anywhere, I don't meet people. I'll never meet a rich man, a man with a car, a car and an apartment. Only the rich marry rich, right?'

A year later Bakytgul' did, however, marry. Her husband comes from her native village and is a childhood friend of hers and a lifetime friend of her brother. He is an army doctor. As of early 2011, the couple were considering various options for their future: an apartment in Astana, according to Bakytgul''s estimates, would cost them some U.S. \$50,000–60,000, whereas one in Karaganda could be bought for U.S. \$10,000–25,000. They also thought of retreating – 'for the time being' – to Semipalatinsk.

Ainura: The Girl Who Played the Accordion

When I met Ainura, she was a junior colleague of Bakytgul''s at the lab. The story of her family over the last two decades brings together many typical elements I heard in other accounts by former rural residents. Both her parents had come from villages in north Kazakhstan, yet through education each had achieved a rather prestigious occupation: Ainura's mother was a doctor, and her father an engineer. Thus, in the late Soviet period they belonged to the upwardly mobile rural elite. They lived in a sovkhoz village 100 kilometres from Tselinograd. However, with the atrophy of the economy in the wake of the dissolution of the USSR in the early 1990s, Ainura's parents suddenly found themselves unemployed, with hardly any prospects for re-employment, and soon – penniless. To make ends meet, Ainura's mother served as a midwife to local women and spent her nights knitting woollen caps for sale. The children, Ainura and her little sister, who had just recently started school, had to wear old, home-repaired clothes and shoes. The father, once a proud senior engineer, remained jobless. Ainura's mother had always seen to the daughters' musical education. Under the harsh new realities, this acquired an unexpected economic dimension: the mother hoped the girls, and the older Ainura in particular, would soon be able to contribute to the family budget by playing for a fee at various gatherings. Therefore, she paid for the girls' music classes with the woollen caps she knitted. The girls dreamed of a piano, but the family could not afford it. One day a family of ethnic Germans from their village who were 'repatriating' to Germany gave them an accordion they no longer needed. Ainura was embarrassed to play it, as the accordion was considered a boy's instrument. However, understanding this was a matter of economic necessity, she became a female accordion player.

In 1996 Ainura's father decided to try his luck in the city. The capital relocation had not taken place yet, but the plan had been announced in 1994, and Aqmola was showing the first signs of economic revival. Anticipating the construction boom of the 2000s, new buildings began to appear around the Soviet-era city centre, such as the Turkish-built high-rise Intercontinental Hotel. Ainura's father found a job as a truck driver at the construction site. Soon the other members of the family reunited with him in the city. They sold their village house, packed all their belongings on a family-owned truck and moved. The family settled in Poselok Internatsional'nyi (usually abbreviated to just Internatsional'nyi), one of the semi-rural fringe settlements within an hour's ride on the slow *marshrutka* bus from the centre of Astana. A couple of years later, Ainura's father quit the job and decided to become a 'private entrepreneur', which in his case, as in the case of many other male migrants, meant unlicensed taxi driving using his private car. The mother soon managed to find a job at the local public clinic in Internatsional'nyi, although the pay in the first few years was quite minimal.

Internatsional'nyi, on the Karaganda road, a few kilometres beyond the south-eastern sleeper districts of Astana, used to be a Korean-dominated rural settlement,[16] incorporated at one point into the administrative boundaries of the city. In the mid to late 1990s, land and houses there were relatively cheap. Ainura's parents bought a plot with a small simple house vacated by a Korean family. For the first several years they kept livestock, including several cows, to make up for the insufficient income from their jobs. Livestock breeding within city limits was finally effectively banned around 2005. More recently, Internatsional'nyi witnessed some measure of development: a local millionaire and former vodka tycoon had a grandiose mosque built at the entry to the settlement from the main road, and dormitories for construction workers, KNB (ex-KGB) officers and students of a local branch of the Kazakh Agro-Technical University appeared nearby. In 2008 the construction of the first multi-storey residential building began, and more or less affluent people from Astana started building their villas (*kottedzhy*). Ainura commented: 'Even we [her family] have raised a big house next to our tiny Korean hut. People have started to live a little bit, to move, right? It's not merely surviving – they've started to hustle, to wheel and deal [*nachali uzhe kak-to vot krutitsia, vertetsia*]. Life has taught everyone a lesson, I guess, so they've all started [to work]'. Much as in central Astana and on the Left Bank, also in Internatsional'nyi construction, though on a different scale, became the sign and catalyst of both economic and moral revival. In the meantime, Ainura continued attending accordion classes at a musical school in the city. For her and her sister, what most profoundly marked the change in their lives associated with the move to Astana was probably the moment when, a few years after settling in Internatsional'nyi, their parents could finally afford to buy them the long dreamed-of piano.

Ainura went to school in the settlement. Much to her comfort, she found that virtually all of her fellow pupils had similar backgrounds: the children of newcomer families from former sovkhoz villages spread within a radius of 100 kilometres or so from Astana – 'middle society', as she reckoned (*'srednee obshchestvo'*). In 2003 the time came for her to decide on her future. She wanted to go to university, and her parents supported her. Initially, Ainura wanted to study psychology at the Eurasian University or dentistry at the Medical Academy, but entry exams for state-funded programmes at both proved too competitive, and self-funded study too expensive. Thus, she had to make do with biotechnology at the Agrarian University. She did not like the idea, for, in her own words, 'anyone could study at the Agrarian – all those sovkhoz lower class, migrants, all, you see, retards [*zachmorennye*]. ... And the Eurasian was elite'. Friends warned her that the Agrarian was a 'dog shelter' where 'all sorts of scum, nobody but kolkhozniki [villagers]' were to be met. Therefore, Ainura was afraid that an agricultural education and association with rural 'lower-class' lifestyles would set her on a life trajectory counter to her expectations of upward mobility achieved through urban residence and occupation. Indeed, she soon found out that among the nineteen students in her class all but six were the children of rural families and lived in university dorms. Those other six counted as Astana 'locals' but, as Ainura commented, they lived 'not really in the city, but in Internatsional'nyi, in Malinovka or in Ugol'naia', the latter two being, respectively, a village some 30 kilometres out of Astana and a street in the city's industrial zone, infamous for its poverty and crime rate. From an outsider's point of view, this could be seen as a 'villager' line-up, with all the negative connotations. Yet Ainura learned to see it differently: those people turned out to be like her in many ways: the children of 'aspiring parents' from the countryside, as she put it.

Soon after graduation, Ainura managed to get a job as a lab technician at the research institute. She had no experience and no connections, so her chances were not very good, she recalls, but she was lucky enough to find a vacancy. When I met her in 2008, she still lived with her parents in Internatsional'nyi, and dreamed of a *magistratura* (MSc) and later a Ph.D. in biotechnology. She had a boyfriend from a northern Kazakhstan rural area. Her father had bought a house in a neighbouring settlement for her to receive in dowry, but her dream was a modern apartment in the Left Bank, 'with three bedrooms, two toilets, a bathtub and all conveniences'. Ainura believed that living in the Left Bank would allow her 'to keep pace with life, to live like others live, not to be a loser'. The 'old city' was for 'the average ones', she reckoned, and the Left Bank for those 'a little higher'. There was one thing Ainura was sure of: 'I will never ever in my life go back to where there is no electricity, no cars, and the buses don't run. And here, in Astana, there's civilization … The elite, they all come to Astana, right?'

Madiar: The Struggling Southerner

The story of Madiar's arrival and subsequent halting integration in Astana can be seen to represent the opposite end of a continuum to that of Kumano's, presented earlier. If Kumano's story belonged to the genre of soon-after-capital-relocation frontier narratives, Madiar's is to some extent typical of the wave of migration to Astana that followed nearly a decade later, around the time of the crisis that struck the construction sector (see Bissenova 2012: 141–58). I met Madiar as a friend of Sultan, the X-ray operator introduced in Chapter 1.

Madiar, twenty-six years old when we met, had been born and raised in a village near the town of Atrar, Shymkent oblast, the heartland of southern Kazakhstan with all of its associated cultural stereotypes. Rural areas in that part of the country are almost entirely Kazakh. Migrants from that region were by default perceived as the purest bearers of rural Kazakhness, ambiguously marked as 'authentic traditionalism' on the one hand, and 'backward' and 'lacking in culture' on the other. Of course, this expectation, which many such migrants justly found unfair and offensive, was often proven wrong by individuals hailing from the remotest mountain villages beyond Shymkent who spoke perfect Russian and demonstrated many cultural skills held to be distinctly urban. However, Madiar's poor command of the Russian language, his strong local accent, his short, unfashionable hairstyle and his bodily posture and attire all stamped him as a quintessential southern Kazakhstani rural newcomer in the streets of Astana. Determined to make it in the capital, he stuck to a company of other southerners and seemed not to notice the contemptuous looks he would often get from other categories of residents, whether Russian or Kazakh.

Madiar had gone to school in the village and later obtained a degree in customs service from the military department of a Shymkent university, which did not stand for a prestigious education, although serving as a customs officer might easily be a very profitable occupation. However, for one reason or another, Madiar failed to obtain a position in the customs service after graduation and soon decided to move to Astana to seek career opportunities there. He did not have any particular plan, other than the general idea that the new capital was a place of opportunity.

The episode of his arrival was as different from Kumano's as could be imagined: confused and buffeted by chance, in contrast to Kumano's celebratory and officially organized welcome. One day in 2006, Madiar, who had previously known Astana only from the highly selective televised representations (cf. Chapter 1), stepped out from a coach at the capital's train station. Carrying his backpack, he saw the bustling crowd and the old, mostly 1950s houses in the area surrounding the station. The relative who was supposed to meet him was nowhere to be found. Madiar tried calling him, but the phone was not working. Thinking he was completely lost, Madiar just sat at a bench in front of the station and waited. Only after several hours had passed and as it was getting dark did his relative suddenly materialize. They walked together to what became Madiar's first accommodation in Astana: an old house in a less than elegant area on Moskovskaia Street, where the newcomer joined ten other men like himself sharing a single rented room. The following day Madiar began working as an unskilled labourer at a nearby construction site.

Migrant labourers tended to stick with their own 'countrymen', and Madiar was no exception. He befriended fellow Shymkentis from the construction crew and even wrote 'Shymkent' on the front of his hard hat to mark his identity. His living conditions improved a little after several months when he moved to a house in the semi-rural chastnyi sektor area in Iugo-Vostok, the south-eastern outskirts of the city. There, he lived in a room with 'only' four other men, strangers to him; there were five such rooms in the house. There was an outside toilet, and in another household a bath was available for a fee. It was a dangerous place: mugging was common among the tenants, and if one was careless enough to leave his boots unwatched at the threshold, they were gone.

Approximately half a year after his arrival Madiar successfully applied for a traffic policeman's job. He received a uniform and a baton and was assigned the task of regulating traffic at the busy junction by the Left Bank shopping mall Mega. The salary was not much, he complained (although he refused to state the exact sum), but this was state service, and there were at least prospects of improved pay at some point.[17] This improvement in his life was matched by another change of accommodation: a friend of a friend, a fellow Shymkenti, took

Madiar on as a subtenant in an apartment he and his family were renting on the ninth floor of a late-Soviet block in one of the 'sleeper districts'. As for so many other migrants, moving into a more comfortable, more unambiguously urban accommodation signified for Madiar an important step in the effortful development of his new Astana self. When we met, things were very much in the midst of development for Madiar, but after an initial period of hardship, he seemed to have reason for relative optimism.

Embodying Identity

Identities are compelling when they are embodied and performed. Against the overly semantic emphasis of the notion of identities as representations, they need to be considered within a framework of material, bodily and also spatial practices. The narratives above are stories of adopting and applying various identities, but fundamentally they are tales of self-making, becoming 'modern' and working to belong in the 'city of the future'. Migrants engaged in those endeavours by drawing on the different resources – financial, social, cultural, educational and so forth – they had at their disposal. They strove, sometimes even desperately, to grasp opportunities that arose, and they faced various challenges.

As expressed most explicitly in one of Bakytgul''s quotations above, owning a suitable apartment was seen as critically important to the successful construction of the desired urban personhood. Migrants' dreams of Left-Bank living seem to echo a familiar story. For instance, Krisztina Fehérváry (2002, 2011) has described how in post-socialist Hungary the materiality of imagined Western-European and North American suburban houses – in particular, baths and kitchens – defined the aspirations of upwardly mobile homemakers to 'middle-class' and simultaneously 'first-world' status. This resonates not only with Ainura's vision of the dwellings and lifestyles of 'those a little higher' but also with the images of 'Europe' and 'America' commonly invoked by my other informants in Astana to articulate their expectations of successful urban living, as mentioned in Chapter 1 (see also Bissenova 2012).

But perhaps for Ainura, Bakytgul' and others, including Sultan from the last chapter, these dreams, rather than being just yearnings, might have a performative function as a part of these persons' efforts to become 'modern', 'urban' subjects. Ainura's suggestion that it was only when they started building new houses that the residents of Internatsional'nyi began to 'live, not just survive' recalls to mind Sultan's comment that despite formal residence within the city he felt he was 'barely living' in Astana. These remarks jibe with an argument made by Caroline Melly (2010) in her ethnography of remittance-funded family house-building in Dakar, Senegal. It is through continuing to build, and thus keeping their future options open, that Senegalese migrants in Europe, wiring remittance back home to finance the ongoing construction, assert their belonging in the city.[18] For, as Ainura seems to have understood too, it is the ability to pursue future goals that makes the difference between merely 'residing' and truly 'living' in a place. 'Belonging is a process that is rooted in both present circumstances and future possibilities', notes Melly (2010: 62). Belonging, moreover, is not a passive state, but rather a performative activity that takes effort. Thus, I suggest that perhaps for migrants in Astana keeping alive their dreams of 'modern' living in the Left Bank was in itself a way to belong – however ambiguously or precariously – in the 'city of the future'. For some, like Sultan or Kirill and Giselle, this was backed by relatively reliable advantages, such as participating in various housing programmes, while others, like Madiar, might have to rely more on their ability to make the most of contingent opportunities.

In this context, the deployment of identities was performative in the linguistic sense of 'doing things with words' (Austin 1962): this was one of the many things migrants did alongside multiple other, more material practices to become more 'modern' and to fit better in the imagined new social environment of Astana. Individuals used 'urban' and 'rural' identities (and various associated terms) to position themselves in relation to others. Like Bakytgul' criticizing the southerners, actors pointed at those whom they saw as more 'rural' (ergo less 'modern' or 'cultured') than themselves to mark what they had achieved and to partly make up for the precariousness of their positions. On the other hand, sometimes rural connections and an otherwise stigmatized 'southern' identity, apparently at odds with the ideals of 'urbanity' and 'modernity', proved to be tactical resources crucial for gaining a foothold in Astana. For example, Madiar got his first job and accommodation upon arrival through his network of rural relatives. He stressed his belonging to a region commonly considered the heart of backwardness by writing 'Shymkent' on his hard hat, and later he managed to advance from the overcrowded chastniy sektor slum to a shared apartment with urban amenities owing to his relations with fellow migrants from the Shymkent countryside.

This points to other important senses in which it is fruitful to think of identities as performative. Identities were not freely played with in a weightless world of words. 'Urbanity' and 'rurality' were embodied as performative bodily competences, 'cultural styles' (Ferguson 1999). Thus, for instance, Bakytgul' and Kirill criticized 'rural' styles, focusing on the southerners' bodily performance, attire, speech or habits such as seed-snapping and squatting. The discourse of urbanity and rurality in Astana became that kind of phenomenon for which Michael Herzfeld (2005: 68–69) has coined the terms 'practical orientalism' and 'practical occidentalism', to highlight the mooring of 'orientalist' stereotyping, in Edward Said's (1978) sense, to everyday material practice. Identities embodied qua cultural styles are performative also in the sense that actors must struggle with available resources and structural determinations to realize imagined models of personhood, to pull off the desired identity. '[E]nacted under a "situation of duress", such styles are motivated, intentional, and performative but not simply chosen or lightly slipped into', Ferguson underscores (1999: 99). Personal traits such as Bakytgul''s shyness or Kirill's communicability impact the performance of cultural styles. There are also material constraints, which can enforce adjustments of one's aspirations and evaluations. For example, Ainura had to redefine the 'kolkhoz scum' who became her university classmates as 'the children of aspiring parents' such as herself, while Bakytgul' and her husband considered giving up on their ambitions of capital living and retreating to Karaganda or Semipalatinsk where apartments were so much more affordable.

Moreover, following how the protagonists of this chapter and the last strove to become different persons by changing their spatial and material environment helps capture the two-way constitutive relationship between places as material-and-imagined constructs and their inhabitants. It thus suggests moving beyond Ferguson's original formulation of 'cultural styles' with an emphasis on individual bodily performance. The stories narrated here suggest that this needs to be complemented by attending to the material environments in which such performance unfolds, as well as by attending to the paraphernalia that help make persons who they are or who they become (Miller 1987). Performing and projecting one's desired identity depends on a sustained relationship with a suitable environment. Thus migrants' aspirations to 'urbanity' were expressed in specific material terms – Ainura's rather detailed vision of her dream apartment offers an evocative example (recall also Oraz and Sultan quoted in Chapter 1). Conversely, 'rurality' and 'backwardness' (the opposite of 'modernity') consisted largely of the lack of certain infrastructures – to cite Ainura again, a situation where there is 'no electricity, no cars, and the buses don't run'. Also the bodily habits of others were so irritating at least partly because human bodies are part of the material environment and so an individual's 'unmodern' performance is imagined to compromise the 'modernity' of the place. The specific qualities of Astana as a place – its being properly 'urban' and 'modern' or rather 'like a village', 'backward' and 'uncultured' – were constructed as much through the development of particular types of infrastructures (housing, transportation and so forth), as through quotidian normative discourses and the performance of cultural styles by residents. Self-making and place-making were in that sense inextricably related.

The place-making dynamics also entailed an important spatio-temporal dimension. That is – built forms, infrastructures, and human bodies with their performative styles, together constituted specific areas of Astana as distinct chronotopes: sites where 'time takes on flesh' and becomes visible (Bakhtin 1981: 84). As we saw in Chapter 1 and as Ainura's dreams in this chapter confirm, the Left Bank was constructed as the locus of 'modernity' and the future. In contrast, Kumano identified certain Soviet-era neighbourhoods as 'reservations' (his exact word) where former tselinogradtsy dwelt, about to go 'extinct'. But the renewed salience of the normative ideals of urbanity and rurality, originally established as part of the conceptual framework of Soviet modernization, was itself one of the ways in which the newly construed future in Astana enmeshed with the Soviet past and future-in-the-past. In the next chapter, the focus shifts to Tselinograd and its former dwellers in Astana to explore the enduring presence of the past in the built environment – in discourses, imaginations and in quotidian practices.

Notes

1. 'Mambet' can also be derived from the name Muhammad, stereotypically associated with southern Kazakh tradition (Svetlana Jacquesson, personal communication).
2. For Kazakhstan, see Akiner (1995); Kaiser and Chinn (1995); Kolstø (1999); Schatz (2000a, 2000b); Wolfel (2002); Cummings (2006); Dave (2007); Danzer (2009); Yessenova (2010). For the former USSR in general, Bremmer and Taras (1993); Brubaker (1994); Smith (1996); Smith et al. (1998); Kolstø (1999); Laitin (1999).
3. I thank Natalie Koch for suggesting this term.
4. There was also a considerable population of Russophone Germans – descendants of tsarist-era colonists and deportees from World War II (Danzer 2009; Sanders 2016).
5. In Kazakhstan in total, the Kazakhs numbered only 39.7 per cent of the population in 1989, with Russians at 33 per cent and 'other European nationalities' making up another 10 per cent (Goskomstat 1992).
6. Migration-driven population growth in Astana has exceeded natural growth by two to three times year by year (Agentstvo 2007: 108, 2011b: 74). As for the internal/foreign immigration rate, in 2004, for instance, there were in Astana 162,000 migrants from within Kazakhstan and only 6,200 immigrants from abroad, including 2,500 *oral-mans* (Tatibekov 2005: 13; the oralmans are ethnic Kazakhs 'repatriating' from China, Mongolia or elsewhere – see Finke 1999; Diener 2005).
7. Approximately a third were between ages fifteen and twenty-four (Tatibekov 2005: 58), and another 40-odd per cent between twenty-five and thirty-nine (ibid.: 39). Zabirova (2002b: 27, 2003: 224) additionally indicates a particularly high percentage of youth among incomers from rural areas: 65 per cent between ages eighteen and twenty-nine and another 32 per cent between thirty and forty-four.
8. Although rings of semi-legal construction sprouted up around major Kazakhstani cities in the 1990s (Gentile 2003: 151–55; Alexander 2007a: 76–78), the existence of quasi-rural built environments and associated types of economic activity and lifestyle within city limits was by no means a new phenomenon. Mud-brick, or *samannye,* houses had been a persistent eyesore to modernizers in this region since tsarist times (M. Pohl 1999: 440; Buchli 2007). Under socialism, the construction of 'modern' and 'properly urban' apartment blocks and the distribution of apartments failed to keep pace with the migration-fuelled growth of the urban population, which contributed to a shortage of housing (Szelenyi 1983; Gentile 2003: 144, 2004: 20). Therefore, the chastnyi sektor (literally, 'private sector') emerged, where individual families erected dwellings for them-selves on available ground as close as possible to industrial workplaces and the urban core. In Tselinograd, such clusters appeared at several locations, roughly encircling the city centre and the adjacent industrial zone. With 'modern' building materials such as bricks or concrete prefabs hard to come by, and hay, clay and mud abundant, the bulk of this 'grass roots' construction was, again, samannye structures.
9. Member of the Komsomol, the Soviet communist youth organization.

10. Kotkin (1995) notes a similar atmosphere at the grand Stalinist construction sites such as Magnitogorsk. He describes the condition that reigned there as 'bacchanalian fluidity' (p. 97).

11. Note the echo of President Nazarbaev's exhortation to the people of the new capital to 'build their future with their own two hands', cited in Chapter 1.

12. *Dom* is Russian for 'house' and 'home', while the Anglicism *lift* means 'elevator'.

13. I became part of his networks through the game Encounter (Chapter 6), when Kirill joined the team I was on.

14. Accusations of nepotism are hardly specific to Astana, appearing in exactly the same form in post-1991 Almaty, for example (Alexander 2009b: 156). Saulesh Yessenova (2003: 25–27) argues that the supposedly collectivist disposition of rural Kazakhs was constructed as part of Kazakhs' perennial ethnic 'nature' by Soviet, Kazakh and Western historians. There is, however, 'no sign that community interests supported migrants' interaction across the urban/rural divide or in the city', and little evidence of cooperation with earlier migrants in the urban setting, even if they were kin (ibid.: 33–34).

15. Note how these words echo Sultan's quote in Chapter 1 about Astana as shown on television versus Astana as actually experienced.

16. About 170,000 Koreans were deported from the Soviet Far East to Kazakhstan and Uzbekistan in 1937 (J. Pohl 1999: 9–19).

17. Of course, one could speculate that the opportunity to extract bribes from drivers was a major advantage of his new position, but Madiar denied that vehemently, not so much on moral or professional grounds but because of the tight controls under which traffic policemen allegedly operated.

18. Tod Hartman (2007) makes a very similar argument for the new villas slowly getting built by Romanian wage migrants.

Chapter 3

Tselinograd

The Past in the 'City of the Future'

During the Soviet period the kitchen had become a favoured place where the most important matters of public concern could be discussed in private, an intimate site for rituals of conversation that helped create the social world (Boym 1994: 147; Ries 1997: 21). For all that has changed in post-Soviet social life, the tradition of long kitchen conversation is alive and well. The kitchen at Mira's place, on the seventh floor of a late-Soviet apartment block hosted numerous *posidelki* (sit-in parties) during which Mira and her friends, often joined by one or both of Mira's parents, would drink endless cups of tea (occasionally some alcohol too) and chat the hours away.

One dark and frosty evening, Mira, her brother, her best friend Margarita and several other friends including myself had gathered around the kitchen table. The radio was quietly playing Soviet rock classics. Suddenly, a curly-haired blonde who went by the nickname Koshka remembered something and exclaimed: 'Have you heard, they've taken Pushkin away! Just like they did Lenin!' She was referring to two monuments that had been displaced. A bronze monument to Lenin used to stand in Tselinograd's Central Square until one night, around the time of the capital relocation, it was driven away by a truck. At first transferred to a less prominent location, it eventually disappeared from the cityscape altogether.[1] As for Pushkin, a modest monument to the great Russian poet used to be situated in a small park near the northern section of the city's Soviet-built main thoroughfare, Pushkin Avenue.[2] In March 2008, shortly before that kitchen gathering, the statue was suddenly removed. Koshka's friends responded to the news of Pushkin's removal with surprise and disbelief, before the topic was changed again. But the disappearance of Pushkin was to resurface in many subsequent conversations among Astana's long-standing residents, preoccupied with the material, social and ideological transformations underway.

Throughout the 1990s and early 2000s, old (usually Soviet-era) monuments were removed and replaced with other symbols and statues in cities across the former Soviet Union (Wanner 1998: 178–91; Forest and Johnson 2002, 2011). This was done to erase previous narratives of the national past and inscribe new interpretations of history, or, as Bruce Grant (2001) argues for a particular set of new monuments in post-Soviet Moscow, to 'suspend' the flow of time and obviate public anxieties as to what the future would bring. But the dismantled monuments, through their very absence, provided material foci for uncertainty over the ongoing redefinition of public values and identities.

The case of the Pushkin monument in Astana fits this broader picture only partly, as of course Pushkin was hardly a specifically Soviet hero, and the monument itself had been installed only in 1999. Yet it was a valued symbol to all those residents of the city who considered Pushkin a part of their cultural legacy: Russians and other Slavs – those whom David Laitin (1995) proposes to call 'the Russian-speaking nationality' – but also Russophone Kazakhs. The monument had become particularly dear to members of Mira and Koshka's generation – the last to be born in Tselinograd, in the 1980s – who, in their high school and university years, used to socialize on the steps of the pedestal, in the shade of the surrounding trees. 'We used to literally drink with Pushkin!' Koshka laughed as she showed me a photograph of a group of her university classmates raising a toast at the foot of the statue. Some residents framed the removal of the monument in terms of national identity. They saw Pushkin's dislocation as related to that of Lenin's and interpreted the two cases as parts of the Kazakh-dominated authorities' agenda to eradicate the new capital's Soviet past and Russian cultural profile. 'Pushkin belongs somewhere in Russia, but in Kazakhstan he doesn't fit, you see?' Koshka reasoned sarcastically. 'Just like Lenin. If Kazakhstan is now an independent state, why would they need him? So they've done away with him'. About half a year later, the Pushkin monument reappeared. This time it was in a recently refurbished university area, next to a large floral composition: an operating clock and letters reading 'Astana 2030', alluding to President Nazarbaev's vision of Kazakhstan's future, the so-called 'Strategy 2030'. Concerns over the erasure of the Russian cultural legacy symbolized by the disappearance of the poet's statue from the cityscape of Astana were thus acquiesced. Yet the monument's relocation still provided a focus of concern about the terms of different groups' belonging in the Kazakhstani capital and about the relationship between the past and the new government-projected future.

This chapter looks at how several generations of long-standing residents, who commonly referred to themselves as *tselinogradtsy*, engaged with the material cityscape to (re)construct Tselinograd as an alternative chronotope (Bakhtin 1981), a 'real-and-imagined' city (Soja 1996; cf. Chapter 1) where they could collectively belong. I examine several ways in which this was done: narratives of building Tselinograd as a modern city; nostalgic projections of community and intimacy; and quotidian spatial practices, such as walking in the Soviet-era neighbourhoods. Multiple pasts not only remained present in the 'city of the future' but were actively produced by residents as bases for alternative configurations of the present and the future. The Pushkin monument had been created after the capital relocation and the introduction of the name Astana. But Tselinograd as constructed by those residents was not fixed within a sharply defined chronological frame – the city as it had 'actually' been up to the fall of the USSR, Tselinograd's renaming as Aqmola or Aqmola's eventual transformation into Astana. Rather, it was a living, changing city, where the continuity of residents' lives and their engagements with the material environment defied the periodization of official history.

Building Tselinograd

One summer day, not far from the site of the displaced monument to Pushkin, the elderly Maria Pavlovna sat on a wooden bench in the shade of an immense 30 metre high wall of grey concrete on whose surface wheat sheaves were painted, and a weather-beaten inscription read, in Russian and Kazakh, 'The Virgin Lands Raised, The Effort Continues!' The building was a grain elevator, originally built in the 1950s, and later expanded to accommodate a record harvest, which the inscription presumably commemorates (Figure 3.1). Although intended for a purely technical role and still in operation, the elevator is now the largest remaining architectural monument to Astana's past as the capital of the Tselina, the Virgin Lands Campaign. As mentioned in the introduction, this Campaign had been an unprecedented effort to turn the steppes of northern Kazakhstan and

Figure 3.1 Soviet-era grain elevator (photo: M. Laszczkowski)

southern Siberia into a grain-producing region, an enterprise comparable in its scope and ideological significance to the great *stroiki* (constructions) of the Stalinist period twenty years earlier (M. Pohl 1999; cf. Kotkin 1995).

Maria Pavlovna, in her seventies, was wearing a simple faded light-grey working gown. A white headscarf and copper-red dyed hair framed her jovial round face; a wedding ring shone on one of her thick fingers. From a plastic bag she pulled two large photo albums in cardboard covers, one grey, the other marine blue, and spread one open on her lap. Black and white photographs featured young women in white gowns checking grain samples for quality in a lab that, as Maria Pavlovna explained to me, was part of the grain elevator facilities. 'I'm going to talk to you in *khokhlatskii*', she smiled a little apologetically, not certain whether I would be able to comprehend that mixed Ukrainian dialect, considerably different from standard Russian. 'After all these years', she added on second thoughts, 'I'm no longer sure what language I speak'. Suddenly, she pointed to a girl in one of the pictures: 'That's me!' she exclaimed, 'I can tell by the blouse, I used to have one exactly like this!' Taking a closer look at the photograph, I realized the person she had pointed out was a very young Maria Pavlovna indeed. A migrant from Ukraine, she had worked at the elevator, mostly at a grain-drying appliance, since 1963. When I asked how it had begun, she laughed wholeheartedly: 'I ran away from my husband!'

Her life story, although in many ways untypical, intertwined with the development of Tselinograd, and thus it offers an opportunity to follow the story of the gradual, reiterative emergence of forms of urban modernity, highlighting the deeply personal dimensions of that process. Maria Pavlovna had lived in a mining town in central Ukraine and worked in a mine since she was sixteen. She was married and had two children, but her husband – a tall, strong and handsome man – soon became a drunkard rather than a breadwinner. When their house burned down, Maria Pavlovna decided to run. She was twenty-four at that time. She gathered her children and a flour sack full of the most vital belongings and headed to the train station. She asked for one-way tickets to Tselinograd. 'Tselinograd?' the woman behind the counter asked, perhaps sensing the young mother's distress. 'My child, do you even know where that is? Why don't you take tickets to the Crimea instead?' Maria Pavlovna had no clue where Tselinograd was, except that it was far away – but that was precisely the point. She had heard the name frequently on the radio. 'If I had gone to the Crimea, my husband would have found me within twelve hours!' she reasoned.

After several days' journey, Maria Pavlovna got off the train in Tselinograd, told her children to sit on their sack and wait, and walked into the town in search of shelter. Nobody seemed willing to take them on, until finally a woman agreed to let them stay in a room in her house, a very modest mud-brick dwelling, in exchange for Maria Pavlovna's help with household chores. Having secured a shelter, Maria Pavlovna took to the streets again to find a job. She came across the grain elevator, back then still only a wooden structure, at the end of a railway track in what was at that time the north-eastern outskirts of the town. She had no experience with this kind of work, so she was doubly surprised when, first, the management agreed to enrol her, and again when her name was not on a layoff list that was put up a month later. Soon she received training in grain-dryer operating, in reward for cleaning the director's office after hours. She also moved to a company-provided room that she and her children were to share with another family in a small brick house nearby.

Her husband knocked on their door half a year after she had arrived in Tselinograd. Maria Pavlovna never learned how he had found her; he must have cried the secret out of Maria Pavlovna's sister, who was the only person to whom she had revealed her new address in a letter. On the doorstep he fell to his knees and begged forgiveness. The kids ran towards him. Maria Pavlovna cried too, and she let him stay. He changed, got employed at a factory and became the model husband to a hard-working Soviet wife. The elevator management arranged for the family to have an entire apartment all to themselves, only needing to share the kitchen with neighbours – such were the residential space norms of the day. Later, those neighbours were evicted for hanging their laundry to dry on a wire stretched across the kitchen: a misuse of communal space.

Maria Pavlovna's husband had a motorcycle accident at age thirty-two and never regained the ability to walk unassisted. Thus, the wife became the sole breadwinner again. In addition to her regular eight-hour shift, she took up other tasks at the elevator facilities: cleaning, whitewashing and so on. She received a garden plot with a small house (dacha) beyond the town limits, and in addition she kept up to a hundred ducks, geese, chickens, rabbits and a few pigs in a garden by their town house. She managed to support her family; she fed the animals with grain she took from the elevator: 'I used to steal grain by the sack!' she laughs. Management probably knew of her theft but turned a blind eye out of sympathy for the brave young woman and in recognition of her very hard labour. Slowly, Maria Pavlovna grew first into a respected worker, then a socialist 'labour heroine'.

The city grew with her. Maria Pavlovna witnessed what was then perceived and today continues to be remembered by many as the most glorious period in its history. Established in 1830 as a tsarist trading outpost called Akmolinsk (Dubitskii 1990), the town had slowly but steadily grown. By 1939 it had become an oblast (regional) capital with a population of 32,000. Akmolinsk gained importance during the Second World War as one of the destinations for industry evacuated from Ukraine and western Russia before the advancing Nazi army. In 1942 the Soviet government decided that a major agricultural-machinery producing complex should be established in Akmolinsk in order to secure supplies for the national agriculture during wartime. Thus was born KazakhSel'Mash (acronym for Kazakhstan Agricultural Machinery), a factory that was to achieve Union-wide importance and remained the city's largest employer until the end of the USSR (Alpyspaeva 2008: 47–48). Other major industrial enterprises in Akmolinsk included a pump factory, railway carriage repair workshops, a sewing factory and a cast iron plant.

In the post-war period, the beginning of the Virgin Lands Campaign, launched in 1954, changed the face of northern Kazakhstan and of Akmolinsk in particular. The campaign involved populating the Kazakh steppes with settlers recruited primarily from the Russian heartland and other Slav areas of the empire to establish farm settlements and crop-processing facilities. By the 1960s, their number totalled up to two million (M. Pohl 1999). The campaign gave rise to a 'colonizing' narrative (Mitchell 1988) according to which Soviet-era settlers had 'built' modern Kazakhstan – constructed the cities, factories, roads and infrastructures where previously there had only been the 'empty' steppe. Half a century later, that narrative would still be invoked – for example, by two elderly ladies who had arrived in Tselinograd as young girls and were living in the same apartment block where I lived during fieldwork:

> Anna Arkadievna: This was the Tselina, there was nothing here. Say, there were such tiny houses and that's it.
> Liubov' Vissarionovna: The Kazakhs used to live in their yurts.
> AA: There was nothing but yurts.
> LV: There were no houses.
> AA: There was nothing. These five-storey, nine-storey buildings – none of them were there. And there were the endless fields …
> LV: … empty!
> AA: And those fields had to be tamed … So from all over Russia, Belarus, Ukraine, settlers came. … They were sent here to tame the virgin lands. And lots and lots of people came. …
> LV: The Kazakhs had never sown anything, had not dug the soil. It was all empty.
> AA: … That was called, conquering the virgin land. There are many songs about it. And there were Russians, Ukrainians, Belarusians, Poles … They all lived together. … And they tamed the land, they tilled, they sowed grain, corn, sunflower and whatever they could. And so, little by little, the cities were born. The construction of the cities began. And all those people came and stayed.

It is striking how this narrative ascribes historic agency exclusively to the Slavic settlers, reducing the Kazakh population literally to a part of the scenery. Similar asymmetry is, of course, typical for the colonial imaginary across the world historical record, for instance with regard to the white settlers' way of seeing – or actually *not* seeing – the native inhabitants of the American West (Brown 2001: 30). It was also a typical optic of Soviet-era 'modernizers' across the enormous non-European expanses of the Union (Martin 2001). In Kazakhstan, in particular, the motif of the 'virgin', 'empty steppe' waiting to be colonized and 'developed' had been a recurrent one at least since the early tsarist excursions in the 1800s (Buchli 2007: 47–48). In Tselinograd, as shall be seen, it returned with each new wave of immigration and construction throughout the post-war decades. Previously existing infrastructures and social forms were repeatedly rhetorically erased to justify and emphasize newer developments. With the relocation of the capital of post-Soviet Kazakhstan, the 'bare steppe' returned in the rhetoric of the Nazarbaev government, as discussed in the introduction. However, at the same time it was also picked up again by those Soviet-era settlers and their descendants who used it to assert their own role as civilization-bearers against the new regime's vision of the past and the present. In this renewed usage, the trope of 'civilization' built amidst wilderness might be expressed in terms of the dichotomy of the 'rural' and the 'urban', as discussed in the previous chapter, or, as in the quotation above, take on an explicitly ethnicized form.

The population of Akmolinsk, as the urban centre of the 'Virgin Lands', rose from 32,000 in 1939 to 85,000 in 1951 and to 140,000 in 1963 (Alpyspaeva 2008: 155). The industrial enterprises established in the 1940s continued to expand, and new factories appeared. These developments were paralleled and largely enabled by the growing role of Akmolinsk as a railway hub (ibid.: 60–67). The Railway Employees' Palace of Culture, a pseudo-classicist structure with a massive colonnaded portico, was built in 1954 in acknowledgement of the Akmolinsk station crew's work.

In the early 1960s, Akmolinsk became Tselinograd. To give a new impulse to the Virgin Lands Campaign, a new administrative unit was created, the Tselinnyi krai, comprised of five northern Kazakhstani oblasts, with Akmolinsk as its capital. In 1961, the city's name was changed. The then Soviet leader Nikita Khrushchev argued that a name that allegedly meant 'white grave' (Kazakh, Aq-Mola) was inauspicious and needed to be replaced with something that 'would be appropriate for the present and the future of [the] city' (Dubitskii 1959: 15; M. Pohl 1999: 430). These events brought Tselinograd into the spotlight in the early 1960s, which very likely explains why the young Maria Pavlovna had heard about the city so often. Khrushchev had proposed that a new city should be erected in a planned manner, 'on a clean slate', next to the pre-existing town. Accordingly, in 1963, the year of Maria Pavlovna's arrival, a new general plan was adopted, based on the then ruling modernist principles of Nikolai Miliutin (French 1995: 39–41; Alpyspaeva 2008: 94). The plan dictated a tripartite zoning of the city: an industrial zone north of the railway tracks, a middle residential zone and southernmost a park belt along the bank of the Ishim.

When we met, Maria Pavlovna remembered that at the time of her arrival Tselinograd was still but a pitiful, small muddy puddle of a town where 'there was nothing but virtual lakes in the streets, puddles and mud', and 'people would step on [wooden] planks [placed on the ground to facilitate walking]'. But soon she witnessed a period of the town's impressive development. The same year 1963 also saw the beginning of construction of a first *mikroraion* (Mikroraion A, later called Tselinnyi), a residential quarter located on previously undeveloped land east of the city centre, designed following the latest theories in urban planning (French 1995: 81–83 for the mikroraion principle; Alpyspaeva 2008: 102–103). Further mikroraiony were to be gradually added throughout the seventies and eighties, unfolding in a south-easterly direction (see Map 1.1; Chapter 1). Also in 1963, the Dvorets Tselinnikov (Palace of the Virgin Landers) was completed, a state-of-the-art venue for mass entertainment, cultural events and assemblies. But the development most often recalled by residents who remember that period was the construction of a grid of new streets between the expanded city centre and the railway station, lined with five-storey standardized apartment buildings (*piatietazhki*, literally 'five-storeys', or *khrushchevki* – from Khrushchev). Those were part of Khrushchev's Union-wide housing programme (French 1995: 75–80; Gerchuk 2000: 86; Alpyspaeva 2008: 91). Some of them were built of prefabricated concrete panels, and the apartments had modern municipal amenities (Figure 3.2).

It was this development that, in the eyes of settlers, turned Akmolinsk/ Tselinograd into a proper modern city: 'When we had first arrived the town was tiny, mainly made up of mud-brick [*samannye*] dwellings', recalls Aleksei Vladimirovich (roughly Maria Pavlovna's age), who had arrived with his parents from Lithuania in 1953, aged seven:

Figure 3.2 Khrushchev-era housing in Prospekt Pobedy (Victory Avenue) (photo: M. Laszczkowski)

And then, after in 1961 Nikita Sergeevich Khrushchev renamed this city Tselinograd ... construction workers came from Ukraine, from Belarus ... The city was established before my eyes. The first street was Karl Marx Street. They got it widened. They gradually demolished the shacks ... And there was also Mira [Peace] Street – these were the first two streets to be reconstructed by builders who came here from all over the Soviet Union. ... I witnessed it all, as they were constructing the first buildings. I contributed to it a little bit too: I used to work in communications after I finished school. ... We put the first TV antennas on the five-storeys, in the 1960s ... And so, gradually, it was all established.

From the 1960s to the 1980s, the number of industrial enterprises in the city grew steadily, including a new grain elevator and several construction factories (Alpyspaeva 2008: 57–59). KazakhSel'Mash (renamed TselinSel'Mash in 1969; Dubitskii 1990: 102) remained a major employer and an engine of urban development, building apartments and infrastructure for the city. Prospekt Tselinnikov (today's southern leg of Prospekt Respubliki) became the city's principal thoroughfare, marked at its southern end by a symmetrical composition of several multi-storey apartment blocks that formed a 'gate' to the city, and whose facades were decorated with wheat-sheaf ornament. A number of other Tselinograd landmarks appeared in the 1970s, such as a tall Lenin statue in front of a new sixteen-storey office tower (*shesnadtsatietazhka*) in the redesigned Central Square (Tsentral'naia ploshchad') and the Monument to the Tselina, featuring a real bright orange K-700 tractor (*kirovets*) and a couple of Herculean statues of Virgin Landers, male and female. Several gems of modernist architecture were added to the cityscape, including the large iceberg-like wedding palace, the glass facade of the Youth Palace (Dvorets molodezhy) and the Central Department Store, Tsentral'nyi univermag (TsUM), opened in 1981 in Central Square. The city's population rose from 180,000 in 1970 to 225,000 seven years later (Alpyspaeva 2008: 156).

Tselinograd's development was not unproblematic, of course. Just as the personal lives of settlers like Maria Pavlovna were often struggles, so the story of Tselinograd was one of continuous struggle to create and maintain a modern urban order. In many ways, Akmolinsk/Tselinograd retained embarrassing marks of 'backwardness' and 'rurality'. Up to the mid 1950s, the built environment consisted mainly of one-storey houses of mud-brick or wood (Alpyspaeva 2008: 87). In 1956 the town had 9,150 dwellings (ibid.), far too few to accommodate the quickly increasing population. Later, construction was often delayed and carried out in a piecemeal manner. Many rundown buildings scheduled for demolition were left standing, while new structures were often poorly and hastily built (ibid.: 103, 106). Moreover, residents' practical interventions deepened the chasm between the plans and reality: storage shacks and garages were located in the backyards of apartment blocks; shops and services opened on ground floors without any overall plan or system; pavements, intra-neighbourhood driveways, curbs and above-ground pipes were placed in an ad hoc manner as needs arose (ibid.: 104). There were few cultural establishments, although a drama theatre was established in 1955. Many roadways remained unpaved, and throughout the 1960s–1980s the city continuously faced problems with water supply, sewerage and drainage (ibid.: 98–100).

Meanwhile, Maria Pavlovna worked hard at the grain elevator and lived modestly in the company-allotted 1950s apartment, with her disabled husband. She received many awards for her work: 'I got a medal, Orden Trudovoi Slavy [Labour Glory], I got other medals … I got eighty-two diplomas … I went to Moscow, to the Kremlin … I took the first place in Kazakhstan in grain-drying … I got a Golden Hands diploma; they gave me a car – a Moskvich … I went to Almaty, they put me on a pedestal and there I stood!' 'I have never done anything better than this elevator', Maria Pavlovna said, but she added quickly: 'Labour used to be valued those days'. Once a journalist from the newspaper *Izvestia* came and interviewed her. A very open and honest person, Maria Pavlovna told the journalist the entire true story: how she had run from her husband and that this was how her 'labour heroine' career had begun. Afterwards, she was afraid that all that she had said would be published and she might get in trouble. But when she got a copy of the paper there was nothing in it but the 'proper' narrative: 'I had expected to see a giant standing between fire and grain', the journalist wrote, 'but there was just this little woman standing there!'

Running counter to the increasingly ossified official image of the Virgin Land settlers in Soviet propaganda from the 1960s to the 1980s as one-dimensional heroes fully committed to the ideological goals set by the leadership (M. Pohl 1999: 82–92), Maria Pavlovna's story highlights the personal motivations, constraints, compromises and hesitations of a Tselinograd labour-heroine. Official representations obscured those personal dimensions, much as they obscured the on-the-ground realities of living in Tselinograd and the city's contingent, uneven and forever incomplete development. In this sense, the history of Tselinograd as told through the biographies of individuals such as Maria Pavlovna is to official Soviet narratives of modernization in the Virgin Lands as the stories of migrants included in Chapters 1 and 2 are to the official post-Soviet discourse about the construction of Astana.

There are further resonances between the histories of building Tselinograd and Astana. It is striking how history seemingly repeated itself when in the late 1990s President Nazarbaev changed the city's name and postulated construction 'on a clean slate', just as Nikita Khrushchev had done forty years earlier. With focus on the individual personal experience, Tselinograd was for Maria Pavlovna what Astana was to become to migrants in the 2000s: a remote place of hope, deliverance from hardship; a place of hard work through which livelihood was secured; where subjecthood was performed and a sense of self-worth was gained. Crucially, in the story just told above, as with the narratives of Astana in the earlier chapters, personal development is intertwined with the gradual, difficult emergence of material forms of urban modernity. In Chapters 1 and 2 we have seen how in Astana 'modernity' was embodied in futuristic landmarks such as Baiterek, but also and at least just as importantly in newly built housing of which migrants dreamed. In Tselinograd, the landmark buildings I have mentioned above had been modernity's exemplars, while the five-storey apartment blocks and asphalted roadways were its more mundane substance, though equally a thing of pride for those who had witnessed and often participated in their making.

Confronted with the transformations to their city and to social life in Kazakhstan generally after the collapse of the Soviet Union and the capital relocation, former tselinogradtsy often invoked a narrative of having 'built the city with their own hands' (or, as is the case with the younger generations, with those of their parents and grandparents).[3] Their sense of local belonging was rooted in the notion that before the settlers' arrival the place had been 'empty' or at least 'tiny' and 'undeveloped'. The identity of the tselinogradtsy stemmed from the sense of being part of the story of a modern city emerging, literally from mud, through settlers' hard labour, and of an endemically deficient built environment reiteratively improved.

Nostalgia and Spatial Intimacy

Alongside the narrative of the creation and maintenance of material urban modernity, Tselinograd's former residents constructed other versions of the city's past. In particular, Tselinograd was reconstructed as a harmonious, almost pastoral community that had been lost – an object of nostalgia. As we chatted over tea one afternoon, Ekaterina Stanislavovna, a woman of Polish descent, in her late fifties, depicted Tselinograd in the following manner:

> Tselinograd used to be tiny ... It used to be Slavic for the most part, Slavic peoples [*slavianskie narody*] used to live here, and very few Kazakhs lived in the city. ... Basically, only related people used to live here [*zdes' zhili v osnovnom-to vse svoi*] ... neighbours, relatives, people [originating] from one village, from one area – they were all friends. All the people were amiable. ... If, say, Karaganda was a bigger city, a miners' city, an industrial one, and more money was put into its development, then Tselinograd was truly an agricultural town [*sel'skokhoziaistvennyi gorod*], with nothing but fields around, and it was more modest, more peaceful, but we lived well anyway. Somehow, it was both merry and amicable. All in all, it was a good city, peaceful and quiet. Say, there weren't that

many cars, we never thought there would ever be traffic jams in our
city. ... We would go by foot everywhere. And still, there were theatres,
and cinemas and the Palace of Culture ...[4]

In this description, Tselinograd was an almost bucolic idyll of close-knit
community and reciprocity, which for all its quasi-rural peacefulness and close-
ness to 'nature' did not lack urban 'culturedness' (*kul'turnost'* – theatres and so
on; see Hoffmann 2003: 15–45). Implicitly, in this view, the town's tranquillity
entailed amicable interethnic relations – safeguarded, as it is so tactfully hinted
at, by the domination of Slavic inhabitants over Kazakhs.[5] But, as Ekaterina
Stanislavovna's account unfolded, the idyll was doomed:

Previously, as I said, Tselinograd was a small town and practically
everyone knew one another. You had gone to school together, worked
together, there were the friends of one's friends and practically you could
meet a friend everywhere. And now it's not so any longer. Many have
left: in the eighties or thereabout, the departure of the Germans began
– many Germans left, then many Poles and many Russians too. And
those who arrived [instead] were people from the villages, from all sorts
of places, an alien kind of people.

The newcomers, Ekaterina Stanislavovna further asserted, brought with
them violence, anomie and moral disorder, expressed for instance in what happened to the suburban dacha garden plots (the once 'private paradises' of socialist
women and men (Lovell 2003)), which were pillaged and occupied by violent
rural migrants in search of free shelter, utensils and foodstuffs. 'In Tselinograd
nobody stole anything from the dachas, smashed anything or burned houses',
Ekaterina Stanislavovna claimed, 'it is only now that people have turned so
rough ... started to loiter and steal'.

Ekaterina Stanislavovna's narrative, echoing familiar tropes of post-Soviet
anomie (cf. Humphrey 2002b; Nazpary 2002), moreover constructs and projects into the past a place, a set of social relations and a moral order in which the
simultaneously projected collective identity of the tselinogradtsy is based – in line
with the observation by Raymond Williams (1973) that images of a supposedly
superior pastoral moral order commonly serve the ideological purposes of groups
losing out in the politico-economic dynamics in the cities. All the ambiguity
inherent in the category of rurality is strikingly brought to the fore in her account.
Latter-day rural migrants are depicted as the agents of chaos and destruction,
while simultaneously the rural-like order of the past is nostalgically praised.

Nostalgia has become a particularly prolific field especially in the anthropology of post-socialism. Diverse phenomena of post-socialist nostalgia have
been described, and various determinants and political ramifications of those

nostalgias have been explored (e.g., Berdahl 1999; Boym 2001; Boyer 2006; Flynn, Kosmarskaya and Sabirova 2014). A sort of general nostalgia not so much for socialism as for lives as they used to be was also expressed by many former Soviet citizens in Astana, especially the elderly. 'The old days' before perestroika and the USSR's break-up were idealized as a time when young families received apartments from their employers, when everyone had a job and there were free holiday vouchers and pioneer camps for the children (cf. Chapter 1). Such discourses construe a generic socialist past as a utopian 'Golden Age' and reverse the temporality vector of post-socialist 'transition', seeing the changes as an Ovidian regression (Alexander 2004: 251). Nostalgic representations of Tselinograd such as the one offered by Ekaterina Stanislavovna easily fit into this broader genre of post-socialist nostalgia.

However, it is fruitful to move beyond the commonalities of post-socialist nostalgias and study nostalgic practices situated in particular contexts (Nadkarni and Shevchenko 2004). The anthropological literature on nostalgia highlights nostalgia's productivity. Debbora Battaglia, for instance, speaks of 'practical nostalgia': a discursive practice 'where the issues for users become, on the one hand, the attachment of appropriate feelings toward their own histories, products, and capabilities, and on the other hand, their detachment from – and active resistance to – disempowering conditions of [social] life' (1995b: 77, emphasis removed). Shaped by context-specific determinants, nostalgic practices produce specific effects. While 'images of the past commonly serve to legitimate a present social order' (Connerton 1989: 3), it is also true that 'nostalgic readings of the past articulate a critique of the present, enabling the imagination of a different future' (Richardson 2008: 149). Nostalgia focused on particular material places or things can create a transformative material link to the past through those objects (Zhang 2006: 461). Thus I argue that nostalgic depictions of Tselinograd were a wager on the future and a critical response to ongoing reconfigurations of social relations. Former tselinogradtsy practised nostalgia to reconstruct Tselinograd as an affectively invested alternative time-space of their collective belonging, as they felt their place in the social order of Astana at present and in the future was being questioned.

While the pastoral is generally one of the most pervasive nostalgic tropes (Williams 1973), nostalgic valuations of Tselinograd's 'rurality' are striking in the context of the ideological emphasis on urban modernity in the Soviet period and after. As discussed earlier in this book, at least since the time of Soviet modernization, rurality carried associations with 'backwardness', the opposite of modernity. The question whether the place is a 'proper city' or just a 'big village' continuously troubled the residents of today's Astana (see Buchli 2007). Despite decades of development, as outlined above, settlers arriving in the 1950s, 1960s or even 1970s repeatedly found Akmolinsk and then Tselinograd a 'village' (if not outright a 'muddy hole') and saw themselves as among those who brought this place up to urban 'civilization' and 'modernity'. Similar to the forever deferred completion of the construction of infrastructure in Soviet subarctic Siberia studied by Ssorin-Chaikov (2003), this perpetual incompleteness of urbanity served as a legitimizing trope to support the settlers' and then their descendants' local belonging. It helped turn the facts of allochtony into the virtue of progress-bearing and creation. And yet in narratives such as Ekaterina Stanislavovna's, Tselinograd was construed as a small, quiet, 'agricultural' town, set amid fields and inhabited by a tightly knit community – evoking fairly rustic associations.

I suggest that in parallel to the narrative of conquering the 'Virgin Lands' and building urbanity, nostalgic constructions of rurality allowed the former tselinogradtsy to strengthen their sense of belonging to a locally rooted community by cultivating what I propose to call 'spatial intimacy'. This term derives from Herzfeld's (2005) more general concept of 'cultural intimacy', but it serves to emphasize space as the main referent of the work done by the actors engaging in that discursive and affective practice. Cultural intimacy in general is a way of creating community drawing on the shared recognition of familiar flaws of common sociality. Those flaws are sources of embarrassment, but precisely by this token they also provide for a sense of an intimate 'fellowship of the flawed' (Herzfeld 2005: 29). Likewise, spatial intimacy refers to embarrassing flaws found in the spatial environment shared by a group of people – for instance, the 'rural' outlook of a city (in contexts where notions of urbanity and rurality are loaded and hierarchized in a way similar to the way they were in Tselinograd/Astana). The recognition of those flaws serves to intensify the sense of connection to the place and to each other.

For example, when I asked a couple of middle-aged local Russians, Natasha and Vladimir, to share their memories of what Tselinograd had looked like towards the end of the Soviet period, they broke into a semi-jocular argument over whether the place had deserved to be called a city at all. Vladimir stated categorically: 'This was a true village, full stop! A big village!' His wife demanded, in a somewhat apologetic voice, 'Vova [diminutive of Vladimir], but it *was* a city …!' to which Vladimir generously conceded: 'Okay, but a tiny one, admit it, it was a tiny town [*malenkii gorodishko byl*]'. He recalled that much of Tselinograd's built environment had been detached samannye (mud and straw) dwellings lining even such prominent roads as Ulitsa Lenina (Lenin Street), and that the most 'modern' buildings had been only two- and five-storey apartment blocks. The same five-storeys of which older residents had been so proud, Vladimir invoked as epitomes of obsolescence. Now the point is that Natasha and Vladimir might seem to be quarrelling, but the tone of their voices and their facial expressions revealed that they were both actually enjoying the exchange. They could enjoy it because they shared an ironic and (as implied by Vladimir's choice of the diminutive '*gorodishko*') at the same time affectionate recognition of Tselinograd's flaws as a 'modern city'.

One more example of this ironic-affectionate attitude can be found in the following words of Mira, recalling her childhood spent in a neighbourhood near the old marketplace and a recent visit she and her childhood friends had made to that area:

> Our neighbourhood used to be merry, with five-storey blocks of apartments. … Somebody used to keep sheep in a shack behind our block, and we'd run and feed the sheep. We would pick twigs from trees, feed the sheep, we would loiter at the garages and climb all the pipes in the neighbourhood.[6] And [recently] we decided to go back to the neighbourhood, look for our old friends. Here I am, and the heating pipes are gone, they've tucked them away somewhere. Then, there used to be such a cool tarmac-covered children's playground – if you fell, your knees were a bloody mash! [laughing] They have replaced it with a real football pitch, with a fence around, well maintained. … Everything's so alien. They've put a decent fence around the kindergarten. … Everything's gotten so unfamiliar [takoe vse ne svoe], I just went away.

The changes Mira describes could be appreciated – after all, the neighbourhood became more 'user-friendly', cleaner and safer for the children. Mira's choice of phrases such as 'a decent fence' and the grotesque implicit in her description of the knee-smashing tarmac-covered playground reveal that she acknowledges the material improvements. Still, the renovated neighbourhood felt alien to Mira – she no longer felt she belonged there. The image she canvasses of the neighbourhood in the past is marked by elements of rurality (the sheep behind the block) and grotesque obsolescence of the infrastructure (the rough playground, as opposed to the new, more 'modern' football pitch). But it was precisely these otherwise embarrassing elements that used to foster an affective sense of belonging.

Despite sentimental tones in the quotations above, especially Mira's, the concept of 'spatial intimacy' is by no means used to essentialize or romanticize place or belonging. Spatial intimacy is a practice, an action. It is primarily an imaginative and discursive practice that selectively draws on the biographical experiences of dwelling in a place and in a time to reaffirm a shared identity, mobilizing sentiment to support it. Since it involves constructing a group by the invocation of a commonality of experience and sentiment, spatial intimacy is in a broad sense a political practice. Its objective is to claim a place.

Cultural intimacy is often expressed in jokes exchanged among 'insiders'. Perhaps the fullest and most concise expression of the tselinogradtsy's spatial intimacy is found in a pun they made on the very name of their city. Instead of Tselinograd ('Virgin Land City') they would sometimes call it Tselinogriaz' – 'Virgin Land Mud'. The trope of mud has already appeared several times in this chapter. Mud was indeed a very conspicuous and extremely persistent element of disorder in Tselinograd/Astana. Thick, oil-black and sticky, it was found virtually everywhere in the city, save perhaps for the recently built brick-covered expanses of the Left Bank. The fertile soil that had become the natural economic base of the region's development since the Virgin Lands Campaign – and so the cornerstone of Tselinograd's growth – now became mud, 'matter out of place' (Douglas 2002 [1966]: 44) when it encroached on the roadways and sidewalks. As the emblematic dark matter of 'rurality' and 'non-modernity' mud was also a suitable medium for spatial intimacy.[7]

Cultural critic Svetlana Boym (2001: 41–56) distinguishes between 'restorative nostalgia' associated with various, usually nationalistic projects of 'revival', and 'reflective nostalgia', which according to Boym is 'ironic and humorous' (ibid.: 49) and does not aim at changing the future but simply values the traces and shadows of what is no more. Tselinograd nostalgia, in the spirit of spatial intimacy, was shot through with a non-partisan, self-directed irony that 'pokes fun at the kind of things that may make us outraged or disempowered, but still … remain important, meaningful, and even dear because we identify with them' (Yurchak 2006: 277). Yet, I argue, blurring Boym's dichotomy, it was a socially constructive imaginative, discursive and affective practice, oriented towards the present and the future as much as towards the past. It helped make shared sense of the changes that had occurred in the city in recent years. Most importantly, it helped project Tselinograd as a chronotope with which the tselinogradtsy could collectively identify.

Walking in Tselinograd

Social space and time are constructed not only through discourses and images, but fundamentally through material practices. Habitual bodily memory and day-to-day repetition of mundane physical practices of dwelling provide continuity between local past and present. The intimate, bodily knowledge of urban space on which spatial intimacy draws derives from such quotidian spatial activities as walking through the city.

The crucial role of dwellers ('users') and their everyday practices (walking in particular) in making space is highlighted, among others, by Michel De Certeau (1984). In tracing trajectories, walking weaves an expansive spatial cloth of what might otherwise remain a mere scattering of points, he argues (1984: 91–110). The walker selectively realizes some of the possibilities for movement built into the spatial layout and invents new paths and patterns. Thus, walking transforms spatial signifiers; it is 'a process of appropriation of the topographical system on the part of the pedestrian' (ibid.: 98). From a phenomenological perspective, Jo Lee and Tim Ingold similarly argue that walking is an act of creating places: 'By creating routes, walkers inscribe their own lives into the city … The meaning of the place is constituted by their bodily presence' (2006: 77). Moreover, by daily repetition, walking blends the past and the present. It reiteratively inscribes the past both in bodies and in the cityscape they traverse, simultaneously regenerating a synchronization between body and place (Bourdieu 1977). Thus the walkers-as-dwellers continually recreate the city as a phenomenological and embodied time-space.

Ethnographically, Tanya Richardson (2008: 139–70) has documented how Odessans participating in walking tours along the streets of their city revealed histories inscribed in those streets and buildings and thus reconstructed Odessa as a particular kind of place, different from what it seemed otherwise. The cosmopolitan Odessa they rediscovered seemed to them a more 'authentic' alternative to the city of the present, which they saw as 'a place eroded by villagers and unfavourable state policies' (Richardson 2008: 146). Adam Reed (2002), in turn, has followed London enthusiasts, who were able to 'animate … plural time-spaces of the city' (2002: 127) by walks during which they imaginatively reconstructed the details of London's topography and built environment in past centuries. In a similar vein, among lifelong dwellers of Tselinograd/Astana, walking and other mundane engagements with space reiteratively reconstructed the city as intimately familiar. Enlivening the past day-to-day, these practices made the city a meshwork of meaningful, eventful paths and places, superinscribed upon the physical landscape and alternative to its official meanings.

One difference from both Richardson's and Reed's research is that while the groups they describe deliberately walked together and in organized ways to act out histories, my present argument concerns mundane walking by residents simply going to work or school, doing their shopping, visiting their friends and relatives or strolling just for leisure. During fieldwork, I often walked with my informants as they went about their daily business. Moreover, to learn more about the meaning of such mundane walking, I asked selected informants to take me on long walks during which we reflected about the places we walked through and the trajectories we followed. Our itineraries would rarely follow the street grid with its straight lines, smooth pavements and right-angle intersections. Rather, we would cross courtyards, passing from one straight into another and rarely coming out to a major street.[8] In Russian, there is a fixed expression for this manner of traversing urban space: *khodit' po dvoram*, literally 'to walk across the courtyards' (Figure 3.3). We would meander between buildings, trees and various elements of courtyard infrastructure; nod politely at elderly neighbours on half-broken benches; circumnavigate smelly dumps; and dodge balls slammed against walls by neighbourhood lads.

Here is a slightly edited extract from my field notes describing one such several-hour walk I took with Margarita:

> Margarita decided to show me the places where she used to hang around when she was a child. We walked across a courtyard between

Figure 3.3 A courtyard (*dvor*) in a Soviet-era *mikroraion* (photo: M. Laszczkowski)

the former textile factory dorm (lengthy rectangular rust-coloured and weather-beaten five-storey blocks built of large concrete plates) and out onto Manasa Street. We crossed the road and headed towards a large building with a green roof. Margarita said this was the former bread factory where she used to fetch fresh bread. The building now houses a car wash, a repair workshop and a billiards room. It reads 'billiards' above the entrance. Margarita said: "It reads 'billiards' nowadays, but there used to be a bakery shop here. It was called Hot Bread. There was just such a narrow steel door". Nowadays the bakery has been replaced with a small grocery store, sporting a rather scarce assortment of food and a heavily loaded shelf with vodka. The bread they sell is brought in from some other place. We bought some plastic-wrapped pastry and left. Margarita commented: 'You see? Even Hot Bread is no longer hot bread'.

We went to the ruins of the textile factory where Margarita's mother used to work. We entered through a hole in the wall on the side of Fabrichnaia Street. Long rows of concrete pillars supporting the collapsed heavy roof high above stood amid piles of broken bricks and litter. Most inner walls and ceilings had been pulled down. The factory had once occupied a huge area: the entire block between the streets Fabrichnaia, Mirzoiana, Manasa and today's Trinadtsataia Magistral'.

We returned to the neighbourhood. Margarita's family moved in 1985 into the apartment block where she and her mother now live. The construction of surrounding buildings came to a halt with the collapse of the Soviet Union and many stood uncompleted and empty for five or even ten years. The neighbourhood kids grew up playing amid that mid-construction landscape – *deti stroek*, 'construction site kids', as they would now occasionally refer to themselves as a generation. 'I know every basement here in and out', Margarita asserted.

We passed the school Margarita used to go to. We walked further on, *po dvoram*, towards 'Orbita' – a part of the neighbourhood that took its name from a large grocery store. There were rows of tall and thick poplars along every building. These were some of the remaining few – poplars, once a dominant feature in the landscape of Tselinograd neighbourhoods, had been chopped down at many locations in recent years. Close to Orbita there is a spacious playground with many ladders and see-saws. Margarita said she used to play there with her sister when they were children. Their grandma lives in one of the five-storeys nearby. Hidden behind the corner of a building, Margarita showed me three big blue boxes, about the size of a telephone booth, with some buttons on the front. I had no clue what they were but Margarita filled me in: old soda-water dispensers, abandoned and forgotten behind the much newer fried chicken booths.

This itinerary reveals complex layers of social and personal past under the surface of the mundane. Walking across the neighbourhoods is a forceful way of daily reaffirming one's intimate familiarity with the built environment's nooks and crannies. It is one of those bodily practices whereby nostalgia acquires tangibility, forging material links to the reconstructed past through the places and things the walker encounters. To lifelong dwellers such as Margarita, each building, courtyard and street corner is a history, affectively charged and viscerally remembered. There are accretions of meaning inscribed in each such spatial form by repeated practices of dwelling over the course of a lifetime: walks to school, games played in courtyards and construction sites, visits to grandmother. There are also marks of social change and continuity: the factory where most of the neighbourhood dwellers used to earn a living turned to ruin; businesses and bazaars where there were none; but also playgrounds as bustling with children at play as ever. Personally, I found particularly revealing the dull, rubbery taste of the plastic-wrapped pastries we chewed as Margarita mused about the smell of the freshly baked produce at the Hot Bread in the old days. This denial of the Proustian madeleine experience highlights the capacity of nostalgia to register social and politico-economic change (such as the collapse of old-time production and distribution networks, their replacement with new market patterns and the accompanying change in the use of the former bakery building) at a sensuous and visceral level.

Exploring industrial ruins of old Tselinograd, such as the textile factory, was a favourite pastime among the Tselinograd-born youth I met during fieldwork (more about this in Chapter 6). Armed with flashlights and cameras, they would head, for example, to the old grain-milling plant or the brick factory and spend hours wandering among the debris and documenting the ruination. Thus, they subverted the spatial-symbolic order of the city, turning sites of abandon into meaningful and eventful places. Exploring ruins implies an excavation of the past and critique of the present and potential future with which the ruin is incompatible (Edensor 2005: 15). The ruin becomes a site of spatial intimacy. Officially neglected and embarrassing, it is rich in scrappy local knowledge to be discovered whole-bodily and shared by the explorers.

Another practice connected to walking that reproduces intimate space is place-naming. Across Astana, street names associated with Russian and Soviet history and ideology were replaced with new names commemorating Kazakh or generically Muslim historical figures. For instance, Karl Marx Avenue became Kenesary Khan, and Five-Year Plan Avenue – Bogenbai Batyr, both named after historic Kazakh military and political leaders. However, long-standing residents habitually used obsolete, Soviet-era place names, especially for smaller streets (see Pilz 2011). Equally often, residents would refer to an entirely different toponymic register altogether: conventional, informal landmark names that could designate a precise location or a broader, loosely defined area. Frequently these unofficial landmark denominations invoked elements of the cityscape that were not even there any longer (cf. Flynn, Kosmarskaya and Sabirova 2014). For instance, '*na vechnom ogne*' ('at the Eternal Flame') meant a square off Prospekt Pobedy (Victory Avenue) where an Eternal Flame used to burn in the Soviet period, but any physical reminder of it had been removed after the capital relocation. Similarly, the department store Moskva, which by the time I began my fieldwork was no more than a memory and a patch of cleared ground behind a tall fence, nonetheless remained a landmark to which residents would often refer. This ghost toponymy created and reproduced a spectral double to Astana. Alongside the topography of the city evident to anyone, with its present material forms and official place names inscribed on address plates, there was also another cityscape that long-standing residents' daily practice constructed of echo-of-the-past place names and shadow landmarks.

For long-term, often Tselinograd-born dwellers, the past was present in the city not only through nostalgic narratives but it imbued mundane material spaces and was enlivened by everyday spatial practices. It was a fundamentally personal, biographical, even visceral past, but at the same time intersubjective, shared. Walking has an exceptional potential for generating shared understandings (Lee and Ingold 2006: 79); the memories it produces are at once bodily and social (Connerton 1989). Walking together, individuals literally share the same outlook, participate in the same process of space-making and so acquire common, bodily knowledge. Among those who frequently walk together or at least routinely walk across the same terrain, particularly visceral ties of sociality may be forged. Hence, walking is a key practice through which 'community' as a phenomenological quality (Appadurai 1996: 178) rooted in a commonality of bodily knowledge is performatively and reiteratively brought into being. As architectural theorist Neil Leach (2002) argues, belonging, in the sense of a relationship between social subjects (individual or aggregate) and space, is a product of repeated bodily practices. Thus walking and related spatial practices, such as the use of obsolete place names, helped construct both a 'community' of the tselinogradtsy and an alternative time-space where they collectively belonged.

Tselinograd's Glory

In Chapter 1 I argued that Astana was constructed as a 'real-and-imagined' place, a 'city of the future'. That construction involved both actual, material building work, and the work of discourses, images and imaginations. Now we have seen that simultaneously old-time residents, through bodily, discursive and imaginative engagements with urban space, constructed Tselinograd as an alternative chronotope – not fixed in a closed past but living on. This served to reaffirm their collective belonging in the city against otherwise dominant discourses that denied 'coevalness' to them and to the values they held.

The resonances and dissonances between the construction of these two real-and-imagined cities (which are in fact one, Tselinograd and Astana) are perhaps best evoked in a music video published on the Internet by a trio of Tselinograd-born musicians living in Astana. The video features a collage of archival footage of people walking in a park, shopping, strolling across a sun-drenched square, or working amidst waving wheat fields and enormous heaps of grain. Other images, some black and white, some colour but bleak and brownish, as if sun bleached, feature broad boulevards, neat rows of rectangular five-storey apartment blocks, a Lenin statue and a monument with a real giant orange tractor on caterpillar tracks. These snapshots of Tselinograd in the 1960s, 1970s and 1980s are mixed with newer images of Astana's Left Bank with its futuristic buildings and spacious avenues. A scratching voice, accompanied by a simple guitar riff, sings lyrics woven around a sequence of names of Soviet-era landmarks and city parts. The song culminates in the chorus: *Khvala rukam, chto pakhnut khlebom! Khvala vsem, kto pomnit eto!* – 'Glory to the hands that smell of bread! Glory to all those who remember that!'

The video evokes the continuity of the idea of representing and materializing 'modernity' in urban built forms and the forms of social life that the built environment enables. Simultaneously, the visual and textual references to Soviet Tselinograd sit a little oddly alongside the pictures of the recent developments in Astana. The clip was probably meant as a story of continuous progress – an attempt to invoke nostalgia in order to 'reappropriate the present' by highlighting and acknowledging the distance from the past (Wilson 1997: 138–39). But the juxtaposition of old and new images inadvertently suggests incongruity between then and now, and between different visions of the future. It invites questions as to the relationship between different politico-economic formations and subsequent versions of modernity. The video ultimately evokes the impossibility of ever materializing the future fixedly against the flux of ever newer dreams, images and materialities that build upon the accumulation of preceding versions of modernity at the same time as they render those earlier forms and ideas always-already obsolete. The questions of how to belong in 'modernity' remain open.

The next chapter explores public squares in Astana as sites where different groups of residents sought answers to those questions, sometimes drawing on the squares' Tselinograd-era history.

Notes

1. A decade later, the site in Central Square vacated by the bronze Lenin was to be filled with another monument – a heavyset, majestic statue of 'the Kazakh national poet' Abai Kunanbaev.
2. The street itself has been renamed too. One-time Prospekt Tselinnikov (Avenue of the Virgin Land Campaigners) and Prospekt Pushkina (Pushkin Avenue), which formed one continuous stretch of road cutting through the city from south to north, have together become Prospekt Respubliki (Republic Avenue).
3. For instance, Margarita's mother told me how especially in the early years after Kazakhstan's independence and the capital relocation she would sometimes quarrel with rural Kazakh newcomers to Astana, who reportedly told her to 'pack up and go back to her mother Russia'. She used to say to them: 'Why should I go? It is you who may go back to your *aul* [Kazakh for village]. I was born here. My parents had come here; they were the ones who built this city, so why should I leave?'
4. The Railway Employees' Palace of Culture, now housing the National Opera and Ballet Theatre.
5. Most other informants would have simply said 'Russian' instead of 'Slavic'. Ekaterina Stanislavovna preferred the latter term, highlighting the presence of other groups than just Russians, because she was an active member of a Polish cultural identity group.
6. Aboveground heating pipes cut across the spaces of many former Soviet cities (see Collier 2004).
7. There was a rich repertoire of other jokes that circulated among the former tselinogradtsy that focused on the material flaws of the built environment. Margarita took pleasure, for instance, in explaining to me that Prospekt Pobedy (Victory Avenue), one of the principal Khrushchev-era thoroughfares, had been known as Archaeologists Avenue for being constantly dug up for underground pipeline conservation. I also heard several times the story of a car and a driver that allegedly had completely disappeared into one of the gaping potholes – an urban legend that matched the best traditions of late-Soviet black humour of the absurd, which had revelled in portraying the USSR as 'Anti-Disneyland', a land of grotesque fairy tale (Ries 1997: 42–43, 49–50; Yurchak 2006: 238–81).

8. One of James Scott's (1998: 74–75) examples of the difference between space as shaped through practical needs and uses of inhabitants and, on the other hand, as produced by a modernist state apparatus is a juxtaposition of two schematic maps: one of paths created by use and topography, and one of a centralized traffic hub. The latter consists of but a few straight lines, crossing at a limited number of points. The former, in contrast, takes the form of a 'network resembling a dense concentration of capillaries' (ibid.), multiple, criss-crossing, irregularly curved and seemingly, yet indeed only seemingly, erratic. Similarly, in a modern city the street grid and planned locations of buildings form a regular, generally rectilinear and relatively simple pattern. If one were, however, to trace the actual movements of pedestrians across the city on a given day, one would have to superinscribe upon this pattern a tangle of irregular itineraries. The relevance here is that Scott discusses not just two different ways of representing space graphically, but rather distinct modes of making space. Walkers in the city construct an alternative real space.

Chapter 4

Celebration and the City

Belonging in Public Space

New Year's Eve 2008 was frosty in Astana. By midnight, the temperature had dropped to around -40°C. Yet, in Central Square, in the right-bank part of the city, a holiday show was on. In front of the city hall, a small stage had been arranged on which singers performed pop songs, ranging from still popular Soviet-era standards to the latest Kazakh and international disco hits. A crowd of perhaps 200 people watched and danced. They seemed almost exclusively rural or small-town Kazakh migrants; families with children, a few larger groups of young Kazakh men and occasionally elderly Slavs.

The musical part of the show was followed, closer to midnight, by a theatrical spectacle that featured Ded Moroz (the Soviet-era Santa-style figure) with his companion snow fairy (Snegurochka), and a bunch of odd colourful creatures: a red cow, green rooster, blue rabbit, an orange lion and so forth. The animals, representing (as the emcee promptly explained) the years that had passed since Kazakhstan's independence according to the Chinese calendar, danced on the stage, while singers sang an optimistic song about Astana's and Kazakhstan's 'bright future'. Suddenly, the music changed. A solemn, triumphant tune introduced to the stage two camels (dressed-up actors) and a man wearing the costume of an ancient Kazakh nomadic sage: a long embroidered coat, an impressive fur cap and long beard. The emcee greeted him as the 'spirit of the ancient town of Bozok', the archaeological settlement discovered near the fringe of today's Astana. With pride, the emcee reported to the spirit: 'Bozok has become the great city of Astana, and caravans set out from here to the north, south, east and west'. The colourful beasts proceeded to boast about the progress made and goals achieved in the development of Astana in 'their' respective years. The spirit congratulated them and said he would give his blessing to the city and all its inhabitants. As he stretched his arms out, the actors on the stage and the spectators in front all fell to their knees, raising their open palms in front of their faces – the traditional Central Asian Muslim gesture of receiving a blessing. I must say, that gesture surprised me, given the light atmosphere of all that had preceded it. The Bozok spirit delivered his blessing in Kazakh (up to that point the show was bilingual, but mostly Russian).

After he and the other actors left the stage, at only a few minutes to midnight, the time came for President Nazarbaev's televised New Year's address – in compliance with a tradition established by Soviet leaders back in the 1970s (Lane 1981: 138). The president's face, with the national flag and a Baiterek vista in the background, appeared on a large screen on one side of the stage. His several-minute speech, first in Kazakh and then in Russian, reiterated the points usually covered by the President's holiday addresses (such as the speech summarized in Chapter 1). After emphasizing Kazakhstan's achievements over the past year – economic growth, new schools and hospitals, housing for thousands of families and so forth – Nazarbaev assured his nation that Kazakhstan was prepared to face the challenges of the coming year as well. He stressed 'peace and accord' and commitment to common goals as the topmost values that should always guide Kazakhstan's people. A lavish fireworks show followed, as if to stress the president's words. Finally, the official part of the celebrations was over, and a disco went on in Central Square for several more hours.

The part with the 'Bozok spirit' could serve as a touchstone for a discussion of the role of representations of remote history and mythology in contemporary regime ideology in Kazakhstan (see Buchli 2007: 59–60). But in this chapter, I take the New Year's Eve show as a point of departure to explore the changing forms, uses and meanings of public space in Astana. Not only did the mix of explicit political ideology – 'invented tradition' (Hobsbawm and Ranger 1983), disco and cartoon-style entertainment – strike me, but there was also something political, I later thought, about the conspicuous absence of Slav urbanites or middle-class Kazakhs with more clearly 'urban' cultural styles (see Chapter 2). Indeed, my local friends had refused to accompany me to the show: I was going to go watch the mambety having a good time, they laughed.

Ongoing scholarly debates on public space have primarily been informed by Western European and North American experience. The Astana case affords a new angle: a perspective on the production and use of space first under Soviet socialism and then under a regime fusing a post-Soviet political centralism with an orientation towards the transnational capitalist market. As mentioned in the introduction, in pronounced contrast to Soviet city planning objectives, leading architects in Astana rejected the idea of public space as socially transformative; they wanted it to be 'liveable', comfortable and pleasurable (Laszczkowski 2011b: 94; see also Bissenova 2014). Their views seemed to evidence the spread into this part of the world of the dominant rhetoric of recent Euro-American urban planning, critiqued by concerned scholars as a factor in the shrinking of the 'public sphere' (Boyer 1994; Low 2000; Mouffe 2002; Thrift 2008: 220–54). Simultaneously, apparently contrarily to the planners' ideas, the Kazakhstani government used public squares to project new collective identities and images of Astana as a 'city of progress'. Public space was thus apparently politically monopolized.

However, in contrast to extant scholarly analyses of mass spectacles in the capital cities of post-Soviet Central Asia (Adams and Rustemova 2009; Adams 2010), whose emphasis is on the formal content of the celebrations and on the ideas that the shows' elite organizers seek to transmit, my focus in this chapter is rather on the audiences. By participating or refusing to participate, targeted members of the public can exert important influence on the actual effects of even the most carefully orchestrated spectacle (cf. Wedeen 1999). As just mentioned, in Astana some urbanites generally refrained from participation in government-organized public events, contesting officially promoted notions of 'modernity', 'urbanity' and collective belonging. The significance and specific qualities of urban 'public' space inscribed during celebrations were thus determined not simply by planners and rulers, but rather by various groups of 'ordinary' users of space, whose practices, ideas and imaginations partly accepted and partly reworked or resisted dominant ideologies.

What is Public Space?

Yael Navaro-Yashin's (2002) *Faces of the State*, an ethnography of 'public life' in Turkey, opens with an invitation to the reader to imagine Istanbul's Taksim Square, or more generically 'a public square in the centre of a metropolis'. It is a space teeming with traffic, crowds and the expressions, some peaceful and others quite violent, of a variety of political passions. Demonstrations by holders of conflicting views meet in this public space, competing claims of representing 'the state' or 'the public' are made, the police intervene, pedestrians and voyeurs speed up or stop to contemplate and perhaps contribute to the action, and the mill of rumour and commentary is running. This image conveys some of the defining characteristics of 'public space' in contemporary Western sociological imagination: public space is a venue for diversity and for the articulation of pluralist politics. 'The public square, so imagined by social theorists as symbol par excellence for the public sphere or for civil society, is a site ... for the production of the political', the anthropologist comments (ibid.: 1).

Scholarly debates about 'public space' are usually structured in terms derived from Jürgen Habermas (1991) or, perhaps less often, Richard Sennett (1978, 1991). To Sennett, public space is primarily where strangers meet, are exposed to each other's gaze and forced to negotiate terms of co-presence and, ideally, cooperation. Vital to sociality and to democracy, this public space is increasingly nullified by monopolizing pressures by the state and compartmentalizing capitalist proprietors (Sennett 1978). Habermas's approach is more formal and more focused on rational debate. He draws attention to the historicity of the notions of 'public' and 'private' sphere. The meaning of 'public space' has undergone transformations over time. Habermas discusses the rise of the 'public sphere' in the West European bourgeois culture of the seventeenth and eighteenth centuries (see also Calhoun 1992). He conceives of the public sphere as the site for rational-critical discourse on matters of public relevance; he does not tie the discussion strictly to material space. Habermas argues that over the course of the nineteenth and twentieth century, the public sphere has gradually deteriorated and disintegrated, leading to a situation where the general public is passive and its role limited to expressing acclamation for agendas devised by corporate actors.

In a similar vein, historian of urbanism M. Christine Boyer (1994) defines public space as space committed to the needs of a political community. Properly public space is one that allows for public assembly, debate and a just representation of the concerns of all inhabitant groups and of the city as a whole.[1] Boyer charts a history of public space in West European and North American cities from early modern times to the late twentieth century. Before the eighteenth century in Europe '"public space" was usually designed as an honorific place celebrating the power of the [sovereign]' (Boyer 1994: 7). Monuments and 'public places' emerged as the 'transcription in stone' of processions and tableaux that were previously used to display relations of authority. The revolutions of the eighteenth and nineteenth centuries subsequently broadened the meaning of 'public space' to include places for public debate and assembly (ibid.). The entire space of the city was then organized to embody a rational public order. The rise of the working class in the nineteenth century led to a polarization of public space between the rich and the poor (ibid.: 8). Elites attempted to transform the space of the city to keep the potentially rebellious poor at a distance and better suit the purposes of controlling and, when necessary, cracking down on demonstrators. Simultaneously, they embellished the city with new places of beauty, in a redoubled effort to impose an aesthetic order. The Haussmannization of Paris under Napoleon III was a prime example of this double offensive (Harvey 2003). The beautification of urban space was supposed to encourage an affective identification with the city and the social order (Boyer 1994: 9). Later, 'high-modernist' planning (Scott 1998) around the middle of the twentieth century, as epitomized most fully in the design of the city of Brasilia, demanded that all outdoor space be public; the private was forced indoors (Holston 1989, 1999). This 'high-modernist' public space, however, was designed to impose a static order rather than encourage debate. Eventually, in Boyer's account, the final decades of the twentieth century in the West saw a gradual denigration of the term 'public' to mean 'bureaucratized', 'corrupt', 'inefficient', 'overly regularized' and 'burdensomely taxed'. Meanwhile, 'private' has risen to denote the exact idealized opposite of that. Private space has become more valued than public space, and the expansion of privately owned and privately managed spaces has come to be seen as the solution to questions of urban development, while no responsibility is taken for the increasingly marginalized minority groups. Those groups are thus deprived of a voice and an arena for raising their concerns, while similarly there is no longer any ground to articulate problems that concern the population as a whole (Boyer 1994: 10). Boyer alerts us to the increasing degradation and commercialization of public space in recent decades, at least in European and North American cities, leading to the constricting of democratic pluralism in the interest of the city's 'marketability', 'imageability' and 'liveability' as defined self-centrically and, Boyer adds, 'myopically' by white middle-class professionals (see also Rutheiser 1996, 1999; Cooper 1999; McDonogh 1999).

The narrative of public space as venue for the pluralist democratic expression of diversity, now increasingly under pressure from the state and from capital, is found also in anthropological writing. One notable example is Setha Low's ethnography of two squares in San Jose, Costa Rica. Low stresses that 'public spaces have important personal meanings for individual users and urban residents' (2000: 238). These meanings emerge out of various forms of 'spatial engagement' that are 'both passive and active, ranging from everyday practices of sitting on benches and talking to friends, to organized street demonstrations, media campaigns, and town meetings' (ibid.: 239). However, Low also highlights the political aspect of public space. Spatial meanings, she notes, are actively manipulated by municipal and national authorities in pursuit of political agendas of domination. In Costa Rica, as Low demonstrates, plazas and other urban spaces have indeed been created with the clear purpose of underwriting the political success of the country's subsequent presidents – a case apparently not far removed from the creation of an entire extensive urban quarter in Astana to perform and manifest President Nazarbaev's agenda. 'The state' attempts to monopolize control over public spaces and even has the capacity to define what counts as important public space in order to maintain a hegemony over the production of social memory and uphold official representations of the past, the present and – as the Astana case shows particularly clearly – the future (Low and Lawrence-Zúñiga 2003: 22). Other pressures come from commercial capital seeking to exploit space as a resource for money-making and to this end attempting to achieve an exclusionary control over space.

Despite these double pressures from the state and capital, Low (2000: 240) argues, 'public spaces, such as the Costa Rican plaza, are one of the last democratic forums for public dissent in a civil society. They are places where disagreements can be marked symbolically and politically or personally worked out'. Public space, then, 'becomes a centre of protest and contestation by providing a place and a culturally charged symbol for expressing social conflict' (ibid.). Drawing on work in urban design (Carr et al. 1992), Low adopts five criteria for 'publicness' of space: unrestricted access; freedom of action; the ability to claim the space and resources in it; freedom of modifying the space; and participatory ownership. Low's emphasis on the centrality of public space as an arena for the articulation of disagreements resonates with the concerns raised recently in political theory about the extinguishing of the political by a liberal 'consensus' and with calls for a rejuvenation of the political by encouraging freer articulation of difference in the public sphere (Mouffe 2002; Amin and Thrift 2002). In this vein, Low (2000: 247) calls for the active defence of public spaces against the pressures of state monopolization and commercializing privatization, since such spaces are vital to retaining democratic practice in society.

The notion of public space derived from West European and North American experience and debates had at best limited applicability to the Soviet Union. There, virtually all space was in some sense public. To the extent at least that ideology was put into practice, the public/private dichotomy was rendered irrelevant for Soviet urban space, which was better understood as communal or 'social' (Kharkhordin 1997: 343; Richardson 2008: 163). It was assumed that there was not, nor should there be, any separation between state and society (Kotkin 1995: 23). The state, in its multiple incarnations as major industrial establishments that were charged, inter alia, with building residential neighbourhoods for their workers, was nearly the exclusive producer of space. Public space was not intended to serve the articulation of diversity, for according to the Marxist-Leninist vision the only true social difference was class difference, and once socialism had been achieved class difference would no longer exist. Thus, the purpose of public space was to manifest the unity and cohesion of state and society. As David Crowley and Susan E. Reid (2002) note in their introduction to a volume on *Socialist Spaces*, that did not mean that the spatial practices of citizens were contained by the 'party-state machine'; but they had to relate to that 'machine's' priorities and strategies (ibid.: 4). The authors argue that spaces of everyday life, such as the residential street or the home, were 'no less important as sites for ideological intervention' (ibid.: 5) than 'grand projects' such as the flagship socialist industrial city Magnitogorsk (Kotkin 1995) or 'exalted spaces' such as monumental parade squares. As pointed out earlier in this book (Introduction), urban space, in its totality as well as in its capillaries, was expected to play a social-transformative role by moulding citizens' consciousness.[2]

As discussed in the introduction and Chapter 1, the changes that swept across the former Soviet Union after 1991 entailed the dissolution of the perceived societal whole, framed by the state, which had linked individuals, collectives, built environment, infrastructure and space. While it is true that spatial inequalities had existed under socialism despite its homogenizing ideology (Szelenyi 1983), with privatization space was fractured in new ways (Andrusz, Harloe and Szelenyi 1996). New kinds of subjects emerged, making new kinds of claims to property or sovereignty over various spaces (Ruble 1995; Humphrey 2002b, 2007). Some spaces, such as formerly expansive enterprises or the urban housing stock, were divided among a host of new owners. Others were converted into private property wholesale, while their form and appearance only changed slightly or slowly – such as the once communal Tsentral'nyi univermag (TsUM) in Astana, which turned into a privately held department store. Entirely new kinds of spaces gradually emerged, including 'gated communities', nouveau-riche villa neigh-bourhoods and Western-style shopping malls (Laszczkowski 2011b). 'Public' space shrank and even ostensibly public venues such as the urban central square were given over to new uses, while the meanings and even the legitimacy of some formerly taken-for-granted public spatial practices became uncertain (Humphrey 2007; Darieva, Kaschuba and Krebs 2011). The divestiture of urban squares of their previous public character was often marked by such clear symbolic gestures as the removal of monuments to Lenin or other Soviet socialist heroes (e.g., Wanner 1998: 171–99; Chapter 3). In former Soviet cities, such as Astana, space was claimed on the one hand by nondemocratic regimes, which continued to use public squares to organize propagandistic mass spectacles (Adams 2010), and on the other by domestic and transnational capitalist forces turning space into commodity (e.g., Darieva 2011).

However, residents in post-Soviet cities find creative ways to use transformed or newly appearing kinds of public space (Darieva, Kaschuba and Krebs 2011).[3] Thus, in Astana central squares became sites of cultural and political dynamics that exceeded elite attempts to design and control public space. As the remainder of this chapter elaborates, drawing on past ideas and practices, citizens managed to evaluate, appropriate and contest officially promoted visions of the present and the future, by the same token subverting official meanings of space and attaching to it qualities that were not foreseen and presumably not desired by planners and government ideologues.

City Squares

Astana's Central Square (Tsentral'naia ploshchad'), also known as Old Square (Staraia ploshchad'), is a rectangle of brick-paved space, approximately 360 metres long by 80 metres wide. Located in the old, right-bank part of the city, a few minutes' walk north from the river embankment, it used to be the very heart of Tselinograd. Given the sense of separateness of the new Left Bank 'centre', around 2010 this area continued to be commonly regarded as Astana's actual centre. The square had been redesigned several times since the early 1960s but retained its central character (Figure 4.1). What follows is a description of the square as of 2009, the time of my main period of fieldwork – since then the square has continued to change little by little.[4]

Central Square is enclosed on the northern side by what used to be Tselinograd's highest building: a sixteen-storey tower, in front of which the Lenin monument used to stand. The building currently houses the ministry of sports and tourism and an educational institute for future cadres of the presidential administration. Like the entire square, it has benefited from the sudden growth in importance in the wake of the capital relocation – it received a facelift and now shines with deep blue glass and light beige-rouge tile. To the left of this

Figure 4.1 May Day 2009 in Central Square (photo: M. Laszczkowski)

building is the massive city hall with a Kazakhstani flag atop the vaguely crystalline-shaped facade. Opposite and across a narrow two-lane roadway, humbler buildings include a pseudo-classicist Soviet hotel and several office buildings in various styles.

This northern part of the square usually serves as parking space for those working in the surrounding offices. In contrast, the square's middle part is more pedestrian-friendly. It is flanked on the west by the two-storey metallic-coloured former TsUM (Central Department Store, now curiously named 'Sine Tempore'), and on the east by an elegant green-roofed nineteenth-century villa. A fountain pool adorns this part of the square in the form of three enormous bowls arranged vertically, each smaller in diameter than the one below, thus forming a tree-shaped structure, supposedly a Tree of Life, with water cascading down the three levels. To the south, Kenesary Avenue (Karl Marx Prospect during the Soviet era), a crucial thoroughfare for the city, cuts through the square. In the warm months, teenagers often play guitars in the underpasses beneath the roadway. Across the road, the square is extended by a small tree-lined space in front of the Congress Hall – the renamed former Palace of Virgin Land Campaigners, Dvorets tselinnikov.

During the long and harsh continental winter, when other open spaces in Astana remained deserted, an ice-skating rink in Central Square enjoyed some popularity. In warmer months, most people would just cross the square on their way to offices, the busy bus stop in front of the Congress Hall or to and from the former TsUM. Family groups and couples could be seen taking leisurely strolls around the pleasantly humming fountain where the air was cooler, and there were always a few photographers or ice-cream vendors around.

There are a few more squares in the right-bank downtown area that can be considered central public sites. One of these, New Square, is immediately behind the town hall building from Central Square. Smaller and quieter, New Square feels more relaxed. There is another Tree of Life fountain in the middle, with a spherical sculpture at the centre. This popular landmark, placed there in the period shortly after the capital relocation, is commonly nicknamed the 'Chupa Chups', after the lollipop, for its shape. Benches are arranged around the fountain, and beyond them there are grass lawns and flower beds. On the eastern side, a handful of trees offer precious shade in the summer, and separate the square from the Presidential Museum, Nazarbaev's first Astana residence, at the back of the city hall. Opposite, across Prospekt Pobedy (Victory Avenue, one of the few main streets in Astana that has retained its Soviet-era name), the dark blue and white wavy facade of the Finance Ministry building ('Minfin') overshadows the square. New Square is at its liveliest on summer evenings, when dozens of residents – families, young couples, pensioners living nearby, loud groups of youths – sit on the benches or the grass lawns. Just as Central Square is the former site of the Lenin Monument, New Square is likewise a Soviet *lieu de memoire* (Nora 1996) now erased, but remembered by the tselinogradtsy (see Chapter 3). Namely, where there is now a rose bed in front of the Presidential Museum, the Eternal Flame burned next to a monument to the fallen of the Civil War (1917–1923).[5] The monument was moved at some point in the 1990s to a cemetery on the city's outskirts, and an Eternal Flame now burns at a new, grandiose monument to the Defenders of the Motherland in the late-Soviet residential area (mikroraiony) in the south-east.

A third central square in right-bank Astana is a fairly small space next to the 1970s Youth Palace, a block east and north from Central Square, across Prospekt Respubliki. Refurbished in 2008 as part of the beautification effort on the eve of the capital relocation jubilee, it now boasts large granite fountains and the official emblems of Astana and Almaty rendered in coloured tile. While this square gets some shade from trees lining the two streets that form one of its corners, Respubliki and Seifullina, there are fewer benches, and it seems less frequented on a typical day than the other two squares. Young couples and elderly residents prefer the benches around the monument to the Friendship of Nations directly across the street, where children splash in the fountain.

The three squares made for relatively pleasurable, accessible spaces for leisure and socializing. They were frequented by diverse groups of residents and thus came as close as anywhere in Astana to the ideal-type public plaza of the kind described by Low for Costa Rica (2000). However, in contrast to the notion of public space as defined by the plurality of expressions of different groups' political views and identities, as summarized above, the main squares in Astana hosted basically only one kind of organized, collective activity: official holiday celebrations. It seemed that just as there was little room for open political debate in the discursive space in Kazakhstan (Olcott 2002; Cummings 2005; Dave

2007; Schatz 2009), pluralism of opinion found virtually no venue for expression in the material public space of the capital. Likewise, the Left Bank's central Nurzhol promenade was designed for pleasurable strolls on summer evenings and for visual consumption. The only organized public events taking place in Nurzhol were the mass celebrations during the evening of Astana Day, when enormous crowds, primarily festival visitors from outside the city, swarmed along the boulevard, and the central concert (actually attended only by a pre-selected elite audience) was broadcast on huge television screens. I now turn to official holiday celebrations in main squares in late-Soviet Tselinograd and in Astana in the 2000s to explore some of those celebrations' possible effects and suggest there might be more ways those events were 'political' than meets the eye.

Public Holiday Celebrations

... in Late-Soviet Tselinograd

The largest Soviet holidays were May Day and the anniversary of the Great October Revolution on 7 November. Both were celebrated with mass parades that went through the city and culminated in the Central Square. Public celebrations were, for the Bolshevik leadership, a potent way to occupy and redefine (particularly urban) space, manifest authority over it and mark centres and peripheries (Rolf 2013: 78–80). The form and content of the parades, however, became gradually ossified as early as the 1920s (Binns 1979: 596–98), and the trend continued in the 1960s, 1970s and 1980s, leading – scholars claim – to a general 'dull uniformity' and 'lack of spirit and passivity [among] the participants' (Lane 1981: 188).[6] Christopher Binns (1980) concludes his analysis of Soviet ceremonies by asserting that in the Khrushchev and Brezhnev periods (that is, from the mid 1950s to the early 1980s), the actual effects of official holidays were, contrary to the authorities' intention, centrifugal, with their actual conduct emphasizing pluralism, individualism and consumption. People 'wrested control' of the festivities from the authorities and appropriated the holidays as occasions for meeting friends and socializing – activities that they enjoyed. The 'ideological content' of the holidays appeared to be 'virtually ignored' (ibid.: 183). In the late Soviet period, many urbanites felt disenchanted by the parades on the two main holidays and preferred to stay at home to party privately with their friends, or to leave the city altogether (Binns 1980; Lane 1981: 186, 249; Wanner 1998: 146).

The memories of my interlocutors from Astana partly corroborate this view. One of my Astana neighbours, the retired driver of construction-work vehicles whom I briefly introduced in Chapter 1, offered a vivid memory of how official holidays – not just the greatest but also a roster of lesser, professional holidays – used to be actually celebrated:

Of the official holidays, there was 7 November – we would booze [*gudeli*], rest at home – the day of the Great October Revolution. ... You'd booze yourself unconscious, call your friends ... On Construction Worker's Day, they'd make a gathering at work, give out awards. Right after that, the boozing started. ... We didn't march the streets with flags. Everyone would start [drinking] at work and finish at home, gather some company together or not. ... Any holiday, really, just any – invariably a drinking bout.

Others recalled the parades nostalgically, especially those on May Day, as joyous, festive occasions. Yet the enjoyment was owed not to the parades' official meaning but rather to the opportunities for socializing and celebratory display they created. Consider, for example, the following account by another neighbour, Svetlana – a Russian woman in her forties – of how May Day used to be celebrated when she was a child:

At home, everyone would lay their table, necessarily prepare something delicious. At half past six in the morning, dad got up, shaved, washed, and at seven he was already by the phone, calling all acquaintances, friends and relatives, even in Russia. ... Then we went to the demonstration; that was obligatory. Do you know what a demonstration is? It's when a crowd marches, but an organized crowd, I wish to say, carrying posters up front, representing their enterprises. We had several of those: the ceramics factory, the TselinSel'Mash, where they used to make the Kamaz trucks, and so on. ,,, And there were the professional schools, the universities, and every single enterprise was there to beautify the march. We didn't have any special outfits; it was usually still cold on 1 May, so we'd be wearing coats. I have a picture somewhere of myself, carrying balloons. A small flag on a wooden rod, as thin as a finger, and a piece of red cloth tied to it, and it read on the cloth: "1 May – Day of the Workers". So I had a small flag like that, two or three balloons, ribbons in my hair, all elegant, and [I was] with my father. ... Fathers would carry their children on their shoulders, with those little flags and balloons, and we would walk across the whole city. Approaching the stands, we would form neat columns. We would walk past our government, I mean, the oblast committee, the First Secretary and others, a lot of them. I would go: "Aaaah!" and wave my arms like a butterfly, so they hurt when we got home. The parents, clearly, wouldn't waste any time; it was cool out in the streets, so they'd have a 50-gram shot each, of course. We would meet a lot of friends, embrace, chat, and then the mutual visiting would begin. We'd go home, the parents would put us to sleep, and then off they went – to their friends again. Off they go, having fun.

It was merry; there were songs, and dances, and the accordion and the guitar. … They used to show the parades on the TV too. By the time we got home, they were only starting the broadcast of the Moscow parade, so we'd turn it on; the whole family gathered together [and] we'd watch Moscow. It was ceremonious, festive, much anticipated, a big holiday for us. … Along the parade route, there were little stalls with sweets or pastries, so the parents would buy something for us. … It was merry, sure, people used to enjoy the holiday.

In the same vein, my friend Margarita's mother remembered May Day as a joyous feast. The children used to enjoy the festive mood of the parades, the new clothes that their parents had bought for them, the ribbons in their hair and so on. The adults appreciated the occasion for social drinking during and after the parade. When the parade was over, families and groups of friends used to go to the Park of Culture and Leisure across the river, where a funfair took place. Margarita's mother emphasized a sense of sociability encouraged by the festivity, and a 'spirit of mutual solidarity', which she believed was later lost in the post-soviet years and which used to be expressed in loud greetings exchanged with the many friends one met at the parade.

Soviet-era celebrations indeed blended 'the public' and 'the private', yet in ways different than Soviet ideologists had apparently intended (cf. Kharkhordin 1997; Crowley and Reid 2002). Instead of infusing the lives of participants with official meanings, public holidays created occasions for unofficial socializing, simultaneously inside and outside the 'public sphere' (what Alexei Yurchak terms 'being *vnye*', 2006: 127–28). The actual festivities extended well before and long after the parade or other official activity, beginning with the early morning phone calls to friends and relatives, and finishing with the private parties that went on long into the night. Former Soviet citizens in Astana would later nostalgically reconstruct precisely those 'deterritorialized' (ibid.) practices of celebration.

The affectively rich socializing the festivities enabled (rather than their formal contents) made them 'authentic' holidays for ordinary participants.[7] 'Soviet commemorations have left a legacy of discredited displays of state power and a public accustomed to disdaining them or remaking them in favour of refashioned, atomized events celebrated at home', concludes Catherine Wanner (1998: 148; see also Rolf 2013: 189–91). This double legacy posed a challenge to post-Soviet governments as they tried to devise new holidays capable of promoting new, coherent national identities.

… and in Astana

As mentioned above, the only organized collective activities in the public squares of Astana were the celebrations of official holidays. At the time of this research, Kazakhstan's official holiday calendar included the following dates: Nauryz, the traditional spring festival of revival on 22 March; the Day of Unity of the People of Kazakhstan on 1 May (the reinterpreted former socialist labour holiday); Victory Day, commemorating the end of the Second World War, on 9 May; Astana Day, celebrated previously on 10 June but since 2008 transferred to 6 July; Constitution Day on 30 August; Republic Day on 25 October; Independence Day on 16 December; and finally the New Year's Eve.

There was some variation in emphasis in the messages conveyed on the different holidays, as well as in the overall presentation of the various celebrations (Adams and Rustemova 2009). Astana Day, as described in Chapter 1, focused on the development of the capital city, its economic role and the benefits of its construction for societal cohesion and state-building. Nauryz is a folk spring holiday known across the Turkic and Iranian world. It was turned into an official holiday by several Soviet republics in the 1960s (Binns 1980: 182; Lane 1981: 136–37). Official Nauryz festivities drew on the myth of spring rebirth, Kazakh legends, traditional games (wrestling, swinging on the *alty-bakan* swing) and seasonal festive dishes, like the sour drink *nauryz kozhe*. Constitution Day and Republic Day emphasized state-building, patriotism and the 'friendship of nations' as the basis of societal harmony in Kazakhstan. The 1 May holiday officially celebrated the 'Unity of the People of Kazakhstan', and so event scenarios focused on the catalogue of officially recognized, essentialized ethnic identities, with performances by various folkloric dance and song groups comprising the bulk of the spectacles. However, much like the socialist May Day celebrations in the Soviet period (Lane 1981: 187), 1 May in Kazakhstan during the 2000s was also a general, colourful spring festivity, emphasizing gaiety and joy.

Astana Day was the largest holiday, celebrated over an extended period with multiple events. In 2008, the festivities were extraordinarily lavish, for that year the tenth anniversary of the capital relocation was celebrated. Big concerts, with bleachers accommodating up to some three thousand spectators, took place in Central Square during the week-long celebrations of Astana Day and on 1 May both in 2008 and 2009. Yet the greatest events were organized not in the right-bank downtown but at the foot of the new Kazakh Land monument, next to the Pyramid (see Chapter 1). These included theatrical spectacles involving thousands of extras, mass choreography and performances by stars such as the Kazakhstani pop diva Roza Rymbaeva, Russia's famous Piatnitskii Choir and the Uzbekistani folk rock band Yalla. Additional Astana Day concerts, involving even bigger international stars, were held at the Left Bank 'Main Square' (Glavnaia ploshchad') by the presidential palace, but access to those was strictly limited to an elite audience. In the week preceding Astana Day 2008, a number of new or thoroughly refurbished squares adorned with sculptural compositions, monuments and fountains were ceremoniously opened, with official speeches and musical performances for audiences of up to several hundred people.[8] Moreover, Astana Day, Nauryz and 1 May were celebrated with numerous

Figure 4.2 Rural vendors on May Day in Astana's Central Square (photo: M. Laszczkowski)

smaller concerts at various sites, such as the above-described New Square and the picturesque river embankment. Enormous crowds descended on the main park, where merry-go-rounds, roller-coasters and so on were running, and there were plenty of vendors – commonly, rural visitors hoping to make a quick buck – squatting on the ground offering candyfloss, ice cream, kites, balloons and other cheap toys out of cardboard boxes (Figure 4.2). This element, called *narodnye guliania* (literally, 'popular entertainment') had become a component of major Soviet official festivities in the mid 1930s and was extended under Khrushchev (Binns 1979: 602, 1980: 171). In contrast to these major holidays, the public celebrations of Constitution Day and Republic Day in Astana were limited to concerts on a relatively small stage in the square next to the Youth Palace, while Independence Day went almost unnoticed, no doubt because of the harsh December weather.

Despite these differences in venue, form and emphasis, all of the holidays had much in common. They all shared a general mood of popular, joyous festivity, with relatively few and usually very simple openly political messages – as exemplified by the New Year's Eve show described in the opening paragraphs of this chapter. The essential format that appeared in all celebrations was a 'concert' featuring soloists, duets and small ensembles with a repertoire mixing adapted folk dances, songs and costumes with pop music. The performers appeared one after another, typically doing only one or two songs or dances each. The emcees – invariably a man in a dark suit and a woman in a ball gown – delivered holiday greetings interlaced with patriotic slogans. Commonly, a concert of this format culminated in a grand finale with all of the artists gathering on stage to perform together an uplifting song, full of optimism about Astana and Kazakhstan's unity and bright future. Many individual songs exploited similar topics, with some popular hits being performed repeatedly at various occasions, such as the disco-style song that ran '*Zdravstvui stolitsa ty vol'naia ptitsa – eto Astana! Zdravstvui strana, eto moi Kazakhstan, zdes' moia zemlia!*' – 'Hello, capital, you're a free bird – this is Astana! Hello, country, this is my Kazakhstan, here's my land!' Speeches by officials and emcees recycled a limited number of themes, emphasizing independence, unity and economic growth, referring to Astana as an 'all-national achievement', 'locomotive of progress', 'fairy tale city' and 'city of dreams' that had 'risen from the bare steppe in a blink of an eye like hope for a happy future'. Invocations to Nazarbaev as the 'dear' or 'beloved' president were also common, especially on Astana Day.

In short, public celebrations communicated a simplified optimistic vision of Astana as the hub of progress and a harbinger of a bright future for the nation. It seemed that the organizers had learned the lesson of the late Soviet festivities, or perhaps they were influenced by the allegedly global trend towards producing public space as aesthetically pleasant and free of explicit ideologizing (Boyer 1994). Emphasis in holiday scenarios was on a limited number of rhetorical tropes from official discourse, promoting not so much specific political arguments as what might be called, borrowing from Milan Kundera (1984), 'categorical agreement with being' (see Laszczkowski forthcoming).

Whose Celebration, Whose City?

A crucial question becomes who attended these celebrations, and who did not. While systematic data is not available, some relevant observations can be made. As mentioned, my local friends – young people of the 'urbanite' type (see Chapter 2), many of whom were Tselinograd-born Russians (Chapter 3) – could hardly be persuaded to join me to attend any of the events, with the possible exception of the most colourful and variegated narodnye guliania on May Day or Astana Day. They actually found my commitment to follow the holiday celebrations peculiar if not ridiculous. The audiences at free-access concerts were almost exclusively Kazakh and dominated by young rural or small-town male migrants. I can only speculate as to what that group got out of attending the celebrations, beyond free entertainment and an opportunity for assembling casually in large groups, or why this particular demographic seemed to be targeted. In any event they made up the bulk of the crowds. Loud and boisterous (though usually non-aggressive), they occupied most of the square, talking, laughing, smoking, snapping sunflower seeds. Sometimes, there would be a few girls in their late teens among them, who would dance to the music or lean against their boyfriends to bounce gently in their arms. Otherwise, women tended to be quieter and stay closer to the fringes of the scene. Plausibly, this gendering of space contributed to the 'urbanites'' view of the celebrations as dominated by 'rural' actors and cultural styles.

Once, during a disco in the square by the Youth Palace on the night of Nauryz, the master of ceremonies encouraged the audience to applaud the performance by asking 'Astana, where are you?', prompting cheers and the shouting of 'Here!' in reply. That, however, apparently failed to satisfy him; he began calling out different groups of spectators by their region of origin. He asked: 'Kostanay? Kokshetau? Arkalyk? Atyrau? Taraz? Taldykorgan?' and so on, and those from each given area screamed in response and raised their arms. The loudest and most enthusiastic response came when the emcee called out 'Shymkent?' – the name of the southern oblast stereotyped as the hotbed of 'rural' Kazakhness (see Chapter 2). He continued to address this heterogeneous, newcomer audience as 'Astana' nonetheless, just as was custom of artists and emcees at other holiday events. On another occasion, in an on-stage dialogue between the compères, the man asked the woman who she was, and she replied she was an 'Astanaian', though she had been born in Karaganda ('*Ia astanchanka, rodilas' v Karagande*').

During holiday events like these, a new collective identity – that of 'Astanaians' – was communicated to migrants. It embraced the variety of regional origins but tacitly excluded the generally absent Russians, other Slavs and 'urban' Russophone Kazakhs (cf. Chapter 2), even while non-Kazakh ethnic groups were represented in essentialized, folkloristic forms on the stage. The exclusionary effect was probably not intended by the organizers. It is worth pointing out that the projection of an 'Astanaian' identity that obscured migrants' rural and regional origins reflected the logic of Soviet celebrations that similarly obfuscated the rural roots of the city and focused on demonstrating the coupling of 'modernity' and 'the urban' (Rolf 2013: 92).

Former tselinogradtsy, especially Slavs, commonly regarded all contemporary official holidays as 'Kazakh' and in one sense or another as contrived and inauthentic. While some might be attracted by the narodnye gulyania or musical performances, especially if Soviet or contemporary international stars were slated to appear, local Russians (and other Russophone urbanites) frequently declared they did not feel they belonged at the celebrations. As an expression of their attitudes towards official holidays, let me quote in extenso a school essay by Stas, the son of my landlady Aleksandra Stepanovna. Stas was in the penultimate grade before graduation and seventeen years old at the time he wrote the following (my translation):

"Where would I wish to be on the day of the Holiday of the Capital?" Undoubtedly, on the day of the Holiday of the Capital, I would like to be as far as possible from the said Holiday and its participants. I generally do not like holidays [*prazdniki*], or, more precisely – celebrations [*prazdnetstva*], festivals, parades and the like, except for folk ceremonies with roots that reach into the depth of the ages. I believe holidays should be spontaneous, and not orchestrated [*mushtrirovannye*] as is the case with all state holidays. I am certain that the parade brings little joy to those parading. And how long do they practice it! How much free, private time this consumes! An overwhelming majority of participants are drawn to the celebration in a voluntary-compulsory manner [*v dobrovol'no-prinuditel'nom poriadke*].

I do not see a particular reason for this holiday. I do not see any history to this date. Most plausibly – this is simply a rest day.

The residents of our city are not distinguished by particular civility [*kul'turnost'*], which can be inferred from seeing the heaps of beer bottles, sweets wrappings, etc.

Let us speak about the good. The state, and more specifically the municipality [*akimat*] of the City of Astana, takes a very responsible approach to the celebration of the Day of the Capital.

Since I do not like these kinds of holidays I do not appear at their epicentre. I will learn about [the celebrations] from reports by my acquaintances, live broadcasts on the television [and] from the newspapers.

So, I reckon, the government does not let the holiday follow its own course but plans all events thoroughly.

Concerts, carnivals, salutes – all of that is not for us, the residents of the glorious city of Astana.

Aleksandra Stepanovna read her son's essay to me, smiling to herself and relishing in the understanding of the text's subversiveness – a feeling she expected me to share. Both she and Stas's aunt, who also listened, took pleasure in the boy's expression of sentiments they shared but would find daring to express so openly (as a half-joke, the aunt mentioned the entire family would have ended up in a camp had this still been Stalin's time).

Not everyone shared Stas's criticism, of course. My observation that those who participated in the public holiday celebrations genuinely enjoyed them was corroborated, for example, by the following testimony offered by Ainura, the northern-Kazakhstani rural incomer girl introduced in Chapter 2:

When I was a second year student, in 2005, they gave us costumes – we were butterflies. We performed. We had green butterfly costumes, with shiny wings. Headscarves, vests and short skirts – it looked cool. And the boys were night butterflies; they wore dark blue hoods. ... There were also clowns, snow queens dressed in white and so forth. And all of us from the Agrarian University ... we all were there, from first-year to third-year students, dressed up – attendance was obligatory; the directors ran through the lists and checked your ID to hand out the costume. And [laughing] dressed up in that special attire, we marched from the uni, along Seifullina Street, then Sary-Arka Avenue, to the stadium. At the stadium, we went through our routine – some butterfly motions, we whirled, we danced, and we moved on towards the Youth Palace … Basically, we celebrated the Day of the City that way. And afterwards we went to hang out with our classmates … and have some beer. … I enjoyed taking part in this. I liked the costumes – so funny and simple. But the costumes are not the point – the point is to participate. I'm such an artistic person, I liked it, and I called all my friends to come along. I invited people to dance and enjoy themselves. I enjoyed performing, I liked it very much.

Ainura's account nearly echoes the memory of the Soviet-era celebration offered by my Astana neighbour Svetlana, quoted above. Although Ainura alludes to what Stas called the 'voluntary-compulsory' manner of mobilizing attendance, she clearly stresses the joy she nonetheless found in participating in the spectacle. That joy, notably, stemmed from two sources: first, the carefree form of the officially arranged parade, and second – again, much as was the case of the Soviet holidays described earlier – the extended unofficial part of the celebration: the drinking and hanging around with friends. The kind of parades Ainura described – known locally as 'carnivals' (*karnaval*) – used to be organized more or less during the first decade following the capital relocation. Subsequently, they gave way to the kind of concerts I have outlined above. The new format, focused on the performances by professional or at least semi-professional musicians, dancers and entertainers, offers considerably less space for active participation by the masses of students, workers and so forth. Ainura actually mentioned this in our conversation about her participation in public holidays – she said she found the concerts relatively less interesting and enjoyed them less than the parades. I can only try guessing why the officials in charge of the celebrations had decided to change the format of the events – perhaps they reckoned the parades resembled too strongly Soviet-era holidays, while the concerts, by channelling the public's attention towards the stage, might have had the additional advantage of allowing them to convey desired messages more efficiently.

Be that as it may, in contrast to the enthusiasm expressed by many participants such as Ainura, long-standing urbanites preferred instead to stay at home during holidays or leave the city altogether, retreating to their dachas or a vacation resort for the period of festivities. Thus they chose to give up the public spaces of the city to whom they called 'kolkhozniki' – recent provincial migrants supported by rural or small-town visitors arriving en masse for the holidays. For instance, Koshka (the Russian girl who told the story of the Pushkin monument in Chapter 3) spent the week of Astana Day in 2008 in Borovoe (a hill resort not far from Astana) for that very reason. 'At first, only some kolkhozniki came', she explained to me, laughing. 'Then they went back to their villages and told all their relatives: "Gosh, you gotta come along next year!" So the following year twice as many kolkhozniki arrived, and the urban people [*gorodskie*] left. And with time the urbanites thought, "Shit, this entire city will be taken over by kolkhozniki, we'd better leave!"'. The trend Koshka jocularly described had been noted in the 1960s and 1970s in Soviet cities (Lane 1981: 159). However, the tension over 'urbanity' and 'rurality' acquired extra salience in Astana during the 2000s (see Chapter 1 and especially Chapter 2).

Corroborating Koshka's view, Margarita, when she agreed to spend time with me on the Left Bank's Nurzhol Boulevard during the evening of Astana Day 2009, easily concluded that – just as she had expected – a vast majority of the crowd were 'rural' visitors. When I asked how exactly she could tell, she said it was mostly by people's attire. The clothes of the 'rural' people were distinctly unfashionable. Their attempts to look elegant did not come off, such as the women's overly formal long skirts and men's démodé suit-like trousers. Margarita pointed out, moreover, that *priezzhie* ('visitors') were those who looked around more and took lots of photos. A local person, even if they came to the boulevard on such a night, would not pose for photographs in front of Baiterek, Margarita remarked. She concluded there was something distinctive about the 'rural' appearance: 'It's not just roughness – it's stupidity. This village look, I mean'.

Likewise, Sputnik, the Almaty-raised Kazakh rock fan (see Chapter 2), kept me company at the evening event on Nauryz 2009, when the master of ceremonies called out members of the audience by their region of origin. After we retreated to my apartment to drink beer and listen to music we both enjoyed, I asked how many of those we had seen in the audience he would have considered mambety at first glance. Sputnik replied: 'You know… how should I put this … all of them, I'm afraid. … And the chief mambet was the one jumping around the stage in the cap!' – implying the emcee himself.

Wanner (1998: 121–40) describes a music festival in Ukraine on the eve of independence during which a section of the audience – local Russians or those Ukrainians who felt there was a visceral link between their nation and Russia that should be preserved – were made to feel uncomfortable by expressions of 'cavalier' anti-Soviet and anti-Russian nationalism on the part of the performers and a majority of other spectators. That part of the audience was made aware of their foreignness in a rapidly redefining national context and felt 'trapped in an amorphous colonial space', 'unsure as to whether they were the colonizers or the colonized' (ibid.: 133). The case at hand from Astana is in some respects similar, yet also different. For one thing, with the passage of nearly two decades, the post-Soviet state had consolidated, nationality relations were more or less settled, and thus the public celebrations no longer possessed the kind of 'liminality' (Turner 1995 [1969]) that Wanner found during the pre-independence

Ukrainian festival. Moreover, the official messages conveyed in the celebrations in Astana were not anti-Russian. While the 'primordial' rights of the Kazakhs in Kazakhstan were asserted, official ideology was inclusivist, calling to harmony and a 'friendship of nationalities'.

However, a politics of inclusion and exclusion works not only on the level of verbal messages, but also on a more embodied level of performance and cultural style (Ferguson 1999; Chapter 2). Local Slavs, as well as Kazakh urbanites like Sputnik, felt they did not belong in the celebrations because the events were dominated by a style that the 'urbanites' interpreted as 'rural'. Clearly, that led to a kind of self-fulfilling prophecy or a Bourdieuan 'structuring structure' (Bourdieu 1977): the stylistic mismatch between the urbanites' self-image on the one hand and the celebratory events and the majority of their audience on the other discouraged the urbanites from attending and thus perpetuated the 'rural' dominance over the holidays. But by scornfully insisting on the 'rural' character of official celebrations and by making a point of their own absenteeism the urbanites drew a boundary separating them from rural migrants.

Public Space Reopened

In line with the common way of seeing post-Soviet urban public space, ostensibly, central squares in Astana were monopolized by the ruling elite as a screen on which to project officially produced imagery of harmony and progress. However, on closer inspection, the squares could be seen to live complex 'social lives' dynamically stretched between alternative versions of the past, the present and the future.

As Nicholas Dirks (1992) has noted with regard to religious rituals in Southern India – which were assumed by their organizers, participants and anthropologists to express hierarchical relationships within the villages – marginalized groups can often assert their collective agency most potently by simply withdrawing from participation. Paradoxically, it is such 'failure' of a public event that renders it especially politically significant by questioning the established order. Similarly, in Astana public holiday spectacles in central squares apparently aimed to reaffirm state ideology focusing on the idealized image of development of the new capital and harmonious social relations. The spectacles conveyed a somewhat vague image of Astana's bright future and communicated a collective identity ('Astanaians') mostly to audiences made up of recent migrants from across Kazakhstan. By their light, festive forms and carefree messages the events left little room for contestation. However, the local Slavs and 'urban' Kazakhs – groups that were relatively marginalized by celebrations tailored to cater rather to small-town and rural migrants – repoliticized the shows, so to speak, by their withdrawal. Against the grain of much scholarly writing on (the demise of) public space (e.g., Sennett 1978; Boyer 1994; Low 2000), absenteeism turned out to be not so much an effect of citizens being 'pressed out' by a government monopolizing space, but an active choice to make a political statement by a group that found itself not represented in officially staged public events.

Moreover, absenteeism and criticism of the holidays were concurrent with the nostalgic idealization of Soviet-era celebrations. Older urbanites, stressing how they used to enjoy the private socializing occasioned by official holidays in the Soviet period, simultaneously emphasized that, in contrast, they found the new post-Soviet holidays 'incomprehensible', 'meaningless' and 'inauthentic'. The idealization of past celebrations helped construct one's distance from the contemporary holidays and the form of national community that those latter-day holidays promoted.

It is an anthropological commonplace since the discipline's earliest days that social groups and collective identities are constructed and reaffirmed through public celebrations (Durkheim 2001 [1912]). However, it is worth pointing out how, in addition to the construction of mutually opposed groups such as the 'urbanites' and the 'rural migrants' or 'kolkhozniki', the dynamics discussed in this chapter entailed the rendering of public space in the city imbued with multiple, divergent qualities. In other words, this was an inherently splintered process of place-making that consisted in an intersection of discourses, imaginations, memories and bodily practices, all anchored in concrete material space and its history. If, as is generally claimed in scholarly literature, 'state' agency tends towards the 'closure' of space – in the sense of the inscription of hegemonic narratives, the drawing of boundaries and the pre-emption of alternative visions – then I would argue that public space in Astana was nonetheless opened up to multiple possibilities of constructing identities and hierarchies of value.

Most basically, mutually incompatible definitions of 'urbanity' (which also implies 'modernity') were put forth: one expressed in the officially promoted imagination of Astana as a city of migrants; the other grounded in narratives of older (Soviet-era) forms of urban sociality. The mutually opposed spatial designations 'urbanity' and 'rurality' were made concrete. Especially the 'rural' – the highly politicized category that served as a vehicle for critiquing the cultural and political economy of the current regime – was articulated in the long-standing urbanites' evaluations of public displays of cultural style by recent migrants. While spectacle scenarios aimed to promote a unifying urban identity, from the point of view of those dissenting urbanites the result was that central sites in the city were increasingly invaded by 'rurality'.

Finally, in connection to the previous chapter, it is worthwhile to highlight how the public spectacles and their critical evaluations allowed for the construction of divergent chronotopes (Bakhtin 1981). The official rhetoric and imagery presented during the celebrations evoked a vague yet nonetheless hope-infused vision of a city without history (despite the occasional reference to a fabled mythical past, as with the Bozok spirit in the New Year's scene with which I opened this chapter), focused on an imagined harmonious future. In a sense, this might be said to resemble the Soviet holiday-organizers' efforts to use newly invented celebrations as a way of colonizing not space alone but also time – erasing all other visions of the past and the future than that promoted by official ideology (Rolf 2013: 72–75). On the other hand, by rejecting the new holidays and remembering Soviet-era feasts, older urbanites reconstructed Tselinograd as a living time-space. Those were very material memories, firmly anchored, that is, in particular streets and squares that continue to exist, physically, in the city. The memories were, moreover, embodied: the 'authenticity' of Soviet holidays was confirmed for instance by the pain in little Svetlana's arms from over-enthusiastic flag-waving, which she could still almost feel as a mature woman thirty years later. That viscerally felt authenticity – constructed through performance, imagination and discourse – seemed to imply, by extension, that it was Tselinograd that was a 'real' city, rather than the officially celebrated 'capital of the future'.

Notes

1. Note the similarity to anthropologists Swartz, Turner and Tuden's (1966: 4–8) notion of public matters as those whose settlement or failure to settle concerns the group as a whole. Thus understood publicness is, according to these authors, one of the key elements defining the political.

2. At various points in Soviet history, such as in the post-revolutionary 1920s, in the 1930s under Stalin (Buchli 2000), and later with Khrushchev's housing drive in the 1950s and early 1960s (Gerchuk 2000; Crowley 2002), domestic space was given particular attention as a crucial determinant of residents' consciousness (Crowley and Reid 2002: 11). This led to what Svetlana Boym (1994) calls 'taste wars', such as the 1929 campaign against 'petit-bourgeois' domestic knick-knacks, when domestic aesthetics were turned into a central ground of political struggle. While in the communal apartment even the most private was subjected to 'public' gaze, which exerted a hierarchical as well as mutual control not unconnected to the control apparatus of the state (Gerasimova 2002), spaces such as the dacha offered privacy on the condition of recognizing public norms and institutional frameworks – what Stephen Lovell (2002) calls 'private publicness'. Also the urban courtyard (*dvor*), designed as a space of everyday leisure, neighbourly small talk and children's play for the inhabitants of several neighbouring blocks of apartments (see Chapter 5), was not only public in the sense of being communal, but also in that within its space official ideology was both embodied and splintered apart (Humphrey 2005). Stalinist architecture in the Soviet Union and elsewhere in the 'socialist bloc', emphasizing the visuality of the facade, subjected the private comfort of the indoors to the public representational function of the outdoors (see Crowley 2002: 184 for an example from Warsaw). Under Khrushchev, the monumental style of Stalinist construction was replaced with uniform, austere, prefabricated mass housing (Gerchuk 2000). Once more, the public goal of enforcing (an appearance of) equality and technocratic 'futurology' (Crowley 2002: 193) ruled the design of buildings. While residents always managed to find ways to organize their homes to express and assert their individuality and even to resist state attempts at regularization (Buchli 2000; Crowley 2002), in all these guises space was a 'socializing project' (Crowley and Reid 2002: 15), public in the sense of goals concerning the whole of society.

3. The arrival of new spatial forms associated with transnational capitalism and consumer culture, such as the shopping mall, seemed to represent the spread of the processes observed in 'the West' – the commercialization of public space and its appropriation by elite interests – to former Soviet cities (Ruble 1995; Czepczyński 2008). The classical critique of commercial space expansion in Western Europe and North America, steadily since the time of the nineteenth-century shopping arcades, has been that when public space was relinquished to private, capitalist ownership, to 'the spectacle of the commodity' and consumption, the effect was depoliticization – the strengthening of domination through the erasure of space for contestation (Harvey 2003: 212, 216). Many authors, including Russian novelist and essayist Viktor Erofeyev, have made a similar argument for some of the post-Soviet states, which applies to Kazakhstan: by allowing and indeed promoting consumerism, the ruling elites discourage citizens from political activity and thus secure complacency (Erofeev 2006; see also Koch 2013). However, cultural forms, including architectural forms such as the shopping mall, do not travel unchanged. Elsewhere (Laszczkowski 2011b), I have analysed a prominent mall in Astana to argue that – contrary to the dominant scholarly view of the shopping mall as a commercial, non-public space par excellence (see Goss 1993; Gottdiener 2000) – it became the venue of significant, if subtle, cultural-political dynamics whereby fundamental values and identities came to be defined. By interacting with cosmopolitan commodities, trademarks and architectural forms, various groups of shoppers – or, often, just viewers – constructed specific images of a global 'modernity' and claimed belonging in that imagined world. By evaluating, moreover, their own and others' comportment in this material and symbolic ambience, they positioned themselves and others in hierarchies of 'worldliness' and 'urbanity' (cf. Chapter 2).
4. For instance, by 2012, a monument to the Kazakh 'national poet' Abai Kunanbaev appeared at the former site of the Lenin statue (Chapter 3), and the fountain mentioned below was removed from the middle of the square.
5. By 2012, a new massive monument to two historic Kazakh khans Zhenibek and Kerei was placed approximately where the Soviet-era Eternal Flame used to be.
6. This seems to have taken place despite the holiday organizers' efforts, especially in the early Soviet decades, to influence participants and audiences not so much through explicit ideologizing but rather through 'festive mood' and the joyfulness of the celebrations (Rolf 2013: 45).
7. Though it should also be kept in mind that, as historian Malte Rolf (2013: 139–40) does well to remind, any retrospective narrative is at best a partial source of knowledge on how participants actually felt about the celebrations – or, for that matter, any other kind of events.
8. Such new sites included a leafy square in Prospekt Pobedy (north of the old-time right-bank centre), another square on Tashenova Street (at a point where the old centre borders the Soviet-built mikroraiony; see Map 1.1, Chapter 1), a small park by the main mosque on the Left Bank and a large fountain at a busy crossroads by the Circus (next to the old Park of Leisure and Culture, on the left bank of the river).

Chapter 5

Fixing the Courtyard

Mundane Place-Making

Five Oktiabrskaia (October) Street, the apartment block where I lived for nine months during my fieldwork in 2008–2009, had been built in the 1970s in a residential area in the centre-north of then Tselinograd, half way between Central Square and the industrial zone.[1] Placed inside a quadrangle of north-south and east-west roads, the block stood away from the street. It was a 'box' of grey brick, with five stories, four entrances and seventy apartments (Figure 5.1). The monotonous facade with square windows was broken by double vertical rows of balconies between each pair of staircases. Residents had glassed-up most of the balconies for protection from wind and frost. In sum, the building looked very much like a typical Soviet apartment block of its period. In front of the building, there was the courtyard (*dvor*) with some trees, a few benches to sit and rest, a children's playground, a laundry-drying area and a tiny grocery store under a steep bright red roof. Across the dvor stood a twin building that had been constructed simultaneously in the 1970s. The dvor was overshadowed by a higher, nine-storey apartment block (*deviatietazhka*), built at a later time, flanking the neighbourhood from the south. The shared courtyard was an object of latent tension between the residents of the three buildings.

Focusing on this narrow, mundane and marginal location – with respect to the prominent public spaces and recently developed spectacular cityscapes discussed in the bulk of this book so far – affords a new perspective on the politics of place-making in Astana. Following the general premise of this book, place-making denotes a dynamic, mutually constitutive relation between local subjects – 'people who think of themselves … as belonging in and to a place' (Raffles 1999: 334) – and their local material environment. Place-making involves the production of 'locality' as a phenomenological quality of place and of a 'situated community' of dwellers, an 'actually existing social form' in which locality is realized ('neighbourhood', in Arjun Appadurai's terms; 1996: 178–79). As this chapter highlights, place-making is a reiterative open-ended

Figure 5.1 The apartment block and courtyard at 5 Oktiabrskaia (photo: M. Laszczkowski)

process of ongoing construction and reconstruction, which consists to a large extent in mundane, ad hoc material maintenance work. It is simultaneously and inextricably a material, ideational and phenomenological process, in which the roles of material things as actants (Latour 2005) are crucial, together with the imaginative and interpretive work of human actors. Local subjects and qualities emerge in engagements with the dynamic material make-up of places. Moreover, places are made through materially mediated connections with other places. Thus they become the terrain of collusions and collisions among individual and collective actors – 'their inhabitants and others' (Raffles 1999: 326).

Place-making is a disorderly process, and its products – places and 'localities' – are unstable. This also implies that place-making is inherently political, 'always a cultural as well as a political-economic activity' (Tsing 2000: 338). Neighbourhoods are subject to change via outside pressures and tensions within. The politics of place-making means that place and locality emerge through multiple, contingent and partly contradictory practices of numerous actors pursuing various projects. Locality denotes not simply a phenomenological quality of familiarity, but also 'a set of relations, an ongoing politics' (ibid.: 324). Likewise, 'community' must not be taken as an entity, least of all a stable or homogeneous one (Creed 2006). Rather, it connotes a relation, marked by a fragile shared sense of belonging derived from quotidian forms of interaction. Just like place, it needs to be performed, recreated ever anew through interactions and material practices. This chapter follows the making and also unmaking of 'locality' and 'community' at 5 Oktiabrskaia.

'Marginal' places offer an analytic potential much valued by anthropology (e.g., Das and Poole 2004). As Anna Tsing argues in a different context, 'marginal perspectives can illuminate both the potency and the limitations of more central visions' (1993: 288). Modern state power aims to produce space as both its object and basis (Lefebvre 1991 [1974], 2003a). It intervenes in place-making to establish scalar and hierarchical relations between 'the state' and those other places that are rendered simultaneously outside and subject to it – which is what the notion of 'local communities' denotes in state discourse (Tsing 1993: 26). The state is made to appear supralocal, positioned above 'society' and encompassing particular places with their resident 'communities' (Ferguson and Gupta 2002). As mentioned in the introduction, one of the technologies of governmentality through which these spatial 'state-effects' (Mitchell 1999) are achieved is urbanism, in the sense of the integrated theory and practice of city planning and management of urban social and material milieus (Rabinow 1989; Scott 1998: 103–17). Urbanism establishes hierarchical and scalar relations between the centres of its production (which are by the same token centres of state power) and those other locales (neighbourhoods) that it treats as objects of design and intervention. But this also means that those very sites that are rendered 'marginal' by urbanism are central to its logic: it is through acting in and upon the capillaries that the 'core' of power is established.

This is clearly visible in the relationship between Soviet urbanism and residential neighbourhoods (Crowley and Reid 2002; Collier 2010). In particular, the urban neighbourhood courtyard (dvor) is a compelling site to study place-making and its politics in Soviet and post-Soviet cities (see Richardson 2008: 119–28). The dvor is not merely the void between buildings. Rather, much like the Latin-American plaza (Low 2000) or the *rua* (street) in Brazil's colonial cities (Holston 1989), the dvor is a spatially constituted social institution, important in generating social action. In Soviet cities, the dvor was – and to some extent remains – that kind of communal space that Tanya Richardson (2008: 125, 163), drawing on the work of Oleg Kharkhordin (1997: 358–59), proposes to call not public but 'social': simultaneously intimate and shared, and deeply politicized. Basic social relations are tied, performed and reproduced in the dvor. It is a site of socializing and of children's socialization under the watchful eye of the retired elders. People meet, greet, talk and sometimes trade in the dvor. Important matters concerning the block or neighbourhood are discussed in the dvor. In common usage, the noun 'dvor' also refers to a group of people brought together by shared use of the courtyard – a neighbourhood 'community'. One can say, for instance, that 'the whole dvor celebrated a holiday together' ('*otmechali vsem dvorom*'). In short, the dvor is the focal site for the production of locality and of local, individual and collective subjects. By the same token, however, the dvor is the site of ongoing politics. In the Soviet Union, the dvor was central to the theory and practice of urbanism. For Soviet city planners and ideologues it was the basic spatial unit through which to define and shape the norms and forms of sociality (French 1995: 62–63), while according to Humphrey (2005) its materiality both transmitted and diffracted ideological intent.

In the post-Soviet period, city planners' attention in Astana shifted away from Soviet-era neighbourhoods and concentrated instead on newly developed areas primarily in the Left Bank. But places such as 5 Oktiabrskaia continued to change and be the loci of social dynamics, the production of local subjects and contests over notions of belonging. Five Oktiabrskaia, as a place, was being made and remade in an ongoing manner through a multiplicity of connections. These included connections to places such as the city hall where the forms of 'scaling' and 'spacing' (Latour 2005: 183–85) state power – that is, power that aims to produce space as its object and establish scalar relations between 'the state' and 'the local' – were being established. The analysis below highlights the roles of mundane material items as 'mediators' (Latour 1993: 77–82) both enabling and inflecting these connections, including the performances of administrative power. It leads me, moreover, to make a case for treating marginality itself as relational and a product of situated claims to define the relationships between what are otherwise equally 'local' places.

Shifting Frameworks

The generation of locality in the cities of post-Soviet Kazakhstan was affected by complex changes inter alia to demography, property relations, legal frameworks and urban administration. As discussed in Chapter 2, the 1990s and 2000s were a period of sweeping demographic change throughout north-central Kazakhstan. In the wake of Kazakhstan's independence, many of the local Russians and other non-Kazakhs (Slavs, Germans) emigrated to Russia, Ukraine, Belarus, Germany and other countries. They were replaced by Kazakh newcomers, often from the countryside. The privatization of housing facilitated mass residential mobility, allowing individuals to buy and sell their apartments (Struyk 1996: 208–10).

These changes were clearly felt at 5 Oktiabrskaia as well. Many former residents had left and were replaced by newcomers. Many apartments had absentee owners and were rented out for shorter or longer periods. Presumably, although I never managed to gain systematic information, some flats had changed owners more than once. I was not able to carry out a precise microsociological survey of the block for reasons to do with the changes in question. In a setting where people frequently came and went, and one knew few neighbours personally, the sight of a stranger on one's staircase did not astonish anyone. On the other hand, it was difficult to solicit knowledge about neighbours since inhabitants knew little about others, and with tenants often changing in many rented apartments even the most inquisitive residents lost track. Moreover, there was a distrust of strangers. Massive steel doors were a symptom of the new attitudes often pointed out by old-time dwellers, and such doors were unlikely to be opened to a person wishing to ask a few questions for a survey. Thus, despite nearly a year's residence in the block, I remained a stranger to many inhabitants – our paths simply failed to cross, a fact that is itself indicative of how loosely integrated a social setting the block as a whole had become.

By the time of my arrival in 2008, more than half of all apartments in the building were occupied by 'new' inhabitants – that is, residents who had not lived there before the onset of changes. In local memory, particular events of the 'long 1990s' – that is, the period from perestroika (late 1980s) and Kazakhstan's independence (1991) to circa 2000, including the early years after the capital relocation – often blurred into an indiscriminate time of change, so it was diffi-cult to assess for how long such residents were considered 'new' at 5 Oktiabrskaia. Probably, it differed from one person to another, depending on their level of involvement in the communal matters of the block and the neighbourhood, as well as on who was giving the assessment. I am constrained to adopt the imprecise category of 'new residents' as deployed by a core group of dwellers who actively participated in the sociality of the dvor and had mostly lived in the building since the Soviet period – some had been among the block's original inhabitants.

The members of that 'core' group (itself rather hazily defined) were between their early forties and mid seventies. They were all Russian or in any case Slav. The eldest had come from various places in European Russia, Siberia, Ukraine and Belarus during the Tselina campaign, from the mid 1950s to mid 1960s (M. Pohl 1999; Chapter 3). The middle aged had been born in Tselinograd or in other towns in north-central Kazakhstan. They had various educational and professional backgrounds: there was the retired construction-machinery opera-tor, already briefly encountered earlier in this book; a truck driver; an accoun-tant; a retired nurse; a tailor; an elderly taxi driver; a retired food-supply worker; a Soviet-era consumer-trade administrative clerk; a retired shop manager; and so forth. Those long-standing residents often complained that they, too, found themselves among strangers in their old familiar building. Their complaints tended to focus on the short-term tenants, usually Kazakh wage migrants from smaller towns, who were commonly stigmatized by long-standing residents as bearers of 'rurality' and 'backwardness' (cf. Alexander 2009b; Chapter 2). In sum, such migrants occupied at least one in every three apartments in the block.

Apart from the presence of numerous newcomers and short-term tenants, residents also had to face other challenges created by the privatization of apart-ments and utility networks. Far from a simple transfer of ownership, this had been a complex process of trying out and negotiating basic rights, roles, norms and relations (Ruble 1995; Struyk 1996; Alexander 2007a, 2009b). Previously, as already noted in Chapter 1, material infrastructures had literally assembled Soviet cities by plugging populations, apartment blocks, factories and so forth together. These infrastructures were seemingly able to reach unproblematically into individual apartments and connect them to nationwide networks (Collier 2004). With privatization, those connections were broken, while households were suddenly burdened with the responsibility for the maintenance of buildings and the end sections of infrastructural networks (such as plumbing).

Importantly, uncertainty was felt equally acutely inside municipal bureaucracies (Alexander 2007a, 2007b; Humphrey 2007) where the changes generated a 'crisis of knowing' (Alexander and Buchli 2007: 3). Since the 1950s, in the Soviet Union an expansive apparatus for the comprehensive planning, management and reform of cities had consolidated (Collier 2010: 84–107). In the 1990s, that totalizing, teleological form of urban governance was over (ibid.: 124). Soviet-era 'executive committees' in Kazakhstan's cities were transformed into city halls, *akimaty* (sing. *akimat*), as local branches of state administration. Their members pondered what their new roles vis-à-vis citizens and infrastructures might be while 'the norms and forms of the social environment' (Rabinow 1989) were in turmoil. One thing in particular that became unknown was who was now responsible for shared spaces within residential units, such as hallways, basements, staircases and courtyards. In sum, the break-up of material and administrative chains of connection left both urban administrators and residents groping for ways to deal with the heterogeneous mass of material elements: buildings, pipes, wires and so on, that had formed an invisible, taken-for-granted background of urban living but were now suddenly brought forth in need for redefinition.

New frameworks were necessary for the maintenance of shared spaces. Initially, maintenance was the responsibility of municipal housing departments (*domoupravlenia*). These were large organizations (only two covered all of Aqmola, as former Tselinograd was called in the 1990s) and largely ineffective. In the late 1990s the so-called Apartment Owners' Committees (*Komitety Sobstvennikov Kvartir* – KSK) were established. A KSK normally comprised the owners of all apartments in a cluster of several neighbouring apartment blocks. KSK members elected a chairperson from their ranks. The committee pooled monthly fees from members, managed maintenance and repair work, and employed an accountant and, funds allowing, a plumber, cleaning personnel and other technicians. Maintenance work was funded from the pool of members' contributions, although the costs of some tasks could be negotiated with municipal authorities.

In a departure from the general pattern, both 5 Oktiabrskaia and the twin block across the dvor had their own separate KSKs – probably in connection to the particular arrangement through which the two buildings had been built and originally populated in the 1970s. In the late-Soviet period urban housing was generally state property. Apartments were distributed either by municipal authorities or (state-owned) major enterprises (Morton 1980). Factory-organized housing was especially prevalent in those cities whose economy hinged on a few 'city-forming enterprises' (Collier 2010: 102).[2] Some employers, however, did not have the capacity to build, distribute and manage housing. Those working, for instance, in the consumer-supply apparatus (*potrebsoiuz*), airlines, healthcare or education could enter a cooperative (*kooperativ*) for the building of apartments. Such apartment blocks were known as 'cooperative houses' (*kooperativnye doma*, sing. *kooperativnyi dom*), built and maintained from resident-members' contributions. The building at 5 Oktiabrskaia and its twin were two cases in point. At the time I lived there, some of the long-standing dwellers would occasionally invoke that historical background to emphasize that the residents of 5 Oktiabrskaia were accustomed to relative independence and responsibility.

Another significant change, next to the replacement of many earlier residents by newcomers and the shift in housing and infrastructure management patterns, was the commercialization of space inside the apartment block and courtyard. In general, attempts by outside entrepreneurs to set up businesses at 5 Oktiabrskaia during the 1990s and early 2000s were received by old-time residents with ambivalence at best, seen as threats to the spatial as well as moral order of the neighbourhood. For instance, one outsider bought a ground-floor apartment in the block, planning to open a computer shop. However, he failed to reach an agreement with the KSK. The man wished to buy basement space underneath his newly purchased property, but the KSK refused. 'How could we sell our legs and be left with all the rest above?' asked one female resident, dragging the edge of her hand across her knees. This metaphor is indicative of how the commercialization of housing was perceived as a threat to the integrity of the body micropolitic, quite literally understood, of the apartment block. In the end, the would-be investor left, and the only trace of his engagement with the block was a steel door he had installed in 'his' staircase. Other entrepreneurs were more successful: a curtain shop and a language school opened in other ground-floor apartments bought by outsiders. It is common to see many more businesses operating in adapted ground-floor flats in other buildings across Astana's Soviet-built neighbourhoods. While this became a taken-for-granted feature of the post-Soviet urban environment, it still sometimes rubs Soviet-formed sensibilities the wrong way. Referring to the post-Soviet shifts in social order in connection primarily to privatization (see Chapter 1), one elderly inhabitant at 5 Oktiabrskaia bickered: 'Everything's been taken apart, nothing's left, but there are five shops in every building!' Another disgruntled neighbour added, evoking the Bolshevik condemnation of commerce: 'This is pure speculation! They used to put you in jail for speculation before ...'

Some businesses particularly offended such older residents' sense of local moral order. In the mid 1990s, an *oralman* (a returning Kazakh from Mongolia or China) entrepreneur opened a billiards bar in a small building (that once housed a fencing club) behind the block. His establishment attracted groups of Kazakh males, presumably rural migrants, for loud sessions of entertainment and drinking every night and especially on weekends, creating noise and the pervasive smells of frying *shashlik*. Residents of 5 Oktiabrskaia often complained about the bar's customers as an alien, unwelcome and potentially threatening presence in the neighbourhood. This example suggests how moral critiques of the commercialization of dvor space intertwined with other spatial imaginaries such as the dichotomy between the 'rural' and the 'urban', with cultural styles, and also with notions of ethnicity. Later in this chapter we will see how the efforts on the part of the group of most committed residents to maintain the 5 Oktiabrskaia block as a place with distinctive characteristics focused, inter alia, on upholding the purity of the imaginary of the dvor as a communal, non-commercial space.

Material Place-Making in the Dvor

Formally speaking, the dvor was municipal property and its maintenance thus a responsibility of the city hall (akimat). However, in practice, residents were left to their own devices with regard to caring for the dvor. Throughout the 1990s and much of the 2000s municipal authorities lacked the capacity or willingness to engage consistently in the maintenance of neighbourhood infrastructures. While new construction was gathering momentum principally in the Left Bank, in many Soviet-era neighbourhoods in Astana akimat involvement was at best sporadically felt. At 5 Oktiabrskaia, the municipality occasionally provided major elements of dvor infrastructure. At some point in the early 2000s, the akimat had the internal roadway surrounding the dvor paved and new curbs installed. On another occasion, a *besedka* (single piece table with benches under a plywood roof) and some ladders and slides for children to play on were placed in the courtyard. However, akimat involvement with the dvor was inconsistent: for instance, an old fence was removed, presumably to be replaced with a new one, yet a new fence never materialized. Everyday maintenance of the dvor was left in the residents' hands. While a group of those to whom I have referred above as the 'core' residents of the block took charge of maintaining their dvor as best they could, the lack of resources and shifting relationships among multiple actors, including individual residents, the KSK, the akimat, the residents of the neighbouring blocks and outside entrepreneurs venturing to set up businesses in the neighbourhood, meant that by the time of my fieldwork the courtyard was a patchy assemblage of broken or dilapidated items and heterogeneous scraps.

My landlady Aleksandra Stepanovna played a leading role in organizing a group of 'activist' residents to assemble the available things in order to maintain the dvor. She was a Russian woman in her forties, a seamstress and the wife of an electronics serviceman. Although raised in Tselinograd, she had not been among the original inhabitants of 5 Oktiabrskaia. In 1998, her family had moved in from a smaller flat elsewhere in the city. Soon, Aleksandra Stepanovna bought another apartment at 5 Oktiabrskaia cheaply from a former resident moving out, and she rented that apartment to long-term tenants (such as me) for a substantial share in her household income. She was not employed by the KSK and held no official function related to the maintenance of the block. Nonetheless, she was often seen busy cleaning or repairing various items in the staircases, the court-yard, or tending the greenery around the building. Aleksandra Stepanovna valued a sense of neighbourly community and was wholeheartedly dedicated to what she saw as the common good of the block (not least, of course, because she owned two flats there – though other owners were not so committed). By the time of my fieldwork she had become the 'core' residents' informal leader in matters of building and courtyard maintenance. At times, she had even been able to de facto appoint and dismiss KSK chairs.

Aleksandra Stepanovna personally painted the fence surrounding the laun-dry-drying area with paint purchased with KSK money. The fence remained unpainted on the side of the other building, as was the case with most items for which the other KSK was responsible. Having leftover red paint, she renovated a concrete camel in the children's playground. The railing around the playground was made of old pipes that had been stored in the basement (probably leftover from some previous maintenance job), their purpose long forgotten. Aleksandra Stepanovna had arranged for the owner of the small grocery shop in the dvor to have the pipes soldered and put up around the playground. Thus the shop owner, a Kazakh woman who had recently moved to Astana, settled her bills for having connected the shop to the block's water supply and sewerage. The shop itself, as an epitome of the commercialization of shared space, was an ambiguous addition to the dvor. The long-standing residents had initially opposed the idea of having it built, on the grounds of Soviet-era principles of social and spatial organization. 'We were used from the Soviet times to the following rule: what's there is there, and nothing extra is needed', Aleksandra Stepanovna commented. Some suspected the shopkeeper had obtained the necessary permits by bribing someone at the akimat.

Next, the small grass patches at each of the apartment block's four entrances had different fences still. Those had once stood in front of the neighbouring nine-storey building, but the owner of a newly opened boutique in the nine-sto-rey had them replaced with fancier fences, simply dumping the old pieces behind the block. Aleksandra Stepanovna would later recall with amusement how together with the then chairman of the 5 Oktiabrskaia KSK she 'stole' the fences under cover of the night. Using the Soviet-era Pioneer Day (19 May)[3] as a pretext, she mobilized a group of male residents of 5 Oktiabrskaia to put up the fences in front of their own block. This was not a professional job, however, so she had to constantly remind people not to sit on the wobbly fences.

For sitting, there were benches by each entrance. Originally, there had been four identical concrete and wood benches. At some point, two of them were replaced by the akimat with more decorative park-style items. Aleksandra Stepanovna could not recall where exactly those had come from or why there were only two; she suspected the other two had simply been stolen before they were even installed. Finally, one of the most long-standing residents, a truck driver, once brought an elegant heavy iron bench, which he had appropriated in circumstances likewise shrouded in the mists of favour-economy and forgetting. However, the bench soon disappeared from outside the block, only to be found in the courtyard of a nearby school. Aleksandra Stepanovna commented with a self-assured tone entirely disregarding the bench's unclear origin: 'Technically, it's ours. We could go and bring it back anytime'.

This account of material place-making highlights a multiplicity of translocal connections and the importance of mundane material items. Place and locality at 5 Oktiabrskaia emerged and were reiteratively remade through the entanglements of multiple agencies – some originating from within the neighbourhood, some from other places – and flows of people and things. Scraps such as old pieces of pipe, leftover paint, discarded fences and other things jerry-rigged, reused, recycled, reappropriated or – in some cases – simply snatched from some other place were brought together through the uncoordinated actions of diverse actors, each pursuing their own situated projects. Aleksandra Stepanovna's coordination was only partial and contingent on available items and coincidental opportunities. Benches, fences and other things appeared and disappeared depending on the often obscure personal deals and exchanges of favours linking residents, entrepreneurs and outsiders.

Importantly, all those diverse items were mediators, in Bruno Latour's sense of the term: things that have the capacity to modify or distort the meaning they were supposed to convey, the project they were meant to help carry out, or alter the course and effect of action and 'make others do unexpected things' (Latour 2005: 39, 106). Old pipes and other such things enabled, constrained and indeed provoked the actions of local inhabitants and other human participants in place-making at 5 Oktiabrskaia. This is not to downplay the agency of residents and other people, but highlighting the roles of things as mediators helps move away from a kind of dualist thinking and scalar assumptions that underlie much anthropological theorizing of place and space.

In most established theories, material elements are assumed to be passive objects of human intervention and interpretation. As archaeologist Bjørnar Olsen (2003: 91) points out, even phenomenological approaches to space and landscape (e.g., De Certeau 1984; Casey 1996) – despite their focus on the body's immersion in space, and hence on materiality, and despite emphasizing mutually constitutive loops between subjects and 'their' environments – nonetheless retain a tendency to limit their view of human engagements with space to subjective mental processes.[4] Anthropologists inspired by this kind of phenomenological theory are primarily interested in how people attach meanings to places and entwine them with memories and narratives (e.g., Bender 1993; Low 2000). This is also implicit in Setha Low's distinction between the material 'production' of space and its 'construction' through individuals' subjective experience and symbolic processes of meaning-making, such as narrativization (cf. Introduction). Connected to this is a distinct temporal sequence: space is apparently first materially 'produced' by 'the state' or other large organizations and subsequently 'constructed' by the individuals who come to inhabit it.

In contrast, the account of place-making at 5 Oktiabrskaia offered above highlights the ongoing, reiterative nature of place-making as a process that is inextricably both material and ideational at the same time. The specific qualities of place emerged as the combined result of its material constitutive elements and what human inhabitants did with them. The residents grouped around Aleksandra Stepanovna took care of repairing and renovating pre-installed infrastructure, and they added new items: benches, fences and so on. These actions were shaped by the availability and particular qualities of those various things. It was through those material acts that the dvor was constructed as a place filled with personal meanings and memories shared among long-time dwellers who had participated and continued to participate in its making.

Moreover, it was the labour of adding and maintaining items in the dvor that simultaneously produced local subjects. Through this labour Aleksandra Stepanovna became a local leader. An acting 'community' was 'performed into being' (Harvey 2005: 128) when residents engaged in installing fences and so forth. A sense of collective local subjecthood – ideally embracing all residents of the block but in practice shared more narrowly among the group of 'activists' – crystallized around particular items: the 'we' in whose name Aleksandra Stepanovna claimed the ownership of the fancy bench (others among the core group of long-standing residents similarly referred to that 'we' and to various items in the dvor as 'ours'). In sum, then, mundane acts of maintenance work – made possible or actually triggered by material mediators – led to the production of both 'locality' as a phenomenological quality and 'neighbourhood' as a group of people defined by particular kinds of interaction (Appadurai 1996: 178–79).

By the same token, the temporal sequence of the 'production' and 'construction' of place is challenged. As Tim Ingold says, 'building ... is a process that is continually going on, for as long as people dwell in an environment' (1995: 78). Five Oktiabrskaia continued to change long after the apartment block had been built back in the 1970s. The boundary between building and maintenance is blurred (Graham and Thrift 2007), and similarly there is no clear dividing line between what Low calls the 'social production' and 'social construction' of space – rather, place-making is a continuous becoming of both the material environment and the subjects who inhabit it.

Furthermore, the dualism of matter versus meaning, 'production' and 'construction', entails a similarly dualistic scalar model of political relations. The dominant, centralized agency of 'the state' is opposed to the multiple dispersed practices of 'ordinary individuals' or 'local communities' who 'reappropriate' space by imbuing it with subjective meanings and memories (De Certeau 1984: 97).[5] Beyond the field of the anthropology of space and place, this kind of dualist thinking has lain at the core of much of the anthropology of resistance (e.g., Scott 1985, 1990), even though, as Mitchell (1990) argues, it reproduces 'the state's' own scalar image as an entity other and larger than, and situated 'above', particular places and groups of people.

But in the account offered above, 'the state' – in the more concrete guise of the akimat – appeared as merely one situated agent, one node among many involved in translocal networks of actions – concatenations of heterogeneous elements that included variously positioned human actors along with rusty pipes and other sorts of things. Each of those elements inflected the outcomes of actions that passed through the network, contributing in various ways to the ongoing transformation of 5 Oktiabrskaia. Mundane items materialized 5 Oktiabrskaia's connections to, and revealed disconnections from, other places and translocal processes such as the relocation of Kazakhstan's capital to Astana, privatization, commercialization of urban space or reform of urban governance. Rather than abstract acts of legal regulation, all these transformations are better understood as material relays of action. Various bits of the patchy infrastructure not only deflected the designs by state planners, as Caroline Humphrey (2005) has argued analysing Soviet courtyards, but rather embroiled the activities of state actors into multi-vector hybrid networks of agency. The akimat's actions within this dynamic context were uncertain and incoherent. The 'activist' residents, committed to caring for the block and its dvor, engaged in 'weaving through things' (Latour 2005: 68) to keep up material place-making at a time when institutionalized urbanism had receded (at least as far as old neighbourhoods such as this were concerned). Their actions were not aimed to resist state power over place but rather to take advantage of the akimat's actions as well as any other arising opportunities, quite literally to patch up the gaps that opened in the material structure of the neighbourhood.

Additionally, it is worth pointing out the distinct temporality of these place-making activities. As discussed in Chapter 1, the utopian project of 'building the future' in Astana rests on a moment of foundation (before which there was 'nothing', or post-Soviet 'chaos'), is teleological and hinges on a 'denial of coevalness' – the necessity to treat the material conditions of the present as 'backward', already past. The temporality of quotidian place-making in old neighbourhoods such as at 5 Oktiabrskaia is very different. Maintenance – simultaneously of infrastructure and of 'locality' – has the broken rhythm of ad hoc interventions. Its durations are those of the particular material elements and their assemblages: when things break, action needs to be taken to repair or replace them. There is no stasis, things change all the time. There is no particular moment of foundation and no teleological future. (The building's origin as a *kooperativnyi dom* is sometimes remembered, but generally the histories of the infrastructure, or even of resident households, get blurred.) In Chapter 3, we have seen how long-term city residents – the former tselinogradtsy – constructed an alternative time-space where they belonged, and that belonged to them, through nostalgic reconstructions of the past. Here we see how the mutually constitutive relationship between individual and collective subjects and place is materially performed in the now, from one contingent instance to the next (cf. Buchli 2000: 4–22).

Digression: Things Make a Difference

Assemblages of specific things make places different, or make different places. Broken fences, pipes and other such elements made 5 Oktiabrskaia a place that residents found entirely different and separate from those areas elsewhere in the city where the government was creating its new capital. This was expressed poignantly in the following comment by one dweller in the building across the dvor from 5 Oktiabrskaia, a Kazakh working-class man in his mid fifties: 'This here is the old city, and Nazarbaev is building a new city there, across the river. ... We are lost, abandoned people. We here are Tselinograd people, and over there are Astana people'. The sense of despair was far less pronounced among those residents who, like Aleksandra Stepanovna, actively took care of their block. But these words indicate how the different material make-up of places produced juxtaposed identities ('Tselinograd people' versus 'Astana people') and a bifurcated sense of spatialized, materialized history where Astana (a 'city of the future') and Tselinograd (construed sometimes as a 'city of the past' – recall Kumano's comments in Chapter 2) were co-present yet incompatible. That implied a particular relation of a neighbourhood such as 5 Oktiabrskaia and local subjects to the state: a relation of 'abandonment', of not belonging together.

In Chapter 1, we have seen how the materiality and aesthetics of the different new and old parts of Astana generated a sense of social, economic and temporal disconnect and alienation among many, especially less affluent yet hopeful migrants. Former tselinogradtsy, who generally continued to live in right-bank old-time neighbourhoods, experienced a similar sense of disparity. However, in stark contrast to the desires of my incomer acquaintances such as Bakytgul', Ainura, Sultan and Oraz (Chapters 1 and 2), to whom the Left Bank was the locus of a dreamed-of future, such residents (including very young people like Mira or Margarita (Chapter 3)) declared they would prefer to live in an old-type apartment in the 'old city' than in a more 'modern' and more spacious apartment in the Left Bank. They commonly described the Left Bank as 'empty', devoid of relevant meanings – essentially a 'non-place' (Augé 1995). 'Emptiness' has been a persistent trope that has served to legitimate modernizing interventions in the region of today's Astana for at least two hundred years – since the tsarist colonization of the steppes of north-central Kazakhstan in the early nineteenth century (Buchli 2007: 45–49). The trope has also already appeared several times earlier in this book. As discussed in Chapter 3, it recurred throughout the Soviet period, from the days of the Virgin Lands Campaign, to empower the narrative of the Soviet state and Slav settlers bringing 'modernity' and indeed 'civilization' into the 'bare' steppe. Later, since the late 1990s, the rhetoric of the post-independence Kazakhstani regime sought to enhance the utopian effect of the construction of Astana by positing that the capital was being built from scratch out of the wilderness (see Introduction and Chapter 1). However, when invoked by former Tselinograd dwellers during the 2000s, the trope of emptiness was simultaneously used to form a critique of the recent production of space in Astana – and implicitly, of the political and economic relations that the construction boom expressed. By saying that the Left Bank was 'empty', those residents of the old right-bank city meant that they had no personal interest in the recent developments. They often pointed out that few if any of their friends or relatives lived in the Left Bank. The critique of the Left Bank simultaneously implied an affirmation of older forms of sociality and locality, nested in old-time neighbourhoods.

Until the later 2000s, there were few shops or service points in the Left Bank to attract residents from across the river. Tellingly, places such as the shopping centre Mega, frequented by crowds of Astana residents representing nearly all population groups (Laszczkowski 2011b), were habitually excluded from the area covered by the term 'Left Bank', despite their undeniably left-bank physical location. However, more fundamentally, the alienating contrast between old-time right-bank neighbourhoods and new residential areas in the Left Bank might have to do with the different spatial layout and material make-up of the respective places. Those were the result of different histories of place-making, entailing both the design by city planners and architects and the ongoing interventions by dwellers.

Differences produced by contrasting paradigms of urban planning can be grasped by comparing the so-called figure-and-ground plans of old and new residential areas. In his study of Brasilia, James Holston (1989: 119–27) introduces to anthropological readership the concept of the organization of the solids and voids in a built environment into figure-and-ground relations. In a densely built town, voids such as streets and squares will be perceived as 'figures' against the 'ground' of the mass of 'densely packed' solids – buildings. Conversely, a church or a monument standing in the middle of an otherwise empty square is a solid that is a figure against a void ground – the square. Holston explains that classic European planning allowed switching between two modalities of figure-ground relations (solids being the ground versus solids being figures against void ground), which was used to mark out particularly important public buildings (cathedrals, town halls). This flexibility was abolished in modernist planning (for example, by Le Corbusier and Oskar Niemeyer), which demanded that all urban space be public, with a private sphere sharply separated and confined indoors (Holston 1989: 127–36). Holston then proceeds to argue that it was this rigid and untraditional spatial paradigm that made the development of traditional forms of social use of space known from other Brazilian cities impossible in Brasilia and thus contributed to the sense of alienation experienced by the new city's residents.

I suggest that the sense of alienating 'emptiness' of the Left Bank compared to the old neighbourhoods in Astana is in part derivative of a similar shift in spatial relations. Earlier in this chapter, I discussed the dvor as a communal space – intimate yet socially shared (Richardson 2008: 125). This kind of space is abolished in the Left Bank in favour of capitalist, compartmentalized space (Lefebvre 1991). This is expressed in different relations between solids and voids in the respective parts of the city. In old-type neighbourhoods even the largest multi-floor

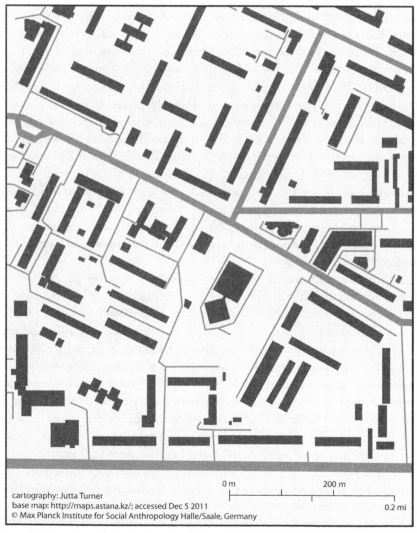

cartography: Jutta Turner
base map: http://maps.astana.kz/; accessed Dec 5 2011
© Max Planck Institute for Social Anthropology Halle/Saale, Germany

0 m   200 m   0.2 mi

Figure 5.2 A section of the Soviet-era *mikroraiony* (figure-and-ground plan)

apartment buildings are solids positioned fairly close to one another over a vast space (see Figure 5.2). As a result of use over time, that space is additionally filled with myriad smaller solids: neighbourhood shops, garages, trees, pipes and so on.

The courtyards generally form a continuous space – ground against which all the buildings and other, smaller items are set as figures. There are multiple openings between buildings that allow for nearly endless combinations of paths to be taken to move across the space. As described in Chapter 3, it is possible to pass directly from one dvor to another over fairly long distances without coming out onto a major street; as mentioned, in casual Russian this mode of movement is called *po dvoram*, literally 'across the courtyards'. Enabling this kind of communication was a deliberate principle of Soviet mikroraion (residential area) design (Gerchuk 2000: 86–87). It allowed residents to craft extensive neighbourhoods as continuous, meaningful places by moving and communicating across and between courtyard clusters.

In the Left Bank one can hardly wander 'po dvoram'. The organization of space is entirely different there (compare Figures 5.2 and 5.3). The principal solids – the housing estates – are relatively few, massive, self-enclosed and far apart. Typically, a Left Bank estate occupies an entire block in the street grid and contains a courtyard, surrounded on all sides by continuous walls. A figure-ground reversal occurs between the relation of the building (solid, figure) to its surrounding space (void, ground) and the relation of the building (solid, ground) to the courtyard it encloses (void, figure). It is impossible to see a neighbouring dvor from inside a dvor, and in order to go from one dvor to another it is necessary to walk along or, *horribile dictu*, cross at least one automobile road. This spatial arrangement induces a sense of compartmentalization and isolation rather than connection to a broader urban fabric. In contrast to the Soviet mikroraion type of spatial organization, it prohibits forms of social activity that link multiple dvory into a larger continuous social space. Walking, for one thing, is considerably constrained.

Beyond contrasts of spatial layout, further differences between old right bank neighbourhoods and new Left Bank residential complexes were produced through the practices of dwelling and day-to-day maintenance. In courtyards such as in 5 Oktiabrskaia, place was continually being remade over years and decades of dwelling. The result was a jumbled place, full of heterogeneous items that were testimonies to a live sociality. Their material presence rendered the place personally meaningful for dwellers and anchored their shared memories. In the Left Bank, although this was probably to change with the passage of time, such evidence of sociality was hard to find. The courtyards there were conspicuously empty, sometimes to the point of eeriness. Surrounded by tall walls of synthetic tile, they felt like the inside of a well. Usually covered with tarmac or concrete, a Left Bank courtyard would sometimes have in the middle a small playground with slides, see-saws and ladders (as in Figure 5.4).

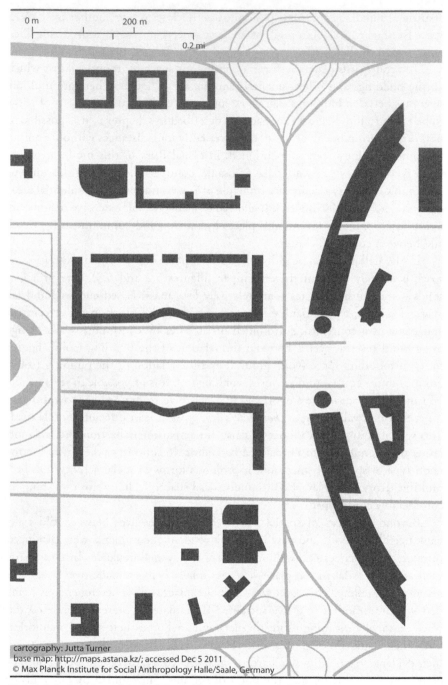

0 m   200 m

0.2 mi

cartography: Jutta Turner
base map: http://maps.astana.kz/; accessed Dec 5 2011
© Max Planck Institute for Social Anthropology Halle/Saale, Germany

Figure 5.3 A section of the Left Bank (figure-and-ground plan)

Figure 5.4 A Left Bank courtyard (photo: M. Laszczkowski)

Correspondingly, as the residents of Soviet-era neighbourhoods would often point out, in the Left Bank the quotidian social habits of dwelling – youths hanging out; old ladies chatting, watching kids at play; neighbours greeting each other and exchanging news, favours, perhaps some household items, foodstuffs and petty cash – had not yet developed, at least not to a degree comparable to the old neighbourhoods. Of course, all of that would come – both the human interactions and the homey material jumbledness. For the time being, however, the evident 'emptiness' of Left Bank courtyards in contrast to the 'thickness' of neighbourhoods such as 5 Oktiabrskaia fostered a sense of the old and the new as radically different kinds of place – mutually incompatible models of material order and social life.

The KSK Takeover

As I returned to the courtyard at 5 Oktiabrskaia one late afternoon in July, after a day spent exploring other parts of the city, I found Aleksandra Stepanovna standing outside the building, engaged in an agitated conversation with the chair of the KSK, Mikhail Petrovich, and two other neighbours – elderly ladies who had lived in the block for many years and could be seen every day chatting on a bench in the courtyard. Mikhail Petrovich was holding a crumpled notebook with columns of handwritten numbers. The women surrounded him and peeped at the notes. As I soon realized, they were discussing accounts for the purchase of valves and pipes to repair the block's plumbing. Mikhail Petrovich had bought the valves with funds pooled from residents' contributions, but somehow it was unclear how many were needed, how many had been bought, how much had been spent, how many valves had been replaced and how much money was left. The man fetched two valves from the basement. The group examined them closely, but they were unable to figure out if they were two of the old broken valves or of the new. Aleksandra Stepanovna and Mikhail Petrovich descended to the basement together, only to see, in the light of the flashlight I held for them, that old and new valves and pipes lay hopelessly jumbled together amid waste and small construction debris. Earlier in this chapter, I outlined the making of place at 5 Oktiabrskaia out of crosscurrents of contingently enmeshed agencies and mutually disjointed projects mediated by mundane material elements not unlike those valves. The events that followed soon after the unsuccessful inspection of the valves highlight the fragility of place and locality as products of such provisionally stabilized confluences of action.

The following day I asked Aleksandra Stepanovna if the point of the discussion had been money. She explained:

> We were not quite counting money. We had given Mikhail Petrovich some money before, he had bought some valves and other stuff, and we wanted to count how much had been spent ... But you see, I was counting, and I don't know these things, then someone else was counting ... We tried to do it all at once, but ... it's very hard to count all this stuff, you need to know these things, and then – I've never done audit, I've never controlled anyone ... And the documents, they always have to be signed by someone [other than the chair, on behalf of the KSK], but he [Mikhail Petrovich] comes when there's nobody to sign the papers, or as it often happens, the grandmas [*babushki*] will sign them [without inspecting] ... He often makes the documents after some time, like it's only now that we see the bill for the stuff he bought in May [two months before], so then it's very hard to figure out what goes with what, if you didn't follow ... Some claim he's a thief, we should get rid of him – but no one wants to do the job ...

In the Soviet period, Mikhail Petrovich had worked at the municipal electricity department and was one of the original members of the housing kooperativ at 5 Oktiabrskaia. More recently, however, he had moved out from the block. He still owned an apartment there, in which his daughter lived. On this account, other long-standing residents trusted him – they had known him for long, and apartment ownership was an incentive to care for the block. On the other hand, he himself did not live there any longer, and according to rumour he owned real estate somewhere in Russia. Like many but far from all Kazakhstani

Russians, Mikhail Petrovich had obtained Russian citizenship, which meant he could emigrate with relative ease. Therefore, the neighbours saw him as not quite in the same boat as the others. They pondered just how strongly committed he actually remained to their common good. Many said Aleksandra Stepanovna should replace Mikhail Petrovich, but she was reluctant. While she had long been practically in charge of the block, she did not want to shoulder the responsibility that came with a formal appointment. Moreover, she felt awkward with regard to Mikhail Petrovich, as she had been the one to put him up for chairman a few years back.

Soon after the day of the inspection of the valves, Mikhail Petrovich decided to retire from the KSK. Nobody seemed ready to replace him, and some residents began to suggest that a thorough report on the KSK's finances should be demanded of him before he was gone. Meanwhile, the KSK chair from the neighbouring nine-storey block, a young and energetic Kazakh man, began to be seen around 5 Oktiabrskaia, along with an akimat representative who aggressively demanded that any meetings among the residents be registered with the municipality and conducted in his presence. Soon, the activist residents at 5 Oktiabrskaia found themselves under pressure from the akimat to give up running their own KSK and to accede to a common KSK with the twin building across the dvor and the nine-storey. Aleksandra Stepanovna and other long-standing inhabitants were upset by what they interpreted as an attempt at suppressing the block's autonomy, the legacy of its cooperative past. They were particularly offended by the nine-storey chairman's plan to clear the basement at 5 Oktiabrskaia, where the residents stored pickles and all sorts of things, to convert it into commercial space. Although outside entrepreneurs, such as the owner of the red-roofed grocery, had been half-heartedly accepted by the old-time residents, the moral imagination of shared spaces in the block and the dvor as non-commercial retained its value and its capacity to catalyse outrage. The neighbours believed that the akimat preferred to group KSKs so as to have fewer of them to deal with and to more easily elicit funds from the residents. They questioned the legitimacy of the akimat's actions.[6]

The merger was effected through a hastily arranged meeting a few weeks later. A small group of apartment owners, in the presence of the akimat representative and the chairman from the nine-storey, voted in favour of abolishing the separate KSK at 5 Oktiabrskaia. The vote was held at very short notice and only twelve voters were present, five of whom voted against the motion. As one of the upset residents pointed out, that was against KSK rules, which required a 30 per cent quorum. Nonetheless, Mikhail Petrovich soon tacitly passed the relevant documents to his counterpart from the nine-storey – an act that disappointed neighbours saw as treason but had no power to oppose.

This story highlights the vulnerability of locality to translocal dynamics and to the pressures of outside actors, always involved in its ongoing production. It

also casts in sharp relief the instability of internal and external relations constituting place. If earlier the focus was on the enabling capacities of material things,
showing how they helped committed residents make and maintain place, the
story just told emphasizes the potential of hybrid human-thing assemblages such
as place for atrophy and their vulnerability to 'flight' – the centrifugal tendency
of their elements (Deleuze and Guattari 1987). I will limit myself to pointing out
only some of the most evident facets.

First, the fuzziness of the KSK as an administrative form proved a liability. Residents lacked the knowledge and resources to guarantee proper care of
the block infrastructure and communal budget. Even the pooling of funds was
not a straightforward affair while some apartment owners and tenants refused to
pay their share. Second, the scrappiness and recalcitrance of the material things
that went into the maintenance of the dvor meant the assemblage they made
up was hard to grasp, sort out and manage – a point powerfully visualized by
the confusing heap of old and new valves and pipes in the basement. Third,
the internal tensions of the neighbourhood 'community' and its contingency on
far-reaching external connections are further exposed if we consider the role of
Mikhail Petrovich. His commitment to 5 Oktiabrskaia was apparently less than
complete, and so was other residents' trust in him as their chairman. As mentioned, this had to do with the Kazakhstani Russians' inconsistent positioning
with regard to the two states – Kazakhstan and Russia – as well as with changing
property regimes on either side of the border. Thus, internal, even interpersonal
dynamics of the local community were influenced by their enmeshing in material
and politico-economic networks spanning thousands of kilometres.

Other aspects of the story of the KSK merger further highlight the contingency of 5 Oktiabrskaia as place on translocal networks of agency. The politics
of place-making involves competing claims by different actors about their position relative to the place in question and their entitlement to control it (Tsing
2000). At 5 Oktiabrskaia, the group of long-standing residents had been out-
numbered by newcomers, whose presence was the result of translocal dynamics
including the commodification of apartments, Kazakhstan's capital relocation,
economic disequilibria between different parts of the country, and migration.
The old-time residents questioned those newcomers' position in locality, just
as they questioned the legitimacy of the akimat's attempt to strengthen its grip
over of the neighbourhood. They saw the akimat representative and the KSK
chairman from the nine-storey as outsiders and usurpers of authority over local
affairs. However, when it came to deciding the fate of 5 Oktiabrskaia's KSK, the
long-term residents were outvoted.

Finally, it is also significant that some of the neighbours interpreted the KSK
merger as part of a Kazakhification agenda by 'the state' (the akimat being a local
branch of state administration). Since independence, the Kazakhstani regime had
been cautious not to alienate the large non-Kazakh as well as Russian-speaking

urban Kazakh populations (Schatz 2000a; Dave 2007). However, as mentioned in Chapter 3, a 'Kazakhification' process had occurred on a symbolic level, expressed for example in the renaming of streets (Oktiabrskaia Street itself officially bore a new, Kazakh name) or the installation of Kazakh historical monuments. Russians and other Slavs had enjoyed a cultural domination in Soviet Kazakhstan (Dave 2007: 50–70) but lost their dominant status after independence. At 5 Oktiabrskaia, the old-time residents were Slav, while the overwhelming majority of recent newcomers were Kazakh, as was the chairman from the nine-storey and the akimat official involved in the KSK merger. A common perception among Slav residents in Astana was that Kazakh newcomers were over-represented particularly in public administration, from top to bottom, partly due to nepotism and partly as the outcome of a deliberate policy to further disempower other nationalities. I do not think that nationalist motives played any role in the akimat-supported move towards the annexation of 5 Oktiabrskaia by the larger neighbouring KSK. But, as Nigel Thrift remarks, 'how things seem is often more important than what they are' (2008: 13). To some residents at least the merger further confirmed their belief in an expanding Kazakh political and cultural domination. Although the KSK takeover was an event that had been produced by a conjuncture of intra-neighbourhood material dynamics and far-reaching processes such as nationwide migration, the actors directly involved operated in close proximity: two neighbouring apartment blocks and an akimat office just a few kilometres away. But actors have at their disposal various means to produce scale and project interactions at different scales (Latour 2005: 184–85). As soon as the long-standing Slav residents perceived their locality as exposed to 'Kazakhification', a kind of rhetorical blow-up effect extrapolated the politics of the KSK merger to nationwide scale. Local administrative change was construed as a matter of 'nationalities policy'.

In the months that followed, little improvement was noted in the actual maintenance of the building or the courtyard. As a matter of fact, the new KSK fired the sweeper at 5 Oktiabrskaia – an impoverished female resident with a drinking problem – which resulted in the courtyard hardly being swept at all, especially since Aleksandra Stepanovna now refused to volunteer her work the way she had often done before. If the building had been 'taken over' by strangers, she reasoned, it was their responsibility now – and theirs only. For the group of 'core' residents at 5 Oktiabrskaia, the KSK takeover meant that now they had even less control over their block and dvor than before. From their point of view, that meant an unmaking of locality. It was brought about by the enmeshing of material and political relations that operated across various distances: from physical contiguity – as between the old and new valves heaped together – to long 'relays' (Latour 2005: 194) of various human and non-human actors linking the local place to the akimat, the state, the nation and international politics (as with the issue of Mikhail Petrovich's citizenship).

Notes

1. Parts of this chapter previously appeared in Laszczkowski 2015. The address '5 Oktiabrskaia' is fictional. A real Oktiabrskaia Street once existed in today's Astana, but it was located in another part of the city.
2. In Tselinograd this role was played by the agricultural machinery producer, TselinSel'Mash (Alpyspaeva 2008: 45–60) and several other factories (see Chapter 3).
3. The Pioneers (*pionery*) had been a Soviet children's organization modelled on the scouts.
4. Despite Olsen's criticism, Tim Ingold's 'dwelling perspective', inspired by the phenomenology of Heidegger, appears an important exception (see Ingold 1995, 2000; cf. Olsen 2010: 15–19).
5. For example, James Holston's (1989) study of Brasilia is organized by a similar kind of dualist logic. The author argues that the purposefully defamiliarizing modernist design of the Brazilian capital was intended to eradicate cultural meanings traditionally inscribed in urban space in Brazil, and led to a kind of semantic deficit that residents expressed as akin to a psychological deprivation – *brasilite*, 'brasilia-itis' (1989: 24–25). But – as Holston describes in a later part of his book – residents found ways to reinscribe personalized meanings into the built environment and thus resisted the design.
6. Aleksandra Stepanovna, for instance, saw the move to merge the KSKs as part of a broader pattern of illegitimate extraction of funds from residents by akimat officials: 'For example, when the akimat people want to go to Almaty to a concert they would tell KSK chairs to collect money for them. The same applies when someone at the akimat dies and a funeral needs to be organized – they raise the money the same way. They're a collective of their own [implying, 'I'll scratch your back, if you scratch mine']'.

Chapter 6

Playing with the City

'Encounter' in Astana

On a November afternoon, it was just getting dark, the sky turning steel grey and a nip in the air portending a frosty night. A crowd of customers dressed in winter jackets – the men wearing fur caps, the women thick woollen scarves and berets – hushed by the chilling dusk, browsed for groceries amid the metal stalls of a small marketplace near Astana's train station square. Suddenly, shouts and laughter broke through the overall hum as a young man dressed entirely in brown, with long neon green paper 'onion sprouts' tied into his dreadlocks, pushed in a wheelbarrow. In the wheelbarrow lay another young man, wearing bright orange overalls and a hood and sporting an enormous pot belly. Yet another young man, the author of these lines, leaped about that weird-looking couple, telling them to pose for a photograph. The incidental witnesses of the scene – the shoppers and vendors – were perplexed: some gathered around and stared; others, realizing they were being caught in the frame, tried to cover their faces with newspapers; many sought to walk away from the scene. Some approached the strange actors and asked if a movie or a commercial was being shot. One big tall man, instinctively sensing the intended jocosity of the situation, joined in and started yelling: 'Don't miss the chance! A photo with real aliens for just 50 tenge!' Another man inquired what kind of politics was behind the incident, which he was sure had to be a 'demonstration'. He refused to believe when one of the young men replied to him earnestly that the weird characters were not demonstrating for anything. 'No way', the shopper insisted, 'that's impossible'. He glanced at the wheelbarrow, assessed the overalls and concluded it had to be about labour and workers.

In this chapter, I will provide, among other things, a solution to the involuntary spectators' puzzlement. The incident they watched and in which they became passive participants was a game of 'Encounter' being played by a team who called themselves Savage (a name they pronounced French). As I explain below, there are various types of Encounter games. The particular game that evening consisted in enacting in the city's streets scenes from a number of fairy tales and Soviet-era children's cartoons. The characters in the above vignette were the onion-man Cipollino and the Orange Baron from a story by the Italian author Gianni Rodari, immensely popular in the Soviet Union. The game scenario stipulated that they had to be photographed at a marketplace, with stalls and chance shoppers in the frame.[1]

'Encounter' is a game that stages unexpected and outlandish scenes, generating stark aesthetic contrasts in public view. It imposes confusion and a sense of the surreal, momentarily transforming various locations into sites of the uncanny, inexplicable and absurd, breathing into space a vivid unusual life. Painter and sculptor Max Ernst defined the primary technique of surrealism – collage – as 'the coupling of two realities, irreconcilable in appearance, upon a plane which apparently does not suit them' (cited in Clifford 1988: 117). Thus Encounter is surrealistic, in the sense of 'an aesthetic that values fragments, curious collections, unexpected juxtapositions – that works to provoke the manifestation of extraordinary realities'; an aesthetic that sees 'culture and its norms … as artificial arrangements susceptible to … analysis and comparison with other possible dispositions' – as James Clifford (1988: 118–19) writes of ethnography. The game casts in sharp relief the capacity of space to germinate multiple, incompatible realities and infuses space with qualities it otherwise does not have or does not exhibit.

Encounter games are played in hundreds of cities across the former Soviet Union and beyond. However, the spatial, aesthetic and social effects the games generate are no doubt largely site-specific. They are particularly interesting in a city such as Astana where the public aesthetics of space have become a matter of highest political concern and, as I argue throughout this book, the pivot of multidimensional processes of social and cultural transformation. Encounter radically destabilizes and alters the meanings of space and built forms, breaking up ideologies, visions of history and the future, and hierarchies of value inscribed in public space and the built environment. With so much symbolic, financial and political capital having been invested into built space in Astana as a state-orchestrated performance of 'the future', Encounter could be seen as a peculiar instance of the 'construction of space' by residents (Low 2000); a particularly expressive act of reappropriation of space by its 'users' (De Certeau 1984).

However, it is important to note that Encounter creates its anti-totalizing, anarchistic effects without the intention to enter any kind of a bipolar dynamic with 'the state', 'capital' or any other 'force' structuring and maintaining social order. Rather than constituting an 'art of resistance' (Scott 1990), the game embraces the radical openness of space (Massey 2005). It is an exceptionally creative practice that does not so much run counter to elite projects as it 'hijacks' urban space and renders those projects irrelevant, creating temporary zones of 'anti-structure' (Turner 1995 [1969]) simultaneously inside and outside ordinary space. The basso continuo of my arguments in this book, following Lefebvre (1991), has been that material-and-imagined space is the basis of all social dynamics, and hence of all politics. Encounter reaches into the very fabric of urban space and alters it. Thus it produces profoundly political effects, despite players' refusal to engage with any specific ideology, as the young people tried to explain to one of the viewers above.

The surreal heterotopias engendered by Encounter are ephemeral, lasting sometimes for as little as a few minutes and hardly ever longer than a night. Yet I shall argue that the game has more durable social effects – building networks, producing memorable experiences and breeding alternative imaginings of space, time and relations among people, things and places. To build this argument, however, requires first an introduction into the world of Encounter and an overview of the various types of games.

What is 'Encounter'?

As concisely put on its central website, world.en.cx, Encounter is an 'international network of active urban games'.[2] It was created in 2004 in Minsk, Belarus. As of late 2011, there were Encounter communities, each with its own website (a so-called 'third-order domain'), scattered across cities in Asia, Europe and North America, although 195 out of the 329 Encounter domains were located in Russia, an additional 59 in Ukraine and 19 in Belarus, with Kazakhstan coming fourth with 9 domains.[3] Usually, there is one domain in each city where there are active Encounter teams, though in large cities, such as Moscow, there can be multiple domains. Each team and every player is registered with a particular local domain – which, however, does not preclude them from guest participation in games on other domains. Anyone who is sufficiently skilled in website management and well versed in all matters pertaining to the game can establish and run a local domain. The domain astana.en.cx was launched in 2006 by Chernii and his girlfriend Margarita. Chernii had become acquainted with Encounter when he was a student in Moscow and decided to transplant the game to Astana when he returned there upon graduation. A second domain, tselina.en.cx, was established in Astana in January 2009 by Flea, another Tselinograd-born Russian girl in her mid twenties, following an argument with Chernii and Margarita about game organization. However, players grouped around the two domains remained on good terms and mutually joined games organized at either domain.

The games are played in the real, physical space of the city (and sometimes its environs) and simultaneously in the virtual space of a domain.[4] Each game has its distinct scenario, which any player with sufficient experience can author. The games played in Astana were generally authored by members of the local Encounter community.[5] Alternatively, Astana-based teams would sometimes join games hosted on other domains (Kazakhstani or foreign, most often Russian) and authored, correspondingly, by players from other cities. This requires, of course, that the particular game be scripted in a manner allowing for it to be played simultaneously in multiple cities, independently from their respective geographies. Such games included national championship tournaments or international games hosted directly on the Encounter network's central website. They are accorded the highest prestige and are often entered by city or national teams in which players who normally compete within their local domains join forces. International games are usually authored by the most experienced players, who submit the scenarios to the administrators of the central worldwide domain. How often a team plays is absolutely up to them. Generally, active teams tend to play all games hosted on their local domain – which means playing once or twice a week – and are free to pick other games available to them as they like.

Depending on the kind of game, on which I elaborate in the next section, its duration can vary, but most games take between eight and forty-eight hours. Players register for a game before it starts, and then, at a fixed time, they log on to the website (the particular domain on which the given game is played) to access the scenario. They stay online until the end of the game to receive successive tasks and monitor their and their competitors' progress. Points are allocated following the criteria established by the authors of the given game, who are also the arbiters in case of controversy – and plenty of controversy often follows after the end of a game, as players' question their opponents' performance and fair play.

Anyone can become an Encounter player. In Astana, most players were between eighteen and thirty years of age.[6] Generally, they were Russophone urbanites, roughly as many Kazakhs as non-Kazakhs, and either native residents of former Tselinograd or migrants who usually came from Almaty or from towns in northern Kazakhstan and had lived in Astana for several years (cf. Chapter 2). Most players were university students or low-tier white-collar workers (sales persons, office clerks, IT specialists, junior managers, aspiring lawyers and many others). Economically, they came from a variety of backgrounds, from working-class to affluent upper middle-class households (insofar as these class denominations apply to the Kazakhstani society – cf. Bissenova n.d.; Daly 2008).

It is difficult to explain why one plays Encounter beyond the enjoyment that pervades the playing itself and also the socializing among players before and after the games. I only very rarely asked players about their motivations, and players did not normally ask that themselves. As a participant in the game, I learned that the excitement involved in playing was reason enough to play, and so it would have felt very awkward (and rather pointless) had I tried more often to doff my 'participant' hat and leave only my 'observer' hat on by verbalizing the question. In the words of one dedicated player, 'one gets *kaif* of Encounter' – 'kaif' meaning an immersive, enjoyable sensation.

Every player registers a personal nickname that is then used to identify the player in all Encounter matters. Upon registration, every player also receives a personal password with which to log on to one's online account and enter particular games. Both individual players and teams earn points for taking part in and winning games. Players' points translate into a hierarchy of military-style ranks, from private (*riadovoi*) all the way to general-colonel (*general-polkovnik*).

Encounter in Astana was a sort of network of networks where everyone seemed to know everyone else, more or less, while new members were admitted all the time. Usually, players remained active for a period of several years. Teams tended to be made up of people who had been friends before joining Encounter and often had known each other from school or university. Players are allowed to occasionally switch from one team to another. During my fieldwork, I initially played for Savage and later joined The ENd [*sic*], a team that was created as a split-off from Savage. Both teams remained on good terms, with a rather fluid mutual membership. From among the persons who have appeared earlier in this book, the combined line-up of the two teams included Mira, Margarita (both Tselinograd-born Russians), Bella (the Kazakh girl from Aktau whose birthday was described in Chapter 2), Kirill and Giselle (the Russian migrants from Almaty also introduced in Chapter 2) and also the son of Sasha and Olga (the engineers from Chapter 1). Mira's and Margarita's parents, as well as the parents of other players, often helped their children's teams, for instance by letting them use the family car or supplying a piece of information useful in solving a game task.

To join a team, one has to be invited by its captain. The number of players on a team is unlimited. On the one hand, though, having too few players makes playing difficult. On the other, too many is not good either, as the sum of points earned by the team is divided among its active players, each of whom thus collects points in the individual rankings. For most games, between six and ten active players on a team is ideal, but each team can have an unlimited number of 'reserve' players beyond the active game squad. Normally, whoever wants and is able to play a particular day's game gets listed in the active squad by the captain. Captains are usually players who have either established their teams or been chosen for this role by their teammates. Any player can become a captain, and captains can change.

To join a game, teams must pay an entry fee to the organizers and domain coordinators (who in turn pass on a margin to the company that owns the Encounter brand). Fees vary significantly in different cities. In Astana, at the time of this research, the individual cost for a player was usually around one to three U.S. dollars per game (and one would normally play one or perhaps two games per week). The two domains in Astana operated on a non-profit principle. The incomes from teams' fees were used to cover the costs of organizing the game (for instance, the purchase of petrol or materials) or for website maintenance.[7]

There is an entire 'culture' to Encounter. Players cultivate a sense of belonging to a distinct community. They refer to themselves as *enshchiki* (pronounced 'yenshchiki' from 'yen', the Russian pronunciation of 'EN', an acronym for

Encounter) or simply *nashi* – 'ours', 'our people'. They often refer to one another by their in-game nicknames also when not playing. The Encounter logo is commonly exposed on players' garments, laptops, car bumpers and so on – this merchandise provides an additional source of income for domains. There is also an insider jargon. Encounter sociality extends well beyond the gaming itself. My apartment, for instance, served my teammates and other players as a place for countless, endless 'sit-in' parties (*posidelki*) with some drinking, a little smoking, much music and lots and lots of talking. All this makes Encounter resemble *tusovka* – the form of non-official, fluid, voluntary sociality that emerged among Soviet urban youth (Yurchak 2006: 141). But the Encounter 'culture' pivots, of course, on the games.

Game Types

The most popular types of Encounter games in Astana at the time of my fieldwork were *skhvatka* ('clash') and *fotoekstrim* ('photo-extreme'). I will begin with the latter, as this was the genre to which the game described in the opening pages of this chapter belonged. Photo-extreme is usually played during one day and may involve somewhere between five and ten tasks. The tasks consist in taking photographs corresponding exactly to detailed requirements, and extra points are awarded for fulfilling so-called 'bonus criteria'. For example, in the fairy tale game, one of the tasks required that a green six-headed, six-tailed dragon be photographed at a public location. If each of the six heads belched fire and if there were more than a certain number of casual pedestrians in the frame the team won extra points. Players are free to take the individual photographs in any order they wish, but time matters: all tasks are released online simultaneously and the fastest team wins. It pays to calculate both the amount of points to be gained by fulfilling the extra criteria and the sum of penalty minutes for not fulfilling some of the basic ones (say, having only a four-headed dragon) against the amount of time it will take to round up all the necessary props, set the scene and so on. Time translates into points and points into time. Quite often, following the completion of a photo-extreme game, heated debates ensue on the online forums, with teams arguing they should be awarded points for various extra elements in their photographs that the referees have failed to recognize, or questioning the fulfilment of particular criteria by their opponents.

The 'extreme' in photo-extreme is the fact that in all such games the photographs depict scenes that are difficult to arrange, are absurd, potentially embarrassing or even dangerous. Examples either from my personal experience or reported by other players include: photographing a naked man covered in bathing foam sitting on an apartment block staircase (a re-enactment of a frame from a well-remembered Soviet movie); a girl holding a man by his ankle and hurling him over the edge of a roof, with other rooftops and streets visible beneath; people walking on ceilings upside down; a Rastafarian sitting in a street in a lotus pose with a tiny green man on each shoulder, whispering into his ears (no dolls or toy figurines allowed!); a flaming ball on human legs; scenes from the *Borat* movie (with 'Borat' wearing nothing but his peculiar swimsuit, socks and shoes, while it was -18°C and snowing in Astana); or a live replica of Delacroix's *Liberty Leading the People*, with bare breasts, a car wreck for the barricade, and flying above the scene an Encounter banner instead of the revolutionary tricolour. Usually, whatever is to be shot must be shot in public, which means that photo-extreme is the kind of Encounter game that introduces the starkest, surrealistic aesthetic clashes into urban space. It temporarily transforms various locations, streets, parks, supermarkets and the like into pockets of the absurd and fantasy.[8]

The original and most recognizable Encounter game format is *skhvatka* ('clash'). Skhvatka is usually played on Saturday nights. It starts in the evening and ends usually in the early hours of the morning, though I have participated in skhvatki that took well until lunchtime to finish. For skhvatka each team divides into a 'field crew' (*pole*) and a 'headquarters' (*shtab*). During the game, field crews cruise the city (and often its rural vicinity) by car, in which they must have a working mobile Internet connection, a good map of Astana and its environs and other equipment that is different for each game but typically including ropes, shovels and compasses.[9] A good flashlight, strong boots and clothes one does not mind ruining and in which one can comfortably run, climb, crawl or even swim are necessary for every field player. The 'headquarters' crew gathers at someone's apartment (mine served this role multiple times for my team) where they need fast Internet (ideally on several computers), maps and sharp, quick-thinking minds. A totally reliable mobile phone connection between the headquarters and the field crew is absolutely vital to success.

When the game is about to start, all of the participating field crews meet at a location chosen by the game's organizers. Traditionally, a small car park at New Square (off Prospekt Pobedy, just out of the strict Soviet-era right-bank city centre), by the Tree of Life fountain known commonly as the Chupa Chups (see Chapter 4), was used for that purpose. There the organizers collect entry fees from the teams and brief the captains about any peculiarities of the game's scenario.

Once the game begins, both field crews and headquarters log on to the website to read the first level task. Only after completing a level is a team promoted to the next. The objective of skhvatka is to complete all levels, proceeding from one to the next as fast as possible. Tasks take the form of complicated riddles, in narrative form, with the use of codes, puzzles, graphics and whatever else the organizers may have devised. Usually, a game scenario follows a plot and all subsequent levels are somehow connected, forming a sort of spy story or quest to solve some mystery. The first thing to do in completing any level is to decipher the exact location where the field crew must go. The headquarters' essential task

Figure 6.1 Playing *skhvatka* (photo: M. Laszczkowski)

is to support their field teammates in figuring that out.[10] Such a location can be almost anywhere; most typically an abandoned factory, a half-ruined former kolkhoz or an incomplete building under construction, but also shops, wells, dams, railway depots, scrapyards, bridge spans, canals, pipes of all sorts, basements in apartment blocks, parks as well as the newest prominent monuments. As soon as the precise location is identified, the field crews rush to it. They can usually tell they have arrived at the right place by the big letters EN and the ordinal number of the particular game being played spray-painted on the surface of the building or other structure in question. Once there, players use their flashlights, ropes and other gear to search the location (Figure 6.1) for codes written in tiny font by the game organizers. The codes have the format of 'xENy', where 'x' stands for the game's ordinal number and 'y' may be any combination of letters (Cyrillic or Latin) and numbers. There may be only one or multiple codes at any location; if there are several, the task is to seek out all of them. Often the location is huge, like a ruined factory or a complex of abandoned farm buildings, and the codes are always hidden from view in hard to access corners, extremely narrow passages, on high ceilings, the undersides of bridge spans, shaky scaffoldings or inside water tanks, empty or full. Having found a code, a player either enters it in the provided field on the website or contacts the headquarters for them to do so. It is also important not to get too excited, as it often happens that more than one team reaches a location more or less simultaneously, so it would be all too easy to reveal the difficult to discover code to one's opponents. When all the codes from a given location are correctly entered on the website, the team advances to the next level; a new riddle appears and the whole procedure starts anew. (Meanwhile, the headquarters are busy solving bonus tasks online – usually all sorts of logical puzzles – for which minutes are subtracted from the team's running time.) Usually, there is between one and two hours provided for each level. If a team fails to solve a level in time, they move on to the next just the same, but as a penalty, significant extra time is added to their final result (the level code is simply revealed on the website when the time is up). Once you complete the final level, the game website treats you to a fireworks screen reading 'Congratulations' and stating the place your team has taken.

Playing skhvatka successfully demands great cooperation among all members of a team; fast, efficient driving; physical skills in running, climbing, jumping, crawling and so on; courage and stamina; excellent knowledge of the topography – present and past – of the city and its environs; the ability to solve riddles quickly; and wide-ranging knowledge, since the tasks may touch upon such diverse topics as the history of Soviet literature, cryptography, computer programming, popular films or advanced mathematics. Skhvatka is definitely the most thrilling Encounter game, but by the same token it is also the most challenging – physically, intellectually and emotionally. As mentioned, skhvatka is a night-long strain. The tension involved in tackling the mind-bending puzzles; the excitement of fast driving; the adrenalin rush of searching for codes in the dark as one climbs half-finished buildings, scrambles over partially collapsed walls, or crawls into pipes and water tanks; the thrill of anticipation as one types in the newly discovered code and awaits the next task – all add up to an enthralling, immersive sensation of extremely focused, sharpened awareness.[11]

'Encounter' as Play

The experience of playing Encounter can be described as 'flow': a 'holistic sensation' of a 'unified flowing from one moment to the next' and a centring of attention on the immediate objectives of action, defined by the rules of the game (Turner 1982: 55–58). According to Victor Turner, flow is a common characteristic of various forms of play – a stimulating game, an entertaining theatre show, an involving ritual. The Dutch historian Johan Huizinga provides a classic, comprehensive definition of play:

> a free activity standing quite consciously outside "ordinary life" as being "not serious", but at the same time absorbing the player intensely and utterly. ... It proceeds within its own proper boundaries of time and space according to fixed rules ... It promotes the formation of social groupings which tend to surround themselves with secrecy and to stress their difference from the common world by disguise or other means. (Huizinga 1955: 13, cited in Turner 1988: 125)

All of the listed characteristics of play can be found in Encounter. It is definitely a 'free activity' in the sense of being voluntary. It is ostensibly 'not serious', as my teammates tried in vain to assure the puzzled public in the game scene with which I opened this chapter. It does absorb players 'intensely and utterly'; without such absorption one would not climb shaky, ice-covered scaffolding 15 metres above the ground in the dead of night or speed 140 kilometres per hour on a frozen, snowed-over mud road just to take third place in a game. Actors immersed in the flow of a game such as Encounter experience a 'loss of ego' and surrender themselves to a commitment to play; flow is its own reward (Turner 1982: 52), and so, as mentioned above, Encounter players play for play's sake. Encounter is set apart from the regular course of 'ordinary' life by rules and the timing of the games. It also sets its own temporary spatial boundaries, arbitrarily occupying selected spaces. Finally, the forms of Encounter 'culture' outlined above suggest the formation of a social grouping whose members tend to emphasize the difference that separates them from, in Huizinga's words, 'the common world'. 'Disguise' is provided under cover of the night and through players' nicknames. 'Other means' include the insider language, in which words such as *uroven* ('level'), skhvatka, *virtualka* (a virtual game, that is, one played entirely online) and even *baian* ('accordion')[12] acquire special meanings; special (mostly military-style) clothes worn during the games; and the ever-growing body of memories and knowledge shared among players. Encounter players' 'secret knowledge' includes a peculiar spectral geography of the city in which the importance of various places is measured by the intensity of shared game memories or the frequency of use in game scenarios. This tends to be very different from topographies more ordinarily taken for granted.

Another classic theory of play is found in the work of Roger Caillois (1961). He distinguishes between two fundamental principles present in varying degrees in every form of play: *paidia* – 'childlike' spontaneity – and *ludus* – a game bounded by rules. Paidia represents turbulence, improvisation, gaiety and freeform fantasy, whereas ludus stands for the conventions that keep paidia in check and provide coherence. Each of these elements can be noted in Encounter. The photo games in particular involve fantasy and improvisation, while in any game it is vital to follow the rules to win. The fun comes from the interplay of these two forces: not taking a game seriously enough and losing badly leaves a team dissatisfied, while taking a game too seriously and focusing solely on winning drains away too much of the joy.

Play does not deserve to be ignored. As Turner points out, play is 'often serious beneath the outward trappings of absurdity, fantasy and ribaldry' (1988: 124). Although it is not structured to code and convey a 'message', play is not meaningless. Drawing on Turner's concepts of 'structure' and 'anti-structure', Richard Schechner (1988b: 17) comments that 'play is ... the "anti-" by means of which all categories are destabilized'. According to Turner, the 'flow' of play 'seems to be one of the ways in which "structure" may be transformed or "liquefied" into communitas' (1982: 58). Thus play can 'perform the liminal function of ludic recombination of familiar elements in unfamiliar and often quite arbitrary patterns' (Turner 1988: 170).

Turner saw play as 'a liminal or liminoid mode, essentially interstitial, betwixt-and-between all standard taxonomic nodes, essentially elusive' (1988: 168). The concept of liminality as developed by Turner (1995 [1969]) with reference to Ndembu rites of passage is well known.[13] 'Liminoid' is a term Turner introduced later, basically meaning 'liminal-like' (1982: 32). Turner intended this derivative of 'liminal' to apply to contexts other than rites of passage in what he called 'tribal and early agrarian societies', and especially to genres of performance characteristic of contemporary Euro-American urban culture, which he saw, nonetheless, as sharing certain characteristics with 'tribal' performances. In contrast to liminal activities proper, liminoid activities are optional, voluntary, plural, fragmentary, entertaining and focused on experimentation rather than on providing the continuity of social structure (Turner 1982: 42–43, 53–55). A 'happening' by a group of hippies is Turner's favoured example (1995 [1969]: 112–13). While classic liminal phenomena refer to Durkheimian 'collective representations' shared by all members of a cultural group, liminoid phenomena, found in large, highly heterogeneous industrial or post-industrial societies, 'tend to be more idiosyncratic, quirky, to be generated by specific named individuals and in particular groups' (Turner 1982: 54). Encounter actions are certainly often 'quirky and idiosyncratic' – recall again the perplexity of the audience of the scene with Cipollino and the Orange Baron, for instance.

I argue that Encounter ought to be analysed as play and a liminoid phenomenon. Now, by evoking 'anti-structure' (Turner 1995 [1969]), play carries culturally transformative potential. Play has the quality of make-believe. As such, it encourages the adoption by players of new, provisional identities and casts alternative meanings upon objects and relations: 'Make-believe asks participants to imagine themselves in new surroundings and to create behaviour appropriate to that environment' (Von Geldern 1993: 147–48). To quote Turner again, 'play, like other liminal phenomena, is in the subjunctive mood. … Subjunctivity is possibility. It refers to what may or might be. It is also concerned with supposition, conjecture, and assumption, with the domain of "as-if" rather than "as-is"' (1988: 169). 'Society in its subjunctive mood' (ibid.: 123) is society as it possibly could or perhaps could not be, yet in any case not as it is or 'must' be. Thus, at its most creative, play could propose alternative models for social living. Play is, at least potentially, socially transformative. Of course, I do not mean to suggest that dressing up as a cartoon character or roaming through abandoned factories with a flashlight by night can offer viable alternatives for the organization of social life. But like other cultural phenomena, from carnival (Bakhtin

1984) to absurd practical jokes (Yurchak 2006) to tribal rites of passage (Turner 1995 [1969]) to hippie 'happenings' (ibid.) and avant-garde theatre (Schechner 1988a), Encounter has the potential to trigger the creative work of imagination and contribute to social change.

Play and Politics: Carnival, Stiob and 'Encounter'

Turner writes of play: 'in its own oxymoronic style it has a dangerous harmlessness, for it has no fear. Its lightness and fleetingness protect it. It has the powers of the weak, an infantine audacity in the face of the strong' (1988: 169). The relationship between play and revolt has often been explored by scholars, especially in studies of carnival following Mikhail Bakhtin's (1984) groundbreaking analysis of late medieval to early modern carnival culture. Bakhtin's is a study of the interface between political power and aesthetics, and in particular an exploration of the force of unofficial aesthetics, of laughter. For Bakhtin, carnival was revolution (Holquist 1984: xviii). In his words, carnival, alongside other manifestations of the folk culture of laughter, 'offered a completely different, nonofficial ... and extrapolitical aspect of the world', a 'second life' (Bakhtin 1984: 6). In this, carnival differed from official festivals, which ultimately served to assert the stability of the dominant order of things. In contrast, 'carnival celebrated temporary liberation from the prevailing truth and from the established order'; it was 'the feast of becoming, change and renewal' (ibid.: 10). These quotes help underline the similarities between carnival and liminal or liminoid phenomena from Ndembu ritual to the hippies' happening. Turner's 'anti-structure' resonates well with Bakhtin's emphasis on the anti-systemic, liberating force of laughter and carnival. Carnival, as an instance of anti-structure, achieves 'ephemeral freedom' (ibid.: 89).

The revolutionary potential of carnival and of play in general has often been evoked to support various kinds of politics. James Von Geldern (1993) studies carnival and other forms of mass festivity during the Bolshevik revolution of 1917–1920 in Russia. For the brief moment of genuinely revolutionary spontaneity, carnivalesque actions served various groups to deconstruct the old world and experiment with visions of the new – until the Bolshevik leadership decided it was time to stifle the anarchistic turmoil of experimentation and seriously get down to the business of rule (see also Stites 1991). Von Geldern (1993: 55) argues that neither in carnival nor in other varieties of festival is there anything inherently revolutionary or conservative; it is the nature of festivity that lends itself to political use by almost any party and can serve various ideas or classes. However, carnivalesque imagery remains a favoured resource for contemporary anarchists and other revolutionaries. Gargantuan puppets, clowns and surrealistic figures such as protesters dressed up as fairies and tickling policemen with feather dusters appear during the mobilizations of what has become known under the misnomer 'anti-globalization movement' (Graeber 2007). There, these images serve the purpose of relieving tension and preventing head-on confrontation, but they also create zones of subjunctivity where imagination is freed to conceive temporary alternative worlds. In these zones, merry-making is freedom-making, for the participants can act as though they are free (Graeber 2004: 74).

Encounter shares many characteristics with carnival. It is a 'free activity' as per Huizinga's definition of play and also in the sense of being merrily oblivious to any constraints the ordinary course of social life puts on individual action and imagination. It is fun and often outlandish as it recombines heterogeneous symbols into absurd configurations. Moreover, as Von Geldern writes, drawing on Bakhtin, 'carnival was discontinuous; it overturned and shattered time and space' (1993: 53). The experience of carnivalesque dissolution and reversion of order was brief, bracketed by the calendric frame of the feast; 'it was a compression of time, a temporary state to be exploited intensively. Carnival was dynamic because it was fleeting' (ibid.). All of this is equally true of Encounter.

The analogies can only be stretched so far, however, and to interpret Encounter it is important to see where it differs from Bakhtin's carnival or from actions such as those of the anarchists. One important difference is that unlike the latter, Encounter lacks a cause; it is about creating liminoid zones beyond the explicitly political – as an end in itself. Moreover, Bakhtin's understanding of carnivalesque culture presumes a bipolar positionality: laughter in this view is directed against authoritative discourse. Also Turner, quoted above, saw play as a 'weapon of the weak' against 'the strong' (see Scott 1985). In an often quoted phrase, Bakhtin (1984: 88) states that laughter 'builds its own world versus the official world, its own church versus the official church, its own state versus the official state'. Bakhtin emphasized the insurrectionary, dissident dimension of his subject – his politics required this dimension, for he was interested in probing how much freedom culture could achieve in the face of Stalinist hegemony (Holquist 1984: xiii–xxiii). In contrast, it would be difficult to argue that Encounter is consciously directed against anything such as 'the state' or 'official discourse'. And certainly it does not aim to create any alternative totalities to replace 'official' order – no world, no church and no state of its own, other than the absurd ephemeral zones it opens up. Rather, Encounter is about opening up space for the free work of imagination in spite of – not against – the political and economic structures of ordinary life. To achieve this, Encounter scavenges for symbols, myths, ideas and images mixing quite freely among the most heterogeneous sources.

Encounter's more direct affinity seems to be to a late-Soviet cultural phenomenon Alexei Yurchak (2006: 238–81) calls 'stiob'. Yurchak argues that from the 1960s to the 1980s, the increasing gap between official discourse and actual social practice led to the formation of an ironic disposition towards just about every aspect of life. That irony became widespread among 'the last Soviet generation' – Soviet urban youth who came of age between the 1970s and mid 1980s. Most Encounter players were born during the final decade of the Soviet Union to parents who belonged to that 'generation'. A particular product of that ironic disposition was a distinct 'humour of the absurd' that reacted to the mundane paradoxes of everyday life by refusing to accept boundaries between 'seriousness and humour, support and opposition, sense and nonsense' (Yurchak 2006: 243). This kind of humour found expression in a range of genres, from the telling of jokes (*anekdoty*) all the way to quite radical forms such as the *provokatsii* ('provocations') staged by a group of Leningrad artists to whom Yurchak refers as 'necrorealists' (ibid.). Yurchak cites examples including mass brawls in the streets, beginning out of the blue and for no apparent reason, and ending just as abruptly; staged public fornication by groups of men in sailors' uniforms with bloodied bandages around their heads; snowball fights among nearly naked men, ending in everyone running off suddenly in different directions; and the severe beating of a mannequin by a group of men in the fifth floor of an under-construction building lacking a facade, ending in the decapitation of the dummy before the eyes of a terrified audience who had no way of knowing this was not an actual human being horrifically murdered (2006: 244–46).

There are clear differences between the necrorealists' actions and Encounter. The necrorealists were not playing a game – there was no 'ludus' dimension to their actions, only a bizarre, grotesque, grim 'paidia' (Caillois 1961). Encounter is rarely that grim. Moreover, the 'provocations' were not part of a network such as Encounter. However, what Encounter does seem to have in common with the necrorealists is a blurring of boundaries between make-believe and reality or between reason and madness. Both Encounter and the provokatsii 'create an unexpected feeling of the uncanny within the ordinary, … dislocate the mundane everyday world, and … make the audience suspect that a whole other dimension might exist within that world' (Yurchak 2006: 247). In other words, both open up urban space to subjunctivity and, crucially, derive fun from doing so.

Stiob was the underlying ironic aesthetic behind the range of practices from anekdoty to provokatsii. Indeed, for many, stiob was a disposition, a lifestyle, even a habitus (Yurchak 1999: 91–92), 'a "total art of living" with its own *stiob* philosophy, language, forms of behaviour, ethical norms, styles of interaction … and so forth' (2006: 250). As a practice, stiob rested on two premises, or more accurately, techniques: overidentification and decontextualization. I argue both are essential also to Encounter. Decontextualization is probably the easier to grasp. Yurchak (2006: 252) defines it as 'the act of placing [a] form in a context that is unintended and unexpected for it'. This is precisely what Encounter does, not only during photographic games but also during skhvatka: it uproots forms found in the cultural world around it and subjects them to unexpected uses in unanticipated contexts. When a fairy tale scene or a Komsomol rally is acted out at a marketplace or in a downtown street (of a city that is no longer socialist), the conventional meanings of both the scene and the setting are changed, and changed beyond interpretation. Likewise, an abandoned factory or a new monument to the nation state ceases to be what it is normally when skhvatka hijacks it and incorporates it in the ephemeral narrative world of the game scenario.

Overidentification, in turn, is 'the precise and slightly grotesque reproduction of [a] form' (Yurchak 2006: 252). As such, it blurs the boundary between subversion and support, endorsement and ridicule. Yurchak's examples include the performances by the Leningrad operatic rock band AVIA (ibid.: 253). On stage, AVIA used to mix the aesthetics of revolutionary utopian art and official Soviet iconography and discourse of the 1970s with elements of punk and cabaret. It was impossible to say whether the band endorsed or resisted the ideology that was normally assumed to be represented in official Soviet aesthetics, for they reproduced the aesthetics' forms to the degree of overidentification. I argue that the principle of overidentification is also found in Encounter. Consider a couple of examples.

The twenty-fifth of October is an official holiday in Kazakhstan – Republic Day. In 2008 it was a Saturday and skhvatka was played that evening. Moreover, the game was special because it marked the second anniversary of Encounter in Astana, with an after-party slated to follow the game's completion. During the pre-game briefing players greeted each other with the casual '*s prazdnikom*', the Russian all-purpose holiday greeting. Did they mean Republic Day or the Encounter anniversary? Republic Day is usually ignored by older non-Kazakh urbanites as one of the 'Kazakh holidays', meaningless to those who prefer to cling to the now abolished Soviet calendar of festivities (see Chapter 4). But what about these young people here, who grew up in the post-Soviet nation state? Or, to reverse the question, is an Encounter anniversary a holiday? There were more of such ambiguities to follow. The first task in the game required teams to find three monuments to the fallen of the Great Patriotic War (Second World War) and lay a bouquet of red carnations at each; an agent waiting there would hand players a slip of paper with a part of the level code when they did so. Finding the three monuments ahead of other teams took a lot of figuring out (two of the three were quite central and obvious, but the third one was an obscure memorial stone within the perimeter of a remote freight railway terminus), fast driving, then running and even climbing fences – skhvatka rush as usual. The three pieces of the code, once assembled, read: 'We remember our War heroes', and this was what one needed to enter on the game website to pass to the next level. Now, was this homage, sacrilege or something in between? What did it mean to include such a task in a game played on Republic Day? Was this an attempt to emphasize Soviet patriotic tradition against the new state nationalism; an act of recognition of the national holiday, although ignorant of the official history behind it (Republic Day commemorates the adoption of the

Declaration on State Sovereignty of the Kazakh SSR on 25 October 1990); or was it just a coincidence, with no special meaning intended?

My next example comes from a photo-extreme game. A game played in February 2009 was titled '*Est cho?* Or, Encounter against drugs'. 'Est cho?', taken literally, is a senseless question ('cho' is not even a word in the Russian language), but is immediately evocative to any participant in contemporary Russian-speaking urban youth subcultures. It could be approximately translated as 'Got stuff?' or, more explicitly, 'Got dope?' Thus, the very pairing of this question with a declaration of an anti-drug stance in the game's title clearly signalled the principle of stiob overidentification at work. Public campaigns against drugs are frequently launched by Kazakhstan's official youth organizations such as Zhas Otan, the youth branch of the ruling Nur Otan party – often likened to the Soviet-era Komsomol. Encounter overidentified with these campaigns. On the one hand, nobody could claim the players were not 'against drugs' or that they were against anti-drug campaigns. And yet, the game had the tone of absurd surrealist humour that completely denied the boundary between support and debasement. The game's online welcome screen presented a very stoned Bob Marley veiled in smoke, and everything was in the Rastafarian tricolour of red, yellow and green. The game had its protagonist – the Rastafarian, who was expected to appear in all pictures, wearing dreadlocks and all of his clothes in the said three colours. One of the tasks required photographing a car full of smoke, with the Rastafarian's face pressed against the windshield inside, parked by a red, green and yellow road sign with a big marijuana leaf and reading 'EST CHO?' (Savage made such a sign and actually used it to replace a real road sign in a street in the monumental area near the Pyramid.) Another task consisted of placing two Rastafarians in front of a real grocery store, smoking huge joints of newspaper (actual flames were to be visible) and holding a real dog in sunglasses on their lap; behind them, there had to stand a policeman with an understandably shocked expression on his face. Yet another photograph needed to feature a street performance by a Komsomol band (white shirts, red scarves, musical instruments and so on) under the direction of the Rastafarian, this time standing on stilts, with at least five random pedestrians in the frame. Savage actually won that game. As a reward they received an elaborate U.S.-made bong.

So, what was it about? In what conceivable sense was this game 'against drugs'? Whom did the players identify with, the Rastafarians or the Komsomol? Whom did they mock? These are of course pointless questions, for the operating principles of surrealist collage and stiob overidentification rendered void the categories of support and resistance, seriousness and ridicule. It was fun, though, and as a participant and an interpreter I feel that it was so precisely for this reason.

Yurchak (2006: 277–81) argues that late-Soviet stiob was a kind of humour that avoided taking any political stance. 'This humour', Yurchak writes, 'did not target some abstract "them" (the system, the dissidents) but looked inside – at those who told the jokes, at their own personal and collective involvement in the paradoxes of socialism' (ibid.: 278). In other words, stiob was an acknowledgement of everyone's involvement in 'authoritative discourse' (Bakhtin 1981) as well as in its thorough displacement. Encounter is similarly anti-ideological. Even if it plays, for instance, with symbols of Kazakh nationalism, it does so in a playful way, without challenging the nation state. Like stiob, Encounter creates in-between zones of blurred categories. However, if stiob, according to Yurchak, was focused on Soviet official discourse, Encounter poaches on whatever discourse or imagery it can open up: Komsomol, Rastafarianism, fairy tale, *Borat*, Soviet movies, folklore, spy pulp, science fiction, Kazakh nationalism, the Virgin Lands, classic art ... and so on. Encounter mixes it all, decontextualizing symbols and overidentifying with clichés only to abandon them the next moment, to produce surrealistically eclectic ephemeral zones of subjunctivity, and having great fun all the while.

As Yurchak (2006: 275–76) notes, when the Soviet Union collapsed and the authoritative discourse of socialism collapsed with it, stiob also waned; this was experienced most clearly in the sudden decline of the once extremely prolific genre of the anekdot. Encounter appears to be stiob's descendant, well adapted to the changed conditions. Just as Yurchak (1999) argues for rave culture in Petersburg and Moscow in the early 1990s, Encounter emerged in the void left after the collapse of late-socialist symbolic order (with all its inherent contradictions and inversions) while remaining connected to late socialism's cultural dynamics.

'Encounter's' Creativity

If I am saying that Encounter, like stiob, is anti-ideological in the sense of not taking a stance, I do not mean to imply that Encounter is socially or culturally or politically inconsequential. Quite the contrary: I argue that it shares with other kinds of liminoid play the capacity for creative effects. What is specific to its creativity is that Encounter uses urban space as the main material of which it crafts its idiosyncratic ephemeral worlds.

Turner calls liminal and liminoid situations 'the seedbeds of cultural creativity' and underscores that the fluid, temporary state of 'anti-structure' they generate 'is the source of new culture'; 'the analysis of culture into factors and their free or "ludic" recombination in any and every possible pattern, however weird, ... is of the essence of liminality' (1982: 28). Such play with various cultural elements lies at the heart of Encounter. This is especially evident in photo-extreme games, where against the background of Astana's streets, squares and supermarkets may be juxtaposed symbols, figures and images from Soviet or Hollywood movies; fairy tales and art classics; Komsomol and Rastafarians; and so forth. However, surrealistic collage operates also in skhvatka, as game scenarios draw on a plethora of myths and Soviet as well as cosmopolitan cultural clichés, turning sites across the city and beyond into stages for apparently incoherent scenes.

Encounter's primary resource for creating its liminoid collages is the city itself. The game cuts loose conventional meanings ascribed to various places and substitutes them with often outlandish alternatives. It reverts the relationships between places, and plays with conventional notions of temporality inscribed in built forms. As is the premise of this book, space is socially produced with differing qualities, invested with values and hierarchies (Lefebvre 1991 [1974]). As I have argued throughout, in Astana, the production of space became the object of exceptional attention from both the ruling elite and the general public ('ordinary citizens') as a pivot of new concepts of identity, modernity and social order. New spaces were produced, laden with enormous doses of symbolism to represent the state and a particular vision of the future. Other areas were heavily transformed (such as the right-bank riverside or the downtown half of Prospekt Respubliki). Still other parts of the built environment were left to decay and oblivion. The city as a whole has been treated as a tabula on which to convey an authoritative narrative about the nation and the modern world. The authoritative narrative in concrete, glass and steel is simultaneously a discourse about time: an attempt at defining the national past, present and future.

Encounter is an exceptionally creative practice of surrealist-style decomposition and recombination of the symbolic spatio-temporal texture of the city, by this token destabilizing also that spatial 'narrative'. Suddenly, the meaning of a prominent architectural symbol such as Baiterek, the Pyramid or the Kazakh Land monument (see Chapter 1) is reduced to a piece in a game. Normally salient meanings become radically irrelevant and replaced, such as that night when an architectural composition in the meticulously designed park around the Pyramid was turned into a fantasy space fashioned after a sci-fi novel, as demanded in the game scenario created by Kirill and Chernii. Or, the carefully arranged picturesque waterfront with the massive shiny facades of elite residential complexes becomes the stage of a clash between a knight in aluminium foil armour and a six-headed dragon. Encounter reshuffles the urban hierarchy of spaces; it disintegrates, reintegrates and reinterprets space and time.

Some of the reversals achieved by Encounter are readily apparent: for instance, Encounter swaps the relation between day and night. Night-time is the setting for skhvatka, Encounter's most engaging variety. Darkness facilitates further transformations, veiling in mystery what could seem dull and mundane in daylight. In night's embrace, abandoned factories or the skeletons of dead kolkhoz infrastructure resurrect, and the city takes on an altered, ghostly other life. Thus Encounter achieves more sophisticated temporal reversals. Since different pasts and futures are arrested in Astana's old and new built forms and spaces, by unbinding and displacing their meanings Encounter liquefies and diffracts dominant narratives of the flow of history. The officially celebrated future may become irrelevant, while the Soviet past – materialized for instance by a factory ruin – is brought to life.

Normally forgotten and abandoned sites and spaces are Encounter's favourite habitat. As Tim Edensor notes, industrial ruins often enjoy their afterlives, hosting various activities that deconstruct and 'confound the normative spacings of things, practices and people' (2005: 18). The ruined sewing factory (see Chapter 3); the enormous abandoned tower of the grain-milling plant; the post-catastrophic landscapes of the industrial zone – all of these are much more familiar to and secretly meaningful to Astana Encounter players than Left Bank plazas and monuments. During skhvatka the meanings of various places as marginal/central, barren/thriving, abandoned/dynamic, rejected/forward-looking and empty/abundant are all reversed.

Moreover, Encounter injects the spaces of the city with alternative temporalities and narrative logics. Some of these escape the linear logic of history, such as when a game follows the storyline of a sci-fi novel or re-enacts scenes from *Alice in Wonderland*. Other temporalities that Encounter conjures, in contrast, enliven Soviet history, when a player dressed up as Lenin delivers a speech to a rally, or when a Komsomol choir gives a performance in front of a supermarket. Many game scenarios draw on the history of Tselinograd and its topography. For instance, the launching game of Astana's second Encounter domain, tselina.en.cx, was called 'Welcome to Tselinograd!' and followed the adventures of three fictional Komsomol activists from Moscow deployed for an agricultural labour campaign to the Virgin Lands. The tasks in that game required, among other things, knowing or figuring out the Soviet-era name of a downtown grocery store, the former location of the Eternal Flame and the names of several peripheral Tselinograd backstreets. Similar motifs were frequently used in other games. Scenarios of this kind literally relive the former topography of the city, rendering meaningful what dominant public discourse on history and collective identity rejects or ignores. Thus Encounter provides a particularly vivid and ingenious form of 'practical nostalgia' for Tselinograd, as introduced in Chapter 3, and places a premium on native residents' intimate knowledge of the city. The game becomes an especially creative, compelling and affectively intense way of fostering and enriching Tselinograd as a chronotope – an alternative time-space parallel to the more ordinary, more ostensible reality of today's Astana.

It is important to point out that also when making explicit references to the Soviet past Encounter remains culturally creative beyond established conventions. As we have seen, far from simply reproducing existing narratives, either inherited from the Soviet period or generated later as fixed retrospectives, Encounter incessantly and emphatically mixes things up. By doing so, the game keeps 'the Soviet' literally alive in the present – and by 'alive' I mean the ability to grow and to change. Re-enlivened in the context of the game, old symbols acquire new meanings; embodied by players, Soviet social roles and subjectivities partake in newly emerging assemblages. In that way, Tselinograd also – despite being only semi-visible and semi-tangible – becomes a living place rather than a fading, dead city on the horizon of collective longing.

Creasing Space

Symbols of various origins are employed in unexpected and indeed unnameable arrangements in Encounter. I remember a game in which my team photographed a Slav male player dressed up in the folkloric costume of a Kazakh girl, waving an Encounter banner and standing inside a supermarket trolley. The trolley was being pulled by two female teammates on all fours, dressed up as rams with sheepskin coats worn inside out, bananas on their heads for horns and lettuce leaves in their mouths – all that amid traffic in a wide scenic new road at the mouth of Prospekt Respubliki (Republic Avenue). While the origin of component symbols could be established with relative ease and precision – the folk costume and the rams being common motifs from romanticized nationalist folkloristic imagery and the shopping trolley likely an attribute of 'consumer culture' – their juxtaposition and the cross-dressing (male/female, Slav/Kazakh, human/ovine) rendered the emerging totality beyond interpretation. This makes the task of description I took up in this chapter more difficult, but in fact the unrestrained freedom of imaginative recomposition of symbols is precisely the point.

In 'anti-structure', writes Turner, is found 'the liberation of human capacities of cognition, affect, volition [and] creativity' (1982: 44). I argue that Encounter affords participants this sort of imaginative freedom. As Chernii, the chief organizer of Encounter in Astana, once remarked, 'Encounter is about bringing it up to people's minds that a different life is possible' – one not bound by the pressures of career-making or institutional politics. Encounter is play, it is fun, but by the same token its effect is to open up the imaginative horizons of possibility. In this lies, I argue, the potential political significance of creative collective practices such as Encounter: without openly challenging authoritative discourse or power relations, they work against hegemony over the imagination. Encounter turns various places into zones of the subjunctive (Turner 1988: 123), 'temporary autonomous zones' (Bey 1991) of the imagination. It opens up what Schechner (1988a: 164) calls 'creases': alternative, liminoid sites for ephemeral, transformative activities, often set up in abandoned urban spaces.[14] According to Schechner, creases 'run through the actual and conceptual centers of society … they signal areas of instability, disturbance, and potentially radical changes in the social topography' (ibid.). Encounter creates temporary, ephemeral zones for the free imaginative recombination of symbols, styles and forms. It opens up enclaves of anti-structure within the material, 'real' space of the city.

This seems particularly important in Astana, given the heightened significance of the aesthetics of urban space in that city for the formation of public identities and notions of order.

'Laughter builds its own world', wrote Bakhtin (1984: 88). Liminal or liminoid cultural practices (Turner 1982, 1995 [1969]) create alternatives to taken-for-granted models of cultural order. Encounter's 'world' extends over digital connections across a large part of the globe, especially the area of the former Soviet Union. It is a network of localized communities of players situated in numerous cities in many countries. They share a sense of belonging to a 'virtual neighbourhood' (Appadurai 1996: 195) expressed through the use of logos, images and jargon, the sharing of ideas and experiences of playing and through transnationally coordinated competitions. The membership in that translocal 'neighbourhood' is open and fluid. At the same time, however, Encounter is intimately grounded in local places. Its world is first of all reproduced through the quirky, idiosyncratic actions players carry out in the material space of their respective cities. Playing the game is a powerful, uncontained and very unconventional way of generating locality.

Throughout this book, I have discussed various modes of space- and place-making as a dimension of processes of social formation – from the elite-orchestrated project of state- and nation-building by means of building a new capital (Chapter 1) to the construction of place by everyday practices such as narrativizing the city nostalgically or walking (Chapter 3) to the roles of mundane material things and contingent connections (Chapter 5). But as Doreen Massey proposes, ordinary material space is radically open to multiplicity, heterogeneity, to 'liveliness indeed' (2005: 13). I argue that Encounter embraces and exploits that openness of space for experimentation with culture. The aesthetic clashes players generate defy stasis and closure of meaning. They turn industrial ruins as well as brand new monumental sites into arenas of surrealistic collage beyond any coherent ideology or representation. Encounter rarely brings about durable material transformations of places, other than leaving its signs and codes spray-painted or written with felt-tip pen on walls and fences. However, creating ephemeral and incongruous 'crease phenomena' (Schechner 1988a), Encounter generates embodied experience and injects various sites with unconventional qualities, thus destabilizing ordinarily taken-for-granted relations between space, time, people and things encoded in built form. In this sense, Encounter is a uniquely imaginative and prolific place-making practice.

Notes

1. Other tasks that evening included photographing Buratino (the Pinocchio-style character known to Kazakh speakers as Saksaul Batyr and thus named in the game) hanging head down on a rope from a tree branch with Alyssa the Vixen and Cat in Boots sitting underneath; Gena the Crocodile – another Soviet-time cartoon character – preparing coffee

on a bonfire in front of a telephone booth; Il'ia Muromets – the Russian fairy tale hero knight – fighting a green six-headed, six-tailed fire-belching dragon amidst casual pedestrians; and three other equally awkward but also hilarious scenes. The team Savage shot the dragon scene on the picturesque riverside promenade, right in front of one of Astana's most expensive, most prominent new housing estates. And the Crocodile scene – with the same 'actor' who also played Cipollino, but dressed this time in a bright red jacket and a wide-brimmed hat, his face painted green and his 'crocodile mouth' an attached juice carton – had to be arranged next to a faux red London telephone box by the entrance to a posh expatriate restaurant. There were simply no other recognizable telephone booths in the city. The players set an actual bonfire in front of the restaurant window.

2. http://world.en.cx/GameHistory.aspx. Retrieved 5 April 2012. The brand Encounter is owned by the limited liability company, 'Энкаунтер' (Russian transliteration of the English word 'Encounter'). The .cx at the end of every Encounter domain name is the code for Christmas Island, where all of the domains are registered.

3. There were two domains in Almaty, two in Ust'-Kamenogorsk and one each in Kokshetau, Pavlodar, Petropavlovsk, Uralsk and Astana. Domains emerge and dissolve, however. During my fieldwork, for instance, there used to exist a domain in Karaganda whose administrators organized Kazakhstan championships in various kinds of Encounter games.

4. With the exception of one type of game that is played entirely online (*virtualka*).

5. Towards the end of my fieldwork, I co-authored a game scenario that followed the adventures of a party of extraterrestrials in Astana. The game attracted numerous teams from the local Encounter community.

6. In general there are no age restrictions for registering as an Encounter player. However, a minimum age is required for particular game types – for instance, only players eighteen years old or older can be admitted to play *skhvatka*, the basic and most popular game variety.

7. Financial arrangements varied across different Encounter communities. In Moscow, for instance, team entry fees might be quite considerable – say, $100 (U.S.) per game. Encounter's main international website tempts prospective local domain organizers with incomes of up to $2,000–3,000 (U.S.) a month in team entry fees.

8. A related genre is 'photo-hunt' (*foto-okhota*). This is probably the most creative kind of Encounter game, in an artistic sense. It consists in taking photographs illustrating particular phrases or expressing particular ideas. A foto-okhota that I remember especially well was organized on the domain world.en.cx and was based on motifs from songs by the Russian poetess and rock singer Zemfira. Lyrics to be illustrated included 'I run over the roofs to you', 'your colour is vitally important to me', 'I feed on miracles', 'there's so little of me for the six billion' or 'each one will come to shore anyway'. In photo-hunt games, the technical quality of photographs and artistic creativity are the criteria of evaluation. There is usually much more time provided for a photo-hunt than for any other kind of game – say, two weeks – and photo-hunts often produce highly artistic entries by serious photographers.

9. Back during my fieldwork, teams would carry laptop computers in their cars to have a big screen and fast Internet – tablets and smartphones were not yet there. You needed room for the laptop and often an adapter to plug the machine to the car's electricity.

10. Knowledge of Soviet history and of the city's past is usually very helpful, for instance to solve riddles that use long-forgotten Soviet-era landmarks. For this reason, the support of the players' parents is often sought in a headquarters. As mentioned, the mothers of

Margarita and Mira – lifelong Tselinograd dwellers – supported our team's headquarters frequently.

11. A similar format but simpler than skhvatka is called *tochki* ('spots'). The riddles to solve are easier and the codes are easy to find, so the game mainly demands fast driving, rushing out of the car and locating the codes within seconds or a few minutes to win. This very dynamic game is a favourite among those who value the 'drive' of the game more than the pleasures of racking one's brain, climbing walls and crawling through pipes. Often played on Friday nights, tochki takes only two to three hours and is sometimes treated as a kind of warm-up before the Saturday skhvatka.

12. In Encounter language, *baian* means a place that has already been used in previous game scenarios, possibly more than once, and now appears again in a new one. The ability to find new, original locations for the game is appreciated in game scenario authors. This usage of the noun 'baian' is akin to a more common informal usage in the Russian language, where the term refers to an old joke or 'old news'.

13. Turner's concept derives from Arnold Van Gennep's classic theory of rites of passage (1960 [1909]). According to that theory, all rites of passage are composed of three stages: separation, margin (or 'limen', Latin for 'threshold') and aggregation. The terms 'liminal' and 'liminality' derive from the word limen. According to Turner (1995 [1969]: 95): '[t]he attributes of liminality or of liminal *personae* ... are necessarily ambiguous, since this condition and these persons elude or slip through the networks of classifications that normally locate states and positions in cultural space. Liminal entities are neither here nor there; they are betwixt and between the positions assigned and arrayed by law, custom, convention, and ceremonial'.

14. Schechner's typical example of a 'crease' would be a theatre studio or art gallery in a post-industrial warehouse scheduled for demolition.

Conclusion

In summer 2013, I returned to Astana. Kirill had great news for me: at long last he and his wife Giselle had received the government-subsidized apartment they had been promised. They had just recently moved in. Kirill clearly sounded very excited on the phone, and I could well understand why. As mentioned in Chapter 2, Kirill and Giselle had spent twelve years living in a dorm, raising first one and later two children. He picked me up in town and we drove to their new place. I had seen the residential complex under construction the year before, but only upon seeing it now in its completed state could I appreciate how impressive it was, comprised of several massive, tall, twelve-storey buildings with a spacious inner courtyard and parking space.

Located in an area east of the Soviet-era core of the city, the estate towered over a landscape of shabby *chastnyi sektor* dwellings and dilapidated two-floor apartment buildings from the 1950s. The new complex's surfaces were of shiny very light grey, almost white tile, and on one side the facade was made of deep blue plate glass. On closer inspection, it turned out that tiles were already broken here and there; there were finger-wide holes around ill-fit window frames from which no one had bothered to pull off the protection tape, and – as in so many other recent buildings in Astana – the staircases and hallways remained unfinished. Likewise, the courtyard looked mid-construction – which, however, did not discourage the kids from roaming in the rough-and-ready playground. None of these shortcomings diminished Kirill and Giselle's enthusiasm for their new home. They showed me around first thing after we entered the flat. It was spacious – a good 120 square metres – with a huge living room with a 10 metre long panoramic window in an arched wall, two bedrooms, two separate bathrooms with large bathtubs, and a large bright kitchen.

Not surprisingly, perhaps, the long-awaited change in their living conditions seemed to have affected Kirill and Giselle's evaluation of the social, political and economic developments in Astana and in Kazakhstan at large. I remembered them several years back, critical and sometimes sarcastic, as they pointed out construction defects that belied the official utopianism of Astana. Now Kirill explained the gaps in their building's facade away, saying they had been left on purpose, for ventilation. He and Giselle praised the government for having finally found a way to bail out struggling developers, get the residential developments completed and deliver flats to people like them, who had patiently waited so long. If before Kirill and Giselle would express their criticism of the government and the direction Kazakhstan was developing by calling Astana a 'village', now they appreciated that Astana was 'all new, all clear and all shiny', while it was the ex-capital (and the couple's former home) Almaty that was becoming a 'dusty and unkempt provincial town' by comparison.

This book opened with an ironical joke told by Kirill about the building boom in Astana. The joke expressed the ambivalent public feelings the emergent new cityscape evoked: spectacular and exciting, the new built forms raised hopes, but at the same time they seemed unreal and unable to change the social landscape of the city and the country at large. So, several years later, is the conclusion that the ambiguities have been resolved? That what had seemed a mirage proved real and that the construction of a new capital to build a better future proved successful? It clearly seemed so to Kirill and Giselle that summer as they were enjoying their new home. They were happy, and I felt happy for them.

As the night wore on, we stepped out to the balcony for fresh air. The view from the seventh floor was breathtaking. We could see almost the entire city, spread out before us. As mentioned, the surrounding area was covered with old, dilapidated houses, which looked even smaller from the balcony high above. They were mostly occupied by impoverished Kazakh rural migrants – a bunch of them was hanging around a late-night alcohol and tobacco kiosk by the bus stop across the street. Further out and immersed in darkness, there were the late-Soviet sleeping neighbourhoods: the *mikroraiony*, with their massive rectangular concrete apartment blocks. Finally, in the distance, the lights of the Left Bank shone under the big silky black sky. We could see the brightly lit blue dome of the presidential palace, the golden globe of Baiterek and the many fancifully shaped and colourfully lit skyscrapers strung out on the horizon. The view reminded me of the immense complexity of Astana's landscape – both in the literal sense of the diversity of built forms and in the more metaphorical sense of the 'landscape' of social action. The story told in this book, full of gaps and loose threads as it necessarily remains, might seem over if, standing at the balcony, one looked inside at the still unfurnished, spacious living room. But one needed only to turn around and cast a glance at the nightly panorama of the city to be reminded that, of course, from myriad other points of view the story was not – could not ever be – quite over. There could be no single answer to the uncertainties expressed in Kirill's joke from several years ago. Built space was a dynamic assemblage, within which countless actors engaged in cross-weaving practices and relations. As has repeatedly become clear in the chapters above, the emergence of new forms of urban order has always implicated the proliferation of material forms and practices that were construed as 'rural'. And any decisive temporal break, a leap into the future, was impossible, for the city was an accumulation of multiple pasts and past futurities that lived on in the spatial, architectural and social fabric; any novel projects could only germinate in that ground.

On a more general level, the experience of Astana points to the tenacity of 'modernity' as a collective 'dreamworld'. Drawing on the work of Walter Benjamin, Susan Buck-Morss defines 'the dreamworlds of modernity – political, cultural, and economic – [as] expressions of a utopian desire for social arrangements that transcend existing forms' (2002: xi). She argues that during the Cold War the two 'sides' at apparent ideological loggerheads were in fact rather similar: the capitalist 'West' and the socialist 'East' shared the fundamental modernist faith that the transformation of the world by means of industrial production of objects and built environments could bring about a better society and provide 'material happiness for the masses' (2002: ix). The term 'postmodern', then, describes the condition when that dream has passed, in 'East' and 'West' alike (see also Lowenthal 1992; cf. Harvey 2000: 195–96).

The case of Astana forcefully suggests that this is not quite so: 'dreamworlds' continue to be constructed, and their making involves planetary exchanges of ideas and practices, as well as creativity in responding to the particularities of each given time and place. As I have argued, Astana is a 'rational and critical utopia' (Holston 1989), akin to earlier modernist dreams of social transformation and 'building the future' by means of constructing cities – though it is also original as a 'performance of worldliness' (Mbembe 2004: 374), as it responds to specific social and historical conditions, drawing on specific legacies, selected borrowed blueprints and local invention. The Astana project has served to revive, for Kazakhstani citizens, the faith in progress and 'modernity' that had been bitterly lost with the atrophy of the Soviet Union (Chapter 1). It has helped mobilize 'the nation' around a government-defined collective goal of development, and became a focus of personal material investments as well as affective engagements for hundreds of thousands of citizens (not counting the millions, perhaps, who stayed where they lived, but to whom Astana became a source of hope, pride and often – through remittance sent by migrant relatives – material improvement; Chapters 1 and 2). But as the chapters above have shown in several ways, things are more complicated than that. Rather than there being just one trajectory of 'progress', socially constructed space in the 'city of the future' harbours plural contingent futures (cf. Collins 2008: 118–23) in diverse relationships with the past (or better said, multiple pasts), and their fulfilment remains an open question.

Ferguson's ethnographically informed view of the fate of the grand 'myth' of modernization is, in some respects, more nuanced that Buck-Morss's. More or less during the final decade of the twentieth century, the narrative of unilinear progress, according to which some societies were simply 'not yet' as 'advanced' (as 'modern') as others, became 'decomposed' (Ferguson 2005). 'Modern' status was uncoupled from historical time, and the world was split into areas that were offered a role in global economic convergence (Ferguson mentions as examples Poland, Turkey and parts of East and South East Asia) and areas that were denied hope and dumped into what Manuel Castells (2000) calls 'the fourth world'. Writing from the perspective of the late 1990s–early 2000s, Ferguson parenthetically notes that many post-Soviet countries were anxiously awaiting their fate between these possibilities (2005: 173–74). But, despite the scepticism (if not outright cynicism) gaining ground in the 'first world' as to the ideals of a global modernity equal for all, the desire to 'modernize' – that is, to progressively transform own selves and environments – remains powerful among postcolonial elites and ordinary citizens, as much in Africa (Ferguson 1999) as in Kazakhstan and elsewhere. 'Modernity' still carries much, often desperate, hope.

The 'decomposition' of the formerly hegemonic unilinear narrative of modernization has not only left people in many places around the world in a desperate state of 'disconnect' and 'abjection', as Ferguson puts it (1999: 234–38), but it has also opened the ground for plural claims as to what defines the forms and meanings of 'modernity'. The beginning of the twenty-first century has seen metropolitan centres in Europe and North America decline into crisis, while emerging cities in the Middle East, the Indian subcontinent, East and South East Asia have been growing in wealth and influence. These shifts in the balance of the global economy have amplified the 'provincialization' of Euro-American paradigms of urban modernity. Cities from Shanghai and Singapore to Dubai and Doha 'have become centres of enormous political investments, economic growth, and cultural vitality, and thus have become sites for instantiating their countries' claims for global significance', challenging formerly established global hierarchies of 'modernity' (Ong 2011: 2). In the introduction, I argued that Astana should be considered a part of this process – a particularly interesting part, because it lies beyond the field of vision of most analyses of the rise of Asian cities and because of its uniqueness in this framework as a formerly Soviet city. If Kazakhstan is one of those places that were suspended between convergence with the centres of the late-capitalist world-system and the abyss of permanent 'underdevelopment' and regression, then with the Astana project local elites clearly seemed to wrest the reigns and assert their ability, through borrowing and innovation, to define the terms of their country's modernity and claim a place on the 'global' stage.

But this is where it becomes possible – indeed compelling – to note more specific implications of this study of Astana for broader concerns with the dynamics of urban social change in today's world. The point is, in a nutshell, that change occurs as a disorderly, largely indeterminate process that involves multiple, partially connected projects, coincidences and improvisations. It is not reducible to the agency of any single apparent entity such as 'the state', 'the government' or 'the elite'. Scholarly texts, including anthropological accounts of rapidly developing (mainly Asian) cities, often focus on the transformative projects undertaken by elites (e.g., Roy and Ong 2011). Applying terms such as 'aesthetic imperialism' (Herzfeld 2006), 'spatial cleansing' (ibid.) or 'the bulldozer state' (Bellér-Hann 2014), anthropologists underscore the aggressive and destructive dimensions of state-led transformation of the built environment. Alternatively, they seek to amplify the voice of resident groups that try to resist those actions (Zhang 2006). But the analysis of the dynamics of change underway in Astana, employing a plurality of situated viewpoints, highlights how multiple actors engage in quotidian, reiterative practices through which they try to lend particular qualities to their selves and their social and material environments. These practices involve various ways of relating to, drawing on, reworking and critiquing the images and utopias projected by others, including by groups such as 'the government' and diverse professional 'imagineers' (Rutheiser 1996) of the future. Moreover, the recalcitrant agency of multiple and heterogeneous material actants in the built environment plays not an insignificant part in the dynamics of transformation (Chapter 5). Altogether, these dynamics exceed the binary logic of domination and resistance – though some of the actors involved may be actively opposing or resisting others. Rather, we are dealing with a multiplicity of forces and contingent projects that collide and collude, and that may stimulate, reinforce or counteract each other in often unpredicted, unacknowledged ways. Change – of personal and local conditions as much as of 'global' socio-economic, political and cultural orders – is generated as an imbroglio of these multiple agencies.

This leads, furthermore, to implications for theorizing state power and the relationship between the state and space. Recent anthropology generally has come to think of 'the state' as an 'as if' reality that emerges and acquires its seeming concreteness out of a plurality of situated practices, discourses, imaginations and performances (e.g., Navaro-Yashin 2002; Krohn-Hansen and Nustad 2005; Reeves, Rasanayagam and Beyer 2014). Yet in scholarly accounts of urban transformation 'the state' often appears as a principal 'producer' of space and an agent of change (Low 2000). Lately, ethnographic studies of state spatialization have begun to challenge this by showing how the spatiality of 'the state', its territorial boundedness and its material presence on the ground (for instance, in the form of various infrastructures and personnel) are fragile and contingent achievements of quotidian, mundane work done by situated actors who undertake it for diverse, context-dependent reasons. These studies follow the time-honoured anthropological method of working through 'marginal' or in some sense 'irregular' places to treat them as heuristic foci for shedding light on more broadly relevant patterns and rules that might otherwise remain overlooked (cf. Tsing

1993; Das and Poole 2004). Thus we find in this vein a study of a bumpy road in the mountains of Peru (Harvey 2005); of a formally non-existent (unrecognized) state in Cyprus (Navaro-Yashin 2012); and of borders in a remote, rugged corner of rural Central Asia (Reeves 2014).

In contrast, this book has highlighted the multiplicity and complexity of space- and place-making relationships in a capital city – a site that is central to the production of state-space (Lefebvre 2003a). The book's conclusion is that the particular qualities and meanings of space in the capital are likewise generated in multiple ways, in complex relationships between human and non-human actants – and hence, the space thus constructed is itself 'multiple', open to heterogeneity, incongruity, contradiction and indeterminacy. If 'state-effects' (Trouillot 2001) are achieved through the production of that space, then first this is the gross outcome of multiple situated forces and interactions, far beyond the realm of institutional 'state' agency; and second, those effects are inherently ambiguous and unstable. This point is of broader relevance, but it seems particularly worth highlighting for the study of Central Asia, a field still generally dominated by state-centric approaches. While some of the most incisive analyses of politics in post-Soviet Central Asia have focused on the spectacular productivity of statecraft (Adams 2010; Cummings 2010), this book has emphasized that 'the spectacular' is always complexly enmeshed with 'the mundane', and it is these multiple relationships that condition the production, the meanings and the effects of spectacular forms.

Bibliography

Abu-Lughod, J. 1961. 'Migrant Adjustment to City Life: The Egyptian Case', *The American Journal of Sociology* 67(1): 22–32.

Abylkhozhin, Zh. 1997. *Ocherki Sotsial'no-Ekonomicheskoi Istorii Kazakhstana. XX Vek.* Almaty: Izdatel'stvo Universiteta Turan.

Adams, L. 2010. *The Spectacular State: Culture and National Identity in Uzbekistan.* Durham, NC: Duke University Press.

Adams, L., and A. Rustemova. 2009. 'Mass Spectacle and Styles of Governmentality in Kazakhstan and Uzbekistan', *Europe-Asia Studies* 61(7): 1249–76.

Agentstvo Respubliki Kazakhstan po statistike. 1999. 'Kratkie itogi perepisi naselenia 1999 goda v Respublike Kazakhstan'. Almaty.

———. 2004. 'Regiony Kazakhstana 2004'. Almaty.

———. 2007. 'Regiony Kazakhstana 2007'. Astana.

———. 2011a. 'Itogi natsional'noi perepisi naselenia Respubliki Kazakhstan 2009 goda. Analiticheskii otchet'. Astana.

———. 2011b. 'Regiony Kazakhstana v 2011 godu'. Astana.

Agnew, J. 1998. 'The Impossible Capital: Monumental Rome under Liberal and Fascist Regimes, 1870-1943', *Geografiska Annaler* 80(B): 229–40.

———. 2005. 'Space: Place', in P.J. Cloke and R. Johnston (eds), *Spaces of Geographical Thought: Deconstructing Human Geography's Binaries.* Thousand Oaks, CA: Sage, pp. 81–96.

Agnew, J.A., and J.S. Duncan (eds). 1989. *The Power of Place: Bringing Together Geographical and Sociological Imaginations.* Boston, MA: Unwin Hyman.

Aitmatov, Ch. 1988. *The Day Lasts More than a Hundred Years,* trans. F.J. French. Bloomington, IN: Indiana University Press.

Akiner, Sh. 1995. *The Formation of Kazakh Identity: From Tribe to Nation-State.* London: Royal Institute of International Affairs.

Alexander, C. 2004. 'Value, Relations, and Changing Bodies: Privatization and Property Rights in Kazakhstan', in K. Verdery and C. Humphrey (eds), *Property in Question: Value Transformation in the Global Economy.* Oxford: Berg, pp. 251–73.

———. 2007a. 'Almaty: Rethinking the Public Sector', in C. Alexander, V. Buchli and C. Humphrey (eds), *Urban Life in Post-Soviet Asia.* London: University College Press, pp. 70–101.

———. 2007b. 'Soviet and Post-Soviet Planning in Almaty, Kazakhstan', *Critique of Anthropology* 27(2): 165–81.

———. 2009a. 'Privatization: Jokes, Scandal and Absurdity in a Time of Rapid Change', in K.M. Sykes (ed.), *Ethnographies of Moral Reasoning: Living Paradoxes of a Global Age.* New York: Palgrave Macmillan, pp. 43–65.

———. 2009b. 'Waste under Socialism and After: A Case Study from Almaty', in H. West and P. Raman (eds), *Enduring Socialism. Explorations of Revolution, Transformation and Restoration.* Oxford: Berghahn Books, pp. 148–69.

Alexander, C., and V. Buchli. 2007. 'Introduction', in C. Alexander, V. Buchli and C. Humphrey (eds), *Urban Life in Post-Soviet Asia.* London: University College Press, pp. 1–39.

Alexander, C., V. Buchli and C. Humphrey (eds). 2007. *Urban Life in Post-Soviet Asia*. London: University College Press.

Alpyspaeva, G. 2008. *Astana v Novoe i Noveishee Vremia*. Astana: Kazakhskii Agrotekhnicheskii Universitet im. S. Seifullina.

Amin, A., and N. Thrift. 2002. *Cities: Reimagining the Urban*. Cambridge: Polity.

Anacker, S. 2004. 'Geographies of Power in Nazarbayev's Astana', *Eurasian Geography and Economics* 45(7): 515–33.

Andrusz, G., M. Harloe and I. Szelenyi (eds). 1996. *Cities after Socialism: Urban and Regional Change and Conflict in Post-Socialist Societies*. Oxford: Blackwell.

Appadurai, A. 1996. *Modernity at Large: Cultural Dimensions of Globalization*. Minneapolis, MN: University of Minnesota Press.

Askew, M. 2002. *Bangkok: Place, Practice and Representation*. London: Routledge.

Augé, M. 1995. *Non-Places: Introduction to an Anthropology of Supermodernity*, trans. J. Howe. London: Verso.

Austin, J.L. 1962. *How to Do Things with Words*. Oxford: Clarendon Press.

Bakhtin, M. 1981. *The Dialogic Imagination: Four Essays*, trans. C. Emerson and M. Holquist. Austin, TX: University of Texas Press.

———. 1984. *Rabelais and His World*, trans. H. Iswolsky. Bloomington, IN: Indiana University Press.

Battaglia, D. 1995a. 'Problematizing the Self: A Thematic Introduction', in D. Battaglia (ed.), *Rhetorics of Self-Making*. Berkeley, Los Angeles and London: University of California Press, pp. 1–15.

———. 1995b. 'On Practical Nostalgia: Self-Prospecting among Urban Trobrianders', in D. Battaglia (ed.), *Rhetorics of Self-Making*. Berkeley, Los Angeles and London: University of California Press, pp. 77–96.

Batuman, B. 2009. *The Politics of Public Space: Domination and Appropriation in and of Kızılay Square*. Saarbrücken: VDM Verlag.

Baudrillard, J. 1983. *Simulacra and Simulation*, trans. S.F. Glaser. Ann Arbor, MI: University of Michigan Press.

Baumann, G. 1996. *Contesting Culture: Discourses of Identity in Multi-Ethnic London*. Cambridge: Cambridge University Press.

Beer, C. 2008. 'The Spatial Accommodation Practice of the Bureaucracy of the Commonwealth of Australia and the Production of Canberra as National Capital Space: A Dialectical and Prosaic History', *Political Geography* 27: 40–56.

Bell, J. 1999. 'Redefining National Identity in Uzbekistan: Symbolic Tensions in Tashkent's Official Public Landscape', *Ecumene* 6(2): 183–213.

Bellér-Hann, I. 2014. 'The Bulldozer State: Chinese Socialist Development in Xinjiang', in M. Reeves, J. Rasanayagam and J. Beyer (eds), *Ethnographies of the State in Central Asia: Performing Politics*. Bloomington, IN: Indiana University Press, pp. 173–97.

Bender, B. 1993. 'Introduction', in B. Bender (ed.), *Landscape: Politics and Perspectives*. Oxford: Berg.

———. 2006. 'Place and Landscape', in C. Tilley, W. Keane, S. Küchler, M. Rowlands and P. Spyer (eds), *Handbook of Material Culture*. Los Angeles: Sage, pp. 303–14.

Benjamin, W. 1999 [1927–1939]. *The Arcades Project*, trans. H. Eiland and K. McLaughlin. Cambridge, MA: The Belknap Press.

———. 2002 [1936]. 'The Work of Art in the Age of Its Technological Reproducibility', trans. E. Jephcott and H. Zohn, in H. Eiland and M. Jennings (eds), *Selected Writings*, Vol. 3. Cambridge, MA: The Belknap Press, pp. 101–33.

Berdahl, D. 1999. '"(N)Ostalgie" for the Present: Memory, Longing, and East German Things', *Ethnos* 64(2): 192–211.

Berman, M. 1988. *All That is Solid Melts into Air: The Experience of Modernity*. New York: Penguin Books.

Bestor, T.C. 1999. *Tokyo's Marketplace: Culture and Trade in the Tsukiji Wholesale Fish Market*. Stanford, CA: Stanford University Press.

Bey, H. 1991. *T.A.Z.: The Temporary Autonomous Zone, Ontological Anarchy, Poetic Terrorism*. New York: Autonomedia.

Beyer, J. 2009. 'According to *Salt*: An Ethnography of Customary Law in Talas, Kyrgyzstan', Ph.D. dissertation. Halle: Martin-Luther-Universität Halle-Wittenberg.

Binns, C. 1979. 'The Changing Face of Power: Revolution and Accommodation in the Development of the Soviet Ceremonial System: Part I', *Man* 14: 585–606.

———. 1980. 'The Changing Face of Power: Revolution and Accommodation in the Development of the Soviet Ceremonial System: Part II', *Man* 15: 170–87.

Bissenova, A. 2012. 'Post-Socialist Dreamworlds: Construction Boom and Urban Development in Kazakhstan', Ph.D. dissertation. Ithaca, NY: Cornell University.

———. 2014. 'The Master Plan of Astana: Between the "Art of Government" and the "Art of Being Global"', in M. Reeves, J. Rasanayagam and J. Beyer (eds), *Ethnographies of the State in Central Asia: Performing Politics*. Bloomington, IN: Indiana University Press, pp. 127–48.

———. N.d. 'Learning to Be Bourgeois: The Rise of the Middle Classes in Post-Soviet Kazakhstan', unpublished manuscript.

Bourdieu, P. 1977. *Outline of a Theory of Practice*, trans. R. Nice. Cambridge: Cambridge University Press.

———. 1984. *Distinction: A Social Critique of the Judgment of Taste*, trans. R. Nice. Cambridge, MA: Harvard University Press.

———. 1990. *The Logic of Practice*, trans. R. Nice. Stanford, CA: Stanford University Press.

———. 2000. *Pascalian Meditations*, trans. R. Nice. Stanford, CA: Stanford University Press.

Bourgois, P. 1995. *In Search of Respect: Selling Crack in El Barrio*. Cambridge: Cambridge University Press.

Bowyer, A. 2008. *Parliament and Political Parties in Kazakhstan*. Washington D.C.: Central Asia – Caucasus Institute & Silk Road Studies Program.

Boyer, D. 2006. '*Ostalgie* and the Politics of the Future in Eastern Germany', *Public Culture* 18(2): 361–81.

Boyer, M.Ch. 1994. *The City of Collective Memory: Its Historical Imagery and Architectural Entertainments*. Cambridge, MA: The MIT Press.

Boym, S. 1994. *Common Places: Mythologies of Everyday Life in Russia*. Cambridge, MA: Harvard University Press.

———. 2001. *The Future of Nostalgia*. New York: Basic Books.

Bozdoğan, S. 2001. *Modernism and Nation Building: Turkish Architectural Culture in the Early Republic*. Seattle: University of Washington Press.

Bremmer, I., and R. Taras (eds). 1993. *Nation and Politics in the Soviet Successor States*. Cambridge: Cambridge University Press.

Bridger, S., and F. Pine (eds). 1998. *Surviving Post-Socialism: Local Strategies and Regional Responses in Eastern Europe and the Former Soviet Union*. London: Routledge.

Brown, K. 2001. 'Gridded Lives: Why Kazakhstan and Montana are Nearly the Same Place', *The American Historical Review* 106(1): 17–48.

Brubaker, R. 1994. 'Nationhood and the National Question in the Soviet Union and Post-Soviet Eurasia: An Institutionalist Account', *Theory and Society* 23(1): 47–78.

Buchli, V. 2000. *An Archaeology of Socialism*. Oxford: Berg.

———. 2007. 'Astana: Materiality and the City', in C. Alexander, V. Buchli and C. Humphrey (eds), *Urban Life in Post-Soviet Asia*. London: University College Press, pp. 40–69.

Buck-Morss, S. 1983. 'Benjamin's Passagen-Werk: Redeeming Mass Culture for the Revolution', *New German Critique* 29: 211–40.

———. 1992. 'Aesthetics and Anaesthetics: Walter Benjamin's Artwork Essay Reconsidered', *October* 62: 3–41.

———. 2002. *Dreamworld and Catastrophe: The Passing of Mass Utopia in East and West*. Cambridge, MA: The MIT Press.

Burawoy, M., and K. Verdery (eds). 1999. *Uncertain Transition: Ethnographies of Change in the Post-Socialist World*. Lanham, MD: Rowman & Littlefield.

Burdick, J. 1993. *Looking for God in Brazil: The Progressive Catholic Church in Urban Brazil's Religious Arena*. Berkeley, CA: University of California Press.

Butler, J. 1999. *Gender Trouble: Feminism and the Subversion of Identity*. New York: Routledge.

Caillois, R. 1961. *Man, Play and Games*, trans. M. Barash. New York: Free Press of Glencoe.

Caldeira, T. 1996. 'Fortified Communities', *Public Culture* 8: 303–28.

Caldeira, T., and J. Holston. 2005. 'State and Urban Space in Brazil: From Modernist Planning to Democratic Interventions', in A. Ong and S.J. Collier (eds), *Global Assemblages: Technology, Politics, and Ethics as Anthropological Problems*. Malden: Blackwell, pp. 393–416.

Calhoun, C. 1992. 'Introduction: Habermas and the Public Sphere', in C. Calhoun (ed.), *Habermas and the Public Sphere*. Cambridge, MA: The MIT Press, pp. 1–48.

Calvino, I. 1978. *Invisible Cities*, trans. W. Weaver. San Diego, CA: Hartcourt Brace.

Candea, M. 2007. 'Arbitrary Locations: In Defence of the Bounded Fieldsite', *Journal of the Royal Anthropological Institute* 13: 167–84.

Carr, S., M. Francis, L. Rivlin and A. Stone. 1992. *Public Space*. Cambridge: Cambridge University Press.

Casey, E. 1996. 'How to Get from Space to Place in a Fairly Short Stretch of Time: Phenomenological Prolegomena', in S. Feld and K. Basso (eds), *Senses of Place*. Santa Fe: School of American Research Press, pp. 13–52.

Castells, M. 1977. *The Urban Question: A Marxist Approach*, trans. A. Sheridan. London: Edward Arnold.

———. 1978. *City, Class and Power*, trans. E. Lebas. New York: St. Martin's Press.

———. 1983. *The City and the Grassroots: A Cross-Cultural Theory of Urban Social Movements*. London: Edward Arnold.

———. 2000. *End of Millennium*, 2nd ed. London: Blackwell.

Central Intelligence Agency. 2011. 'CIA World Factbook'. Retrieved 26 November 2011 from https://www.cia.gov/library/publications/the-world-factbook/geos/kz.html

Chikanaev, A. 2008. *Astana: Arkhitekturnaia Simfonia Velikoi Stepi*. Astana: Delovoi Mir.

Çınar, A. 2007. 'Imagined Community as Urban Reality: The Making of Ankara', in A. Çınar and T. Bender (eds), *Urban Imaginaries: Locating the Modern City*. Minneapolis, MN: University of Minnesota Press, pp. 151–81.

Clifford, J. 1986. 'Introduction: Partial Truths', in J. Clifford and G. Marcus (eds), *Writing Culture: The Poetics and Politics of Ethnography*. Berkeley, CA: University of California Press, pp. 1–26.

————. 1988. *The Predicament of Culture: Twentieth-Century Ethnography, Literature, and Art*. Cambridge, MA: Harvard University Press.

Cohen, M. 1989. 'Walter Benjamin's Phantasmagoria', *New German Critique* 48: 87–107.

Collier, S.J. 2004. 'Pipes', in S. Harrison, S. Pile and N. Thrift (eds), *Patterned Ground: Entanglements of Nature and Culture*. London: Reaktion Books, pp. 50–52.

————. 2010. *Post-Soviet Social: Neoliberalism, Social Modernity, Biopolitics*. Princeton, NJ: Princeton University Press.

Collins, S.G. 2008. *All Tomorrow's Cultures: Anthropological Engagements with the Future*. New York: Berghahn Books.

Connerton, P. 1989. *How Societies Remember*. Cambridge: Cambridge University Press.

Coole, D., and S. Frost (eds). 2010. *New Materialisms: Ontology, Agency, and Politics*. Durham, NC: Duke University Press.

Cooper, M. 1999. 'Spatial Discourses and Social Boundaries: Re-Imagining the Toronto Waterfront', in S. Low (ed.), *Theorizing the City: The New Urban Anthropology Reader*. New Brunswick, NJ: Rutgers University Press, pp. 377–99.

Creed, G.W. 2006. 'Reconsidering Community', in G.W. Creed (ed.), *The Seductions of Community: Emancipations, Oppressions, Quandaries*. Santa Fe: School of American Research Press, pp. 3–22.

Cresswell, T. 2011. 'Place. Part I', in J. Agnew and J.S. Duncan (eds), *The Wiley-Blackwell Companion to Human Geography*. Malden: Wiley-Blackwell, pp. 235–44.

Crook, S. 2000. 'Utopia and Dystopia', in G. Browning, A. Halcli and F. Webster (eds), *Understanding Contemporary Society: Theories of the Present*. London: Sage, pp. 205–18.

Crowley, D. 2002. 'Warsaw Interiors: The Public Life of Private Spaces', in D. Crowley and S.E. Reid (eds), *Socialist Spaces: Sites of Everyday Life in the Eastern Bloc*. Oxford: Berg, pp. 181–206.

Crowley, D., and S.E. Reid. 2002. 'Socialist Spaces: Sites of Everyday Life in the Eastern Bloc', in D. Crowley and S.E. Reid (eds), *Socialist Spaces: Sites of Everyday Life in the Eastern Bloc*. Oxford: Berg, pp. 1–22.

Cummings, S.N. 2005. *Kazakhstan: Power and the Elite*. London: I.B. Tauris.

————. 2006. 'Legitimation and Identification in Kazakhstan', *Nationalism and Ethnic Politics* 12: 177–204.

Cummings, S.N. (ed.). 2010. *Symbolism and Power in Central Asia: Politics of the Spectacular*. London: Routledge.

Czepczyński, M. 2008. *Cultural Landscapes of Post-Socialist Cities: Representation of Powers and Needs*. Aldershot: Ashgate.

Daly, J.C.K. 2008. 'Kazakhstan's Emerging Middle Class', Silk Road Paper. Washington D.C.: Central Asia – Caucasus Institute & Silk Road Studies Program, Johns Hopkins University.

Danzer, A.M. 2009. 'Battlefields of Ethnic Symbols. Public Space and Post-Soviet Identity Formation from a Minority Perspective', *Europe-Asia Studies* 61(9): 1557–77.

Darieva, T. 2011. 'A "Remarkable Gift" in a Postcolonial City: The Past and Present of the Baku Promenade', in T. Darieva, W. Kaschuba and M. Krebs (eds), *Urban Spaces after Socialism: Ethnographies of Public Places in Eurasian Cities*. Frankfurt: Campus Verlag, pp. 153–80.

Darieva, T., W. Kaschuba and M. Krebs (eds). 2011. *Urban Spaces after Socialism: Ethnographies of Public Places in Eurasian Cities*. Frankfurt: Campus Verlag.

Das, V., and S. Poole (eds). 2004. *Anthropology in the Margins of the State*. Santa Fe: School of American Research Press.

Dave, B. 2007. *Kazakhstan: Ethnicity, Language and Power.* London: Routledge.

De Certeau, M. 1984. *The Practice of Everyday Life*, trans. S. Rendall. Berkeley, CA: University of California Press.

Deleuze, G., and F. Guattari. 1987. *A Thousand Plateaus: Capitalism and Schizophrenia*, trans. B. Massumi. Minneapolis, MN: University of Minnesota Press.

Denison, M. 2009. 'The Art of the Impossible: Political Symbolism, and the Creation of National Identity and Collective Memory in Post-Soviet Turkmenistan', *Europe-Asia Studies* 61(7): 1167–87.

Diener, A.C. 2005. 'Problematic Integration of Mongolian-Kazakh Return Migrants in Kazakhstan', *Eurasian Geography and Economics* 46(6): 465–78.

Dirks, N.R. 1992. 'Ritual and Resistance: Subversion as a Social Fact', in D.E. Haynes and G. Prakash (eds), *Contesting Power: Resistance and Everyday Social Relations in South Asia.* Berkeley, CA: University of California Press, pp. 213–38.

Donahoe, B., J. Eidson, D. Feyissa, V. Fuest, M.V. Hoehne, B. Nieswand, G. Schlee and O. Zenker. 2009. 'The Formation and Mobilization of Collective Identities in Situations of Conflict and Integration', Working Paper No. 116. Halle: Max Planck Institute for Social Anthropology.

Douglas, M. 2002 [1966]. *Purity and Danger: An Analysis of Concept of Pollution and Taboo.* London: Routledge.

Dubitskii, A.F. 1959. *Akmola, Gorod Slavnii: Istoricheskii Ocherk.* Akmolinsk: Oblastnoe Izdatel'stvo.

———. 1990. *Proidemsia po Ulitsam Tselinograda: Kraevedcheskie Zametki.* Tselinograd: Tselinogradskoe Oblastnoe Otdelenie Sovetskogo Fonda Kul'tury.

Durkheim, E. 2001 [1912]. *The Elementary Forms of Religious Life*, trans. C. Cosman. Oxford: Oxford University Press.

Dzhaksybekov, A. 2008. *Tak Nachinalas Astana: Zapiski Pervogo Akima Stolitsy.* Astana: Valeri-ART.

Edensor, T. 2005. *Industrial Ruins: Space, Aesthetics and Materiality.* Oxford: Berg.

Epstein, D. 1973. *Brasilia, Plan and Reality: A Study of Planned and Spontaneous Urban Development.* Berkeley: University of California Press.

Erofeev, V. 2006. *Russkii Apokalipsis: Opyt Khudozhestvennoi Eskhatologii.* Moskva: Zebra E.

Fabian, J. 2002 [1983]. *Time and the Other: How Anthropology Makes Its Object.* New York: Columbia University Press.

Fauve, A. 2015. 'A Tale of Two Statues in Astana: The Fuzzy Process of Nationalistic City Making', *Nationalities Papers: The Journal of Nationalism and Ethnicity*, DOI: 10.1080/00905992.2014.981745.

Fehérváry, K. 2002. 'American Kitchens, Luxury Bathrooms, and the Search for a "Normal" Life in Postsocialist Hungary', *Ethnos* 67(3): 369–400.

———. 2011. 'The Materiality of the New Family House in Hungary: Postsocialist Fad or Middle-Class Ideal?', *City & Society* 23(1): 18–41.

Feld, S., and K. Basso (eds). 1996. *Senses of Place.* Santa Fe: School of American Research Press.

Ferguson, J. 1999. *Expectations of Modernity: Myths and Meanings of Urban Life on the Zambian Copperbelt.* Berkeley, CA: University of California Press.

———. 2005. 'Decomposing Modernity: History and Hierarchy after Development', in A. Loomba, S. Kaul, M. Bunzl, A. Burton and J. Esty (eds), *Postcolonial Studies and Beyond.* Durham, NC: Duke University Press, pp.166–81.

Ferguson, J., and A. Gupta. 2002. 'Spatializing States: Toward an Ethnography of Neoliberal Governmentality', *American Ethnologist* 29(4): 981–1002.

Fernandez, J. 2003 [1984]. 'Emergence and Convergence in Some African Sacred Places', in S. Low and D. Lawrence-Zùñiga (eds), *The Anthropology of Space and Place: Locating Culture*. Malden: Blackwell, pp. 187–203.

Findley, L. 2005. *Building Change: Architecture, Politics and Cultural Agency*. London: Routledge.

Finke, P. 1999. 'The Kazaks of Western Mongolia', in I. Svanberg (ed.), *Contemporary Kazaks: Cultural and Social Perspectives*. Richmond: Curzon, pp. 103–47.

Flynn, M., N. Kosmarskaya and G. Sabirova. 2014. 'The 'Place' of "Memory" in Understanding Urban Change in Central Asia: The Cities of Bishkek and Ferghana', *Europe-Asia Studies* 66(9): 1501–24.

Forest, B., and J. Johnson. 2002. 'Unravelling the Threads of History: Soviet-Era Monuments and Post-Soviet National Identity in Moscow', *Annals of the Association of American Geographers* 92(3): 524–47.

———. 2011. 'Monumental Politics: Regime Type and Public Memory in Post-Communist States', *Post-Soviet Affairs* 27(3): 269–88.

Foucault, M. 1977. *Discipline and Punish: The Birth of the Prison*, trans. A. Sheridan. London: Allen Lane.

———. 1983. 'Afterword: The Subject and Power' in H.L. Dreyfus and P. Rabinow (eds), *Michel Foucault: Beyond Structuralism and Hermeneutics*, 2nd ed. Chicago: The University of Chicago Press, pp. 206–26.

———. 1986. 'Of Other Spaces', trans. Jay Miskowiec, *Diacritics* 16(1): 22–27.

———. 1991. 'Governmentality', in G. Burchell, C. Gordon and P. Miller (eds), *The Foucault Effect: Studies in Governmentality*. Chicago: The University of Chicago Press, pp. 87–104.

Fox, R. 1972. 'Rational and Romance in Urban Anthropology', *Urban Anthropology* 1: 205–33.

———. 1977. *Urban Anthropology: Cities in Their Cultural Settings*. Englewood Cliffs: Prentice Hall.

French, R.A. 1995. *Plans, Pragmatism and People: The Legacy of Soviet Planning for Today's Cities*. Pittsburgh, PA: University of Pittsburgh Press.

Fukuyama, F. 1992. *The End of History and the Last Man*. New York: Free Press.

Geertz, C. 1980. *Negara: The Theatre State in Nineteenth-Century Bali*. Princeton, NJ: Princeton University Press.

———. 1998. 'Deep Hanging Out', *The New York Review of Books*, 22 October.

Gell, A. 1992. *The Anthropology of Time: Cultural Constructions of Temporal Maps and Images*. Oxford: Berg.

Gentile, M. 2003. 'Delayed Underurbanization and the Closed-City Effect: The Case of Ust'-Kamenogorsk', *Eurasian Geography and Economics* 44(2): 144–56.

———. 2004. 'Studies in the Transformation of Post-Soviet Cities: Case Studies from Kazakhstan', Ph.D. dissertation. Uppsala: Uppsala University.

Gerasimova, K. 2002. 'Public Privacy in the Soviet Communal Apartment', in D. Crowley and S.E. Reid (eds), *Socialist Spaces: Sites of Everyday Life in the Eastern Bloc*. Oxford: Berg, pp. 207–30.

Gerchuk, I. 2000. 'The Aesthetics of Everyday Life in the Khrushchev Thaw in the USSR (1954-64)', in S.E. Reid and D. Crowley (eds), *Style and Socialism: Modernity and Material Culture in Post-War Eastern Europe*. Oxford: Berg, pp. 81–100.

Gleick, J. 1988. *Chaos: Making a New Science.* London: Cardinal.

Goskomstat Respubliki Kazakhstan. 1992. *Itogi Vsesoiuznoi Perepisi Naselenia 1989 Goda.* Almaty.

Goss, J. 1993. 'The "Magic of the Mall": An Analysis of Form, Function, and Meaning in Contemporary Retail Built Environment', *Annals of the Association of American Geographers* 83(1): 18–47.

Gottdiener, M. 2000. 'The Consumption of Space and the Spaces of Consumption', in M. Gottdiener (ed.), *New Forms of Consumption: Consumers, Culture, and Commodification.* Oxford: Rowman & Littlefield, pp. 265–85.

Graeber, D. 2004. *Fragments of an Anarchist Anthropology.* Chicago: Prickly Paradigm Press.

———. 2007. 'On the Phenomenology of Giant Puppets: Broken Windows, Imaginary Jars of Urine, and the Cosmological Role of the Police in American Culture', in *Possibilities: Essays on Hierarchy, Rebellion, and Desire.* Oakland: AK Press, pp. 375–417.

Graham, S., and N. Thrift. 2007. 'Out of Order: Understanding Repair and Maintenance', *Theory, Culture & Society* 24(3): 1–25.

Grant, B. 2001. 'New Moscow Monuments, or, States of Innocence', *American Ethnologist* 28(2): 332–62.

———. 2014. 'The Edifice Complex: Architecture and the Political Life of Surplus in the New Baku', *Public Culture* 26(3): 501–28.

Gulick, J. 1989. *The Humanity of Cities: An Introduction to Urban Societies.* Granby, MA: Bergin & Garvey.

Gupta, A., and J. Ferguson. 1992. 'Beyond "Culture": Space, Identity, and the Politics of Difference', *Cultural Anthropology* 7(1): 6–23.

———. 1997. 'Discipline and Practice: "The Field" as Site, Method, and Location in Anthropology', in A. Gupta and J. Ferguson (eds), *Anthropological Locations: Boundaries and Grounds of a Field Science.* Berkeley, CA: University of California Press, pp. 1–46.

Habermas, J. 1991. *The Structural Transformation of the Public Sphere: An Inquiry into a Category of Bourgeois Society,* trans. T. Burger and F. Lawrence. Cambridge, MA: The MIT Press.

Hall, P. 2002. *Cities of Tomorrow: An Intellectual History of Urban Planning and Design in the Twentieth Century.* Malden: Blackwell.

Hann, C. (ed.). 2002. *Postsocialism: Ideals, Ideologies and Practices in Eurasia.* London: Routledge.

Hannerz, U. 1969. *Soulside: Inquiries into Ghetto Culture and Community.* New York: Columbia University Press.

———. 1980. *Exploring the City: Inquiries Toward an Urban Anthropology.* New York: Columbia University Press.

Hartman, T. 2007. 'Moral Vectors, Transitional Time, and a "Utopian Object of Impossible Fullness"', *Social Anthropology/Anthropologie Sociale* 15(2): 187–203.

Harvey, D. 1973. *Social Justice and the City.* Oxford: Basil Blackwell.

———. 1985a. *Consciousness and the Urban Experience.* Oxford: Basil Blackwell.

———. 1985b. *The Urbanization of Capital.* Oxford: Basil Blackwell.

———. 1989. *The Urban Experience.* Baltimore, MD: The Johns Hopkins University Press.

———. 2000. *Spaces of Hope.* Edinburgh: Edinburgh University Press.

———. 2003. *Paris, Capital of Modernity.* New York: Routledge.

Harvey, P. 2005. 'The Materiality of State-Effects: An Ethnography of a Road in the Peruvian Andes', in C. Krohn-Hansen and K.G. Nustad (eds), *State Formation: Anthropological Perspectives.* London: Pluto Press, pp. 123–41.

Herzfeld, M. 1991. *A Place in History: Monumental and Social Time in a Cretan Town.* Princeton, NJ: Princeton University Press.

———. 2005. *Cultural Intimacy: Social Poetics in the Nation-State*, 2nd ed. New York and London: Routledge.

———. 2006. 'Spatial Cleansing: Monumental Vacuity and the Idea of the West', *Journal of Material Culture* 11(1/2): 127–49.

———. 2009. *Evicted from Eternity: The Restructuring of Modern Rome.* Chicago: The University of Chicago Press.

Hillier, B., and J. Hanson. 1984. *The Social Logic of Space.* Cambridge: Cambridge University Press.

Hobsbawm, E., and T. Ranger (eds). 1983. *The Invention of Tradition.* Cambridge: Cambridge University Press.

Hoffmann, D. 2000. 'European Modernity and Soviet Socialism', in D. Hoffmann and Y. Kotsonis (eds), *Russian Modernity: Politics, Knowledge, Practices.* London: Macmillan Press, pp. 245–60.

———. 2003. *Stalinist Values: The Cultural Norms of Soviet Modernity, 1917–1941.* Ithaca, NY: Cornell University Press.

Holm-Hansen, J. 1999. 'Political Integration in Kazakstan', in P. Kolstø (ed.), *Nation-Building and Ethnic Integration in Post-Soviet Societies: An Investigation of Latvia and Kazakstan.* Boulder: Westview Press, pp. 153–226.

Holquist, M. 1984. 'Prologue', in M. Bakhtin, *Rabelais and His World*, trans. H. Iswolsky. Bloomington, IN: Indiana University Press, pp. xiii–xxiii.

Holston, J. 1989. *The Modernist City: An Anthropological Critique of Brasilia.* Chicago: Chicago University Press.

———. 1999. 'The Modernist City and the Death of the Street', in S. Low (ed.), *Theorizing the City: The New Urban Anthropology Reader.* New Brunswick, NJ: Rutgers University Press, pp. 245–76.

Hubert, H. 1999 [1905]. *Essay on Time: A Brief Study of the Representation of Time in Religion and Magic*, trans. R. Parkin and J. Redding. Oxford: Durkheim Press.

Huizinga, J. 1955. *Homo Ludens: A Study of the Play Element in Culture.* Boston: Beacon Press.

Humphrey, C. 1984. 'Some Recent Developments in Ethnography in the USSR', *Man* (N.S.) 19(2): 310–20.

———. 1998. *Marx Went Away – But Karl Stayed Behind.* Ann Arbor, MI: The University of Michigan Press.

———. 2002a. 'Does the Category "Postsocialist" Still Make Sense?', in. C. Hann (ed.), *Postsocialism: Ideals, Ideologies and Practices in Eurasia.* London: Routledge, pp. 12–15.

———. 2002b. *The Unmaking of Soviet Life: Everyday Economies after Socialism.* Ithaca, NY: Cornell University Press.

———. 2005. 'Ideology in Infrastructure: Architecture and Soviet Imagination', *Journal of the Royal Anthropological Institute* (N.S.) 11: 39–58.

———. 2007. 'New Subjects and Situated Interdependence: After Privatization in Ulan Ude', in C. Alexander, V. Buchli and C. Humphrey (eds), *Urban Life in Post-Soviet Asia.* London: University College Press, pp. 175–207.

Ingold, T. 1993. 'The Temporality of the Landscape', *World Archaeology* 25(2): 152–74.

———. 1995. 'Building, Dwelling, Living: How Animals and People Make Themselves at Home in the World', in M. Strathern (ed.), *Shifting Contexts: Transformations in Anthropological Knowledge.* London: Routledge, pp. 57–80.

————. 2000. *The Perception of the Environment: Essays on Livelihood, Dwelling and Skill.* London: Routledge.

Jackson, P. 1985. 'Urban Ethnography', *Progress in Human Geography* 9: 157–76.

James, W., and D. Mills. 2005. 'Introduction: From Representation to Action in the Flow of Time', in W. James and D. Mills (eds), *The Qualities of Time: Anthropological Approaches.* Oxford: Berg, pp. 1–18.

Jones Luong, P. (ed.). 2004. *The Transformation of Central Asia: States and Societies from Soviet Rule to Independence.* Ithaca, NY: Cornell University Press.

Kaiser, R., and J. Chinn. 1995. 'Russian-Kazakh Relations in Kazakhstan', *Post-Soviet Geography* 36(5): 257–73.

Kandiyoti, D. 2002. 'How Far Do Analyses of Postsocialism Travel? The Case of Central Asia', in C. Hann (ed.), *Postsocialism: Ideals, Ideologies and Practices in Eurasia.* London: Routledge, pp. 238–57.

Kharkhordin, O. 1997. 'Reveal and Dissimulate: A Genealogy of Private Life in Soviet Russia', in J. Weintraub (ed.), *Public and Private in Thought and Action: Perspectives on a Grand Dichotomy.* Chicago: University of Chicago Press, pp. 333–63.

————. 1999. *The Collective and the Individual in Russia: A Study of Practices.* Berkeley, CA: University of California Press.

King, A.D. (ed.). 1980. *Buildings and Society: Essays on the Social Development of the Built Environment.* London: Routledge.

Kislov, D. 2011. 'Kazakhstan, Zhanaozen: Prazdnik isporchen. Est zhertvy', *Fergana News*, 16 December 2011. Retrieved 26 February 2012 from http://www.fergananews.com/article.php?id=7211

Koch, N.R. 2010. 'The Monumental and the Miniature: Imagining 'Modernity' in Astana', *Social & Cultural Geography* 11(8): 769–87.

————. 2012a. 'The City and the Steppe: Territory, Technologies of Government, and Kazakhstan's New Capital', Ph.D. dissertation. Boulder, CO. University of Colorado.

————. 2012b. 'Urban "Utopias". The Disney Stigma and Discourses of "False Modernity"', *Environment and Planning A* 44: 2445–62.

————. 2013. 'Technologizing Complacency: Spectacle, Structural Violence, and "Living Normally" in a Resource-Rich State', *Political Geography* 37: A1–A2.

————. 2014. '"Building Glass Refrigerators in the Desert": Discourses of Urban Sustainability and Nation Building in Qatar', *Urban Geography* 35(8): 1118–39.

————. 2015a. 'Domesticating Elite Education: Raising Patriots and Educating Kazakhstan's Future', in M. Ismayilov and M. Ayoob (eds), *Identity and Politics in Central Asia and the Caucasus.* New York: Routledge, pp. 82–100.

————. 2015b. 'The Violence of the Spectacle: Statist Schemes to Green the Desert and Constructing Astana and Ashgabat as Urban Oases', *Social & Cultural Geography*, http://dx.doi.org/10.1080/14649365.2014.1001431

Koch, N.R., and K. White. Forthcoming. 'Cowboys, Gangsters, and Rural Bumpkins: Constructing the "Other" in Kazakhstan's "Texas"', in M. Laruelle (ed.), *Kazakhstan beyond Economic Success: Exploring Social and Cultural Changes in Eurasia.* Lanham, MD: Lexington Books.

Kolstø, P. 1998. 'Anticipating Demographic Superiority: Kazakh Thinking on Integration and Nation Building', *Europe-Asia Studies* 50(1): 51–69.

Kolstø, P. (ed.). 1999. *Nation-Building and Ethnic Integration in Post-Soviet Societies: An Investigation of Latvia and Kazakhstan.* Boulder, CO: Westview Press.

Kotkin, S. 1995. *Magnetic Mountain: Stalinism as Civilization*. Berkeley, CA: University of California Press.

Krohn-Hansen, C., and K.G. Nustad (eds). 2005. *State Formation: Anthropological Perspectives*. London: Pluto Press.

Kuhn, T.S. 1970. *The Structure of Scientific Revolutions*, 2nd ed. Chicago: University of Chicago Press.

Kundera, M. 1984. *The Unbearable Lightness of Being*, trans. M.H. Heim. New York: Harper & Row.

Kurokawa, K. 1997. *Each One a Hero: The Philosophy of Symbiosis*. Tokyo: Kodansha International.

Laitin, D. 1995. 'Identity in Formation: The Russian-Speaking Nationality in the Post-Soviet Diaspora', *Archives Européennes de Sociologie* 36(2): 281–316.

———. 1999. 'The Cultural Elements of Ethnically Mixed States: Nationality Re-formation in the Soviet Successor States', in G. Steinmetz (ed.), *State/Culture: State-Formation after the Cultural Turn*. Ithaca, NY: Cornell University Press, pp. 291–320.

Lane, C. 1981. *The Rites of Rulers: Ritual in Industrial Society – The Soviet Case*. Cambridge: Cambridge University Press.

Laszczkowski, M. 2011a. 'Building the Future: Construction, Temporality, and Politics in Astana', *Focaal – Journal of Global and Historical Anthropology* 60: 77–92.

———. 2011b. 'Superplace: Global Connections and Local Politics at the Mega Mall, Astana', *Etnofoor* 23(1): 85–104.

———. 2014. 'State Building(s): Built Forms, Materiality, and the State in Astana' in M. Reeves, J. Rasanayagam and J. Beyer (eds), *Ethnographies of the State in Central Asia: Performing Politics*. Bloomington, IN: Indiana University Press, pp. 149–72.

———. 2015. 'Scraps, Neighbors, and Committees: Urbanism, Place-Making, and Material Things in an Astana Apartment Block', *City & Society* 27(2): 136–59.

———. 2016. '"Demo-Version of a City": Buildings, Affects, and the State in Astana', *Journal of the Royal Anthropological Institute* 22(1): 148–65.

———. Forthcoming. 'Shrek Meets the President: Magical Authoritarianism in a Fairy-Tale City', in M. Laruelle (ed.), *Kazakhstan beyond Economic Success: Exploring Social and Cultural Changes in Eurasia*. Lanham, MD: Lexington Books.

Latour, B. 1993. *We Have Never Been Modern*, trans. C. Potter. Cambridge, MA: Harvard University Press.

———. 2005. *Reassembling the Social: An Introduction to Acton-Network Theory*. Oxford: Oxford University Press.

Law, J. 2004. *After Method: Mess in Social Theory*. New York: Routledge.

Lawrence, D., and S. Low. 1990. 'The Built Environment and Spatial Form', *Annual Review of Anthropology* 19: 453–505.

Leach, N. 2002. 'Belonging: Towards a Theory of Identification with Space', in J. Hillier and E. Rooksby (eds), *Habitus: A Sense of Place*. Aldershot: Ashgate, pp. 281–95.

Lee, J., and T. Ingold. 2006. 'Fieldwork on Foot: Perceiving, Routing, Socializing', in S. Coleman and P. Collins (eds), *Locating the Field: Space, Place, and Context in Anthropology*. Oxford: Berg, pp. 67–85.

Lefebvre, H. 1991 [1974]. *The Production of Space*, trans. D. Nicholson-Smith. Oxford: Blackwell.

———. 2003a. 'Space and the State', in N. Brenner, B. Jessop, M. Jones and G. MacLeod (eds), *State/Space: A Reader*. Malden: Blackwell, pp. 84–100.

————. 2003b [1970]. *The Urban Revolution*, trans. R. Bononno. Minneapolis, MN: University of Minnesota Press.

Lemon, A. 2011. 'Afterword for Urban (post)Socialisms', in T. Darieva, W. Kaschuba and M. Krebs (eds), *Urban Spaces after Socialism: Ethnographies of Public Places in Eurasian Cities*. Frankfurt: Campus Verlag, pp. 307–14.

Li, T.M. 2005. 'Beyond "the State" and Failed Schemes', *American Anthropologist* 107(3): 383–94.

Liu, M. 2007. 'A Central Asian Tale of Two Cities: Locating Lives and Aspirations in a Shifting Post-Soviet Cityscape', in J. Sahadeo and R. Zanca (eds), *Everyday Life in Central Asia: Past and Present*. Bloomington, IN: Indiana University Press, pp. 66–83.

Lovell, S. 2002. 'Soviet Exurbia: Dachas in Postwar Russia', in D. Crowley and S.E. Reid (eds), *Socialist Spaces: Sites of Everyday Life in the Eastern Bloc*. Oxford: Berg, pp. 105 22.

Low, S. 1999a. 'Introduction: Theorizing the City', in S. Low (ed.), *Theorizing the City: The New Urban Anthropology Reader*. New Brunswick, NJ: Rutgers University Press, pp. 1–36.

————. 1999b. 'Spatializing Culture: The Social Production and Social Construction of Public Space in Costa Rica', in S. Low (ed.), *Theorizing the City: The New Urban Anthropology Reader*. New Brunswick, NJ: Rutgers University Press, pp. 111–37.

————. 2000. *On the Plaza: The Politics of Public Space and Culture*. Austin, TX: University of Texas Press.

Low, S., and D. Lawrence-Zúñiga. 2003. 'Locating Culture', in S. Low and D. Lawrence-Zúñiga (eds), *The Anthropology of Space and Place: Locating Culture*. Malden: Blackwell, pp. 1–47.

Lowenthal, D. 1992. 'The Death of the Future', in S. Wallman (ed.), *Contemporary Futures: Perspectives from Social Anthropology*. London: Routledge, pp. 23–35.

McDonogh, G. 1999. 'Discourses of the City: Policy and Response in Post-transitional Barcelona', in S. Low (ed.), *Theorizing the City: The New Urban Anthropology Reader*. New Brunswick, NJ: Rutgers University Press, pp. 342–76.

McMann, K. 2007. 'The Shrinking of the Welfare State: Central Asians' Assessments of Soviet and Post-Soviet Governance', in J. Sahadeo and R. Zanca (eds), *Everyday Life in Central Asia: Past and Present*. Bloomington, IN: Indiana University Press, pp. 233–47.

Malkova, I., P. Kolstø and H. Melberg. 1999. 'Attitudinal and Linguistic Integration in Kazakstan and Latvia', in P. Kolstø (ed.), *Nation-Building and Ethnic Integration in Post-Soviet Societies: An Investigation of Latvia and Kazakstan*. Boulder, CO: Westview Press, pp. 227–80.

Marat, E. 2010. 'Nation Branding in Central Asia: A New Campaign to Present Ideas about the State and the Nation', in S.N. Cummings (ed.), *Symbolism and Power in Central Asia: Politics of the Spectacular*. London and New York: Routledge, pp. 39–52.

Marcus, G.E. 1995. 'Ethnography in/of the World System: The Emergence of Multi-sited Ethnography', *Annual Review of Anthropology* 24: 95–117.

Marston, S.A. 2000. 'The Social Construction of Scale', *Progress in Human Geography* 24(2): 219–42.

Martin, T. 2001. *The Affirmative Action Empire: Nations and Nationalism in the Soviet Union, 1923–1939*. Ithaca, NY: Cornell University Press.

Massey, D. 1984. 'Introduction: Geography Matters', in D. Massey and J. Allen (eds), *Geography Matters! A Reader*. Cambridge: Cambridge University Press, pp. 1–11.

————. 1994. *Space, Place, and Gender*. Minneapolis, MN: University of Minnesota Press.

————. 2002. 'Don't Let's Counterpose Place and Space', *Development* 45(1): 24–25.

————. 2005. *For Space*. Los Angeles: Sage.

Massey, D., and J. Allen (eds). 1984. *Geography Matters! A Reader*. Cambridge: Cambridge University Press.

Matveeva, A. 2009. 'Legitimising Central Asian Authoritarianism: Political Manipulation and Symbolic Power', *Europe-Asia Studies* 61(7): 1095–121.

Mbembe, A. 2004. 'Aesthetics of Superfluity', *Public Culture* 16(3): 373–405.

Medeuova, K. 2008. 'Astana i Karta', *Psikhologia, Sotsiologia, Politologia* 6: 13–19.

Melly, C. 2010. 'Inside-out Houses: Urban Belonging and Imagined Futures in Dakar, Senegal', *Comparative Studies in Society and History* 52(1): 37–65.

Merleau-Ponty, M. 1962. *The Phenomenology of Perception*. London: Routledge.

Metcalf, T. 1989. *An Imperial Vision: Indian Architecture and Britain's Raj*. Berkeley, CA: University of California Press.

Miller, D. 1987. *Material Culture and Mass Consumption*. Oxford: Blackwell.

Mitchell, J.C. 1969. 'The Concept and Use of Social Networks', in J.C. Mitchell (ed.), *Social Networks in Urban Situations: Analyses of Personal Relationships in Central African Towns*. Manchester: Manchester University Press, pp. 1–50.

Mitchell, T. 1988. *Colonising Egypt*. Berkeley, CA: University of California Press.

———. 1990. 'Everyday Metaphors of Power', *Theory and Society* 19: 545–77.

———. 1991. 'The Limits of the State: Beyond Statist Approaches and Their Critics', *The American Political Science Review* 85(1): 77–96.

———. 1999. 'Society, Economy, and the State Effect', in G. Steinmetz (ed.), *State/Culture: State-Formation after the Cultural Turn*. Ithaca, NY: Cornell University Press.

Mol, A. 2002. *The Body Multiple: Ontology in Medical Practice*. Durham, NC: Duke University Press.

Mol, A., and J. Law. 2002. 'Complexities: An Introduction' in J. Law and A. Mol (eds), *Complexities: Social Studies of Knowledge Practices*. Durham, NC: Duke University Press, pp. 1–22.

Moore, S.F. 1987. 'Explaining the Present: Theoretical Dilemmas in Processual Ethnography', *American Ethnologist* 14(4): 727–36.

Morton, H. 1980. 'Who Gets What, When and How? Housing in the Soviet Union', *Soviet Studies* 32(2): 235–59.

Mouffe, C. 2002. 'Which Kind of Public Space for a Democratic Habitus?', in J. Hillier and E. Rooksby (eds), *Habitus: A Sense of Place*. Aldershot: Ashgate, pp. 93–100.

Nadkarni, M., and O. Shevchenko. 2004. 'The Politics of Nostalgia: A Case for Comparative Analysis of Post-Socialist Practices', *Ab Imperio* 2: 487–519.

Navaro-Yashin, Y. 2002. *Faces of the State: Secularism and Public Life in Turkey*. Princeton, NJ: Princeton University Press.

———. 2012. *The Make-Believe Space: Affective Geography in a Postwar Polity*. Durham: Duke University Press.

Nazarbaev, N. 2005. *V Serdtse Evrazii*. Astana: Atamura.

———. 2006. *Kazakhstanskii Put'*. Karaganda.

Nazpary, J. 2002. *Post-Soviet Chaos: Violence and Dispossession in Kazakhstan*. London: Pluto Press.

Nora, P. 1996. *Realms of Memory: Rethinking the French Past*, trans. A. Goldhammer. New York: Columbia University Press.

Odgaard, K., and J. Simonsen. 1999. 'The New Kazak Elite', in I. Svanberg (ed.), *Contemporary Kazaks: Cultural and Social Perspectives*. Richmond: Curzon, pp. 17–45.

Olcott, M.B. 2002. *Kazakhstan: Unfulfilled Promise*. Washington, D.C.: Carnegie Endowment for International Peace.

Olsen, B. 2003. 'Material Culture after Text: Re-membering Things', *Norwegian Archaeological Review* 36(2): 87–104.

———. 2010. *In Defence of Things: Archaeology and the Ontology of Objects*. Lanham, MD: AltaMira.

Ong, A. 1999. *Flexible Citizenship: The Cultural Logics of Transnationality*. Durham, NC: Duke University Press.

———. 2011. 'Introduction: Worlding Cities, or the Art of Being Global', in A. Roy and A. Ong (eds), *Worlding Cities: Asian Experiments and the Art of Being Global*. Malden: Blackwell, pp. 1–26.

Ortner, S. 1984. 'Theory in Anthropology since the Sixties', *Comparative Studies in Society and History* 26(1): 126–66.

Park, R. 1968 [1925]. 'The City: Suggestions for the Investigation of Human Behavior in the Urban Environment', in R. Park, E. Burgess and R. McKenzie, *The City*. Chicago: The University of Chicago Press, pp. 1–46.

Pelkmans, M. 2003. 'The Social Life of Empty Buildings: Imagining the Transition in Post-Soviet Ajaria', *Focaal – European Journal of Anthropology* 41: 121–35.

Pilz, M. 2011. 'Tbilisi in City-Maps: Symbolic Construction of an Urban Landscape', in T. Darieva, W. Kaschuba and M. Krebs (eds), *Urban Spaces after Socialism: Ethnographies of Public Places in Eurasian Cities*. Frankfurt: Campus Verlag, pp. 81–106.

Pohl, J. 1999. *Ethnic Cleansing in the USSR, 1937–1949*. Westport, CT: Greenwood Press.

Pohl, M. 1999. 'The Virgin Lands between Memory and Forgetting: People and Transformation in the Soviet Union, 1954–1960', Ph.D. dissertation. Bloomington, IN: Indiana University.

Rabinow, P. 1989. *French Modern: Norms and Forms of the Social Environment*. Chicago: Chicago University Press.

Radio Free Europe. 2012. 'OSCE Monitors Criticize Kazakh Vote Failings', *Radio Free Europe – Radio Liberty*, 16 January. Retrieved 11 March 2012 from http://www.rferl.org/content/kazakhstan_three_parties_win_entry_to_parliament/24452861.html

Raffles, H. 1999. '"Local Theory": Nature and the Making of an Amazonian Place', *Cultural Anthropology* 14(3): 323–60.

Redfield, R. 1969 [1947]. 'The Folk Society', in R. Sennett (ed.), *Classic Essays on the Culture of Cities*. New York: Meredith Corporation, pp. 180–205.

Redfield, R., and M. Singer. 1969 [1954]. 'The Cultural Role of Cities', in R. Sennett (ed.), *Classic Essays on the Culture of Cities*. New York: Meredith Corporation, pp. 206–33.

Reed, A. 2002. 'City of Details: Interpreting the Personality of London', *Journal of the Royal Anthropological Institute* (N.S.) 8: 127–41.

Reeves, M. 2014. *Border Work: Spatial Lives of the State in Rural Central Asia*. Ithaca, NY: Cornell University Press.

Reeves, M., J. Rasanayagam and J. Beyer (eds). 2014. *Ethnographies of the State in Central Asia: Performing Politics*. Bloomington, IN: Indiana University Press.

Richardson, M. 1982. 'Being-in-the-Market versus Being-in-the-Plaza: Material Culture and the Construction of Social Reality in Spanish America', *American Ethnologist* 9(2): 421–36.

Richardson, T. 2008. *Kaleidoscopic Odessa: History and Place in Contemporary Ukraine*. Toronto: University of Toronto Press.

Ries, N. 1997. *Russian Talk: Culture and Conversation during Perestroika*. Ithaca, NY: Cornell University Press.

Rodman, M.C. 1992. 'Empowering Place: Multilocality and Multivocality', *American Ethnologist* 94(3): 640–56.

Rolf, M. 2013. *Soviet Mass Festivals, 1917–1991*, trans. C. Klohr. Pittsburgh, PA: University of Pittsburgh Press.

Roy, A. 2011. 'Conclusion: Postcolonial Urbanism: Speed, Hysteria, Mass Dreams', in Roy, A. and A. Ong (eds), *Worlding Cities: Asian Experiments and the Art of Being Global*. Malden: Blackwell, pp. 307–35.

Roy, A., and A. Ong (eds). 2011. *Worlding Cities: Asian Experiments and the Art of Being Global*. Malden: Blackwell.

Ruble, B. 1995. *Money Sings: The Changing Politics of Urban Space in Post-Soviet Yaroslavl*. Cambridge: Cambridge University Press.

Rushdie, S. 2006 [1988]. *The Satanic Verses*. London: Vintage Books.

Rutheiser, C. 1996. *Imagineering Atlanta: The Politics of Place in the City of Dreams*. London: Verso.

———. 1999. 'Making Place in the Nonplace Urban Realm: Notes on the Revitalization of Downtown Atlanta', in S. Low (ed.), *Theorizing the City: The New Urban Anthropology Reader*. New Brunswick, NJ: Rutgers University Press, pp. 317–41.

Sanders, R. 2016. *Staying at Home: Identities, Memories and Social Networks of Kazakhstani Germans*. New York: Berghahn Books.

Sanjek, R. 1991. 'The Ethnographic Present', *Man* (N.S.) 26(4): 609–28.

Said, E. 1978. *Orientalism*. New York: Pantheon Books.

Schatz, E. 2000a. 'Framing Strategies of Non-conflict in Multi-ethnic Kazakhstan', *Nationalism & Ethnic Politics* 6: 71–94.

———. 2000b. 'The Politics of Multiple Identities: Lineage and Ethnicity in Kazakhstan', *Europe-Asia Studies* 52: 489–506.

———. 2004a. *Modern Clan Politics: The Politics of "Blood" in Kazakhstan and Beyond*. Seattle: University of Washington Press.

———. 2004b. 'What Capital Cities Say about State and Nation Building', *Nationalism and Ethnic Politics* 9: 111–40.

———. 2009. 'The Soft Authoritarian Tool Kit: Agenda-Setting Power in Kazakhstan and Kyrgyzstan', *Comparative Politics* 41(2): 203–22.

Schechner, R. 1988a. *Performance Theory*. New York: Routledge.

———. 1988b. 'Victor Turner's Last Adventure', in V. Turner, *The Anthropology of Performance*. New York: PAJ Publications, pp. 7–20.

Schlee, G. 2008. *How Enemies are Made: Towards a Theory of Ethnic and Religious Conflicts*. New York: Berghahn Books.

Schröder, P. 2010. '"Urbanizing" Bishkek: Interrelations of Boundaries, Migration, Group Size, and Opportunity Structure', *Central-Asian Survey* 29(4): 453–67.

Schwenkel, C. 2013. 'Post/Socialist Affect: Ruination and Reconstruction of the Nation in Urban Vietnam', *Cultural Anthropology* 28(2): 252–77.

Scott, J. 1985. *Weapons of the Weak: Everyday Forms of Peasant Resistance*. New Haven, CT: Yale University Press.

———. 1990. *Domination and the Arts of Resistance: Hidden Transcripts*. New Haven, CT: Yale University Press.

————. 1998. *Seeing Like a State: How Certain Schemes to Improve the Human Condition Have Failed*. New Haven, CT: Yale University Press.

Sennett, R. 1969. 'An Introduction', in R. Sennett (ed.), *Classic Essays on the Culture of Cities*. New York: Meredith Corporation, pp. 3–19.

————. 1978. *The Fall of Public Man*. New York: Alfred A. Knopf.

————. 1991. *The Conscience of the Eye: The Design and Social Life of Cities*. New York: W. W. Norton.

Shatkin, G. 2011. 'Planning Privatopolis: Representation and Contestation in the Development of Urban Integrated Mega-Projects', in A. Roy and A. Ong (eds), *Worlding Cities: Asian Experiments and the Art of Being Global*. Malden: Blackwell, pp. 77–97.

Simone, A. 2001. 'On the Worlding of African Cities', *African Studies Review* 44(2): 15–41.

————. 2004. *For the City Yet to Come: Changing African Lives in Four Cities*. Durham, NC: Duke University Press.

Simmel, G. 1969 [1903]. 'The Metropolis and Mental Life', in R. Sennett (ed.), *Classic Essays on the Culture of Cities*. New York: Meredith Corporation, pp. 47–60.

Smith, G. (ed.). 1996. *The Nationalities Question in the Post-Soviet States*. London: Longman.

Smith, G., V. Law, A. Wilson, A. Bohr and E. Allworth. 1998. *Nation-Building in the Post-Soviet Borderlands: The Politics of National Identities*. Cambridge: Cambridge University Press.

Sneath, D. 2005. 'The Rural and the Urban in Pastoral Mongolia', in O. Bruun and L. Narangoa (eds), *Mongolians from Country to City: Floating Boundaries, Pastoralism and City Life in the Mongol Lands*. Honolulu: Hawaii University Press, pp. 140–61.

Soja, E.W. 1996. *Thirdspace: Journeys to Los Angeles and Other Real-and-Imagined Places*. Cambridge, MA: Blackwell.

'Sotsial'no-Ekonomicheskii Pasport Goroda Astany'. 2012. Retrieved 11 March 2012 from http://www.astana.kz/ru/taxonomy/term/50

Spengler, O. 1969 [1922]. 'The Soul of the City', in R. Sennett (ed.), *Classic Essays on the Culture of Cities*. New York: Meredith Corporation, pp. 61–88.

Ssorin Chaikov, N. 2003. *The Social Life of the State in Subarctic Siberia*. Stanford, CA: Stanford University Press.

Stewart, S. 1984. *On Longing: Narratives of the Miniature, the Gigantic, the Souvenir, the Collection*. Baltimore, MD: The Johns Hopkins University Press.

Stites, R. 1991. *Revolutionary Dreams: Utopian Vision and Experimental Life in the Russian Revolution*. New York: Oxford University Press.

Stoler, A.L. (ed.). 2013. *Imperial Debris: On Ruins and Ruination*. Durham, NC: Duke University Press.

Strathern, M. 1995. 'Foreword: Shifting Contexts', in M. Strathern (ed.), *Shifting Contexts: Transformations in Anthropological Knowledge*. London: Routledge, pp. 1–12.

————. 2002. 'On Space and Depth', in J. Law and A. Mol (eds), *Complexities: Social Studies of Knowledge Practices*. Durham, NC: Duke University Press, pp. 88–115.

————. 2004. *Partial Connections*, updated ed. Walnut Creek, CA: AltaMira Press.

Street, A. 2012. 'Affective Infrastructure: Hospital Landscapes of Hope and Failure', *Space and Culture* 15(1): 44–56.

Stronski, P. 2010. *Tashkent: Forging a Soviet City, 1930–1966*. Pittsburgh, PA: University of Pittsburgh Press.

Struyk, R. 1996. 'Housing Privatization in the Former Soviet Bloc to 1995', in G. Andrusz, M. Harloe and I. Szelenyi (eds), *Cities After Socialism: Urban and Regional Change and Conflict in Post-Socialist Societies*. Oxford: Blackwell, pp. 192–213.

Svanberg, I. 1996. 'Kazakhstan and the Kazakhs', in G. Smith (ed.), *The Nationalities Question in the Post-Soviet States*. London: Longman, pp. 318–33.

Swartz, M., V. Turner and A. Tuden. 1966. 'Introduction', in M. Swartz, V. Turner and A. Tuden (eds), *Political Anthropology*. Chicago: Aldine Press, pp. 1–41.

Szelenyi, I. 1983. *Urban Inequalities under State Socialism*. Oxford: Oxford University Press.

Šír, J. 2008. 'Cult of Personality in Monumental Art and Architecture: The Case of Post-Soviet Turkmenistan', *Acta Slavica Iaponica* 25: 203–20.

Tatibekov, V.L. (ed.). 2005. *Migranty v Novoi Stolitse Kazakhstana*. Astana: International Organization for Migration.

Thrift, N. 2008. *Non-Representational Theory: Space, Politics, Affect*. London: Routledge.

Tresch, J. 2001. 'On Going Native: Thomas Kuhn and Anthropological Method', *Philosophy of the Social Sciences* 31(3): 302–22.

Trevisani, T. 2014. 'The Reshaping of Cities and Citizens in Uzbekistan: The Case of Namangan's "New Uzbeks"', in M. Reeves, J. Rasanayagam and J. Beyer (eds), *Ethnographies of the State in Central Asia: Performing Politics*. Bloomington, IN: Indiana University Press, pp. 243–60.

Trouillot, M.-R. 2001. 'The Anthropology of the State in the Age of Globalization: Close Encounters of the Deceptive Kind', *Current Anthropology* 42(1): 125–38.

Tsing, A. 1993. *In the Realm of the Diamond Queen: Marginality in an Out-of-the-Way Place*. Princeton, NJ: Princeton University Press.

———. 2000. 'The Global Situation', *Cultural Anthropology* 15(3): 327–60.

Tuan, Y.-F. 1977. *Space and Place: The Perspective of Experience*. Minneapolis, MN: University of Minnesota Press.

Turner, V. 1982. *From Ritual to Theatre: The Human Seriousness of Play*. New York: PAJ Publications.

———. 1988. *The Anthropology of Performance*. New York: PAJ Publications.

———. 1995 [1969]. *The Ritual Process: Structure and Anti-Structure*. New York: Aldine de Gruyter.

Van Gennep, A. 1960 [1909]. *The Rites of Passage*, trans. M. Vizedom and G. Caffee. Chicago, IL: Chicago University Press.

Von Geldern, J. 1993. *Bolshevik Festivals, 1917–1920*. Berkeley, CA: University of California Press.

Wanner, C. 1998. *Burden of Dreams: History and Identity in Post-Soviet Ukraine*. University Park, PA: The Pennsylvania State University Press.

Weber, M. 1978 [1905]. 'The City (Non-legitimate Domination)', in G. Roth and C. Wittich (eds), *Economy and Society: An Outline of Interpretive Sociology*, trans. E. Fischoff, H. Gerth, A.M. Henderson, F. Kolegar, C. Wright Mills, T. Parsons, M. Rheinstein, G. Roth, E. Shils and C. Wittich. Berkeley, CA: University of California Press, pp. 1212–372.

Wedeen, L. 1999. *Ambiguities of Domination: Politics, Rhetoric, and Symbols in Contemporary Syria*. Chicago, IL: The University of Chicago Press.

West, H.G., and P. Raman (eds). 2009. *Enduring Socialism: Explorations of Revolution and Transformation, Restoration and Continuation*. New York: Berghahn Books.

Weszkalnys, G. 2010. *Berlin, Alexanderplatz: Transforming Place in a Unified Germany*. Oxford: Berghahn Books.

Williams, R. 1973. *The Country and the City*. Oxford: Oxford University Press.

Wilson, E. 1997. 'Looking Backward: Nostalgia and the City', in S. Westwood and J. Williams (eds), *Imagining Cities: Scripts, Signs, Memory*. London: Routledge, pp. 127–39.

Wirth, L. 1969 [1938]. 'Urbanism as a Way of Life', in R. Sennett (ed.), *Classic Essays on the Culture of Cities*. New York: Meredith Corporation, pp. 143–64.

Wolfel, R. 2002. 'North to Astana: Nationalistic Motives for the Movement of the Kazakh(Stani) Capital', *Nationalities Papers* 30(3): 485–506.

Wright, G. 1991. *The Politics of Design in French Colonial Urbanism*. Chicago, IL: The University of Chicago Press.

Yessenova, S. 2003. 'The Politics and Poetics of the Nation: Urban Narratives of Kazakh Identity', Ph.D. dissertation. Montreal: McGill University.

———. 2010. *The Politics and Poetics of the Nation: Urban Narratives of Kazakh Identity*. Montreal: Lambert Academic Publishing.

Yurchak, A. 1999. 'Gagarin and the Rave Kids: Transforming Power, Identity, and Aesthetics in Post-Soviet Nightlife', in A.M. Barker (ed.), *Consuming Russia: Popular Culture, Sex, and Society since Gorbachev*. Durham, NC: Duke University Press, pp. 76–109.

———. 2006. *Everything Was Forever, Until It Was No More: The Last Soviet Generation*. Princeton, NJ: Princeton University Press.

Zabirova, A.T. 2002a. 'Astana: A City Like Others or a Catalyst of Changes?', *Central Asia and The Caucasus* 5(17): 169–74.

———. 2002b. *Migratsia, Urbanizatsia i Identifikatsia u Kazakhov: Case Study Astana*. Almaty: NITs Ghylym.

———. 2003. *Identichnost' Kazakhov: Mezhdu Traditsiei i Sovremennostiu*. Almaty: NITs Ghylym.

Zhang, L. 2001. *Strangers in the City: Reconfigurations of Space, Power, and Social Networks within China's Floating Population*. Stanford, CA: Stanford University Press.

———. 2006. 'Contesting Spatial Modernity in Late-Socialist China', *Current Anthropology* 47(3): 461–84.

Zukin, S. 1992. 'Postmodern Urban Landscapes: Mapping Culture and Power', in S. Lash and J. Friedman (eds), *Modernity and Identity*. Oxford: Blackwell, pp. 221–47.

Žižek, S. 1999. *The Ticklish Subject: The Absent Centre of Political Ontology*. London: Verso.

Index